Autofiction and Advocacy in the Francophone Caribbean

UNIVERSITY PRESS OF FLORIDA

Florida A&M University, Tallahassee
Florida Atlantic University, Boca Raton
Florida Gulf Coast University, Ft. Myers
Florida International University, Miami
Florida State University, Tallahassee
New College of Florida, Sarasota
University of Central Florida, Orlando
University of Florida, Gainesville
University of North Florida, Jacksonville
University of South Florida, Tampa
University of West Florida, Pensacola

Autofiction and Advocacy in the Francophone Caribbean

Renée Larrier

University Press of Florida
Gainesville Tallahassee Tampa Boca Raton
Pensacola Orlando Miami Jacksonville Ft. Myers Sarasota

Copyright 2006 by Renée Larrier
All rights reserved
Published in the United States of America

First cloth printing, 2006
First paperback printing, 2020

25 24 23 22 21 20   6 5 4 3 2 1

A record of cataloging-in-publication data is available from the Library of Congress.

ISBN 978-0-8130-3005-0 (cloth)
ISBN 978-0-8130-6823-7 (pbk.)

The University Press of Florida is the scholarly publishing agency for the State University System of Florida, comprising Florida A&M University, Florida Atlantic University, Florida Gulf Coast University, Florida International University, Florida State University, New College of Florida, University of Central Florida, University of Florida, University of North Florida, University of South Florida, and University of West Florida.

University Press of Florida
2046 NE Waldo Road
Suite 2100
Gainesville, FL 32609
http://upress.ufl.edu

For my mother Naomi, sister Diane,
nephew Matthew, and niece Melanie

Contents

Acknowledgments ix

Introduction. Caribbean *I*dentity Poetics: Subjectivity, *I-mage*, Collage 1
1. "To Get Around the Rule of Silence": Performing Masculinity as *Détour* 30
2. "*I* Spy": Curators, Translators, and In-trust Narrators 55
3. Secrets and Silence, Displacement and *Délivrance* 79
4. Travelers' Trees and Umbilical Cords: Embodying Dyaspora, Renegotiating Home 101
5. A Roving *I*: Autofiction(s) and Subversions 126
Conclusion 146

Notes 151
Bibliography 167
Index 181

Acknowledgments

I greatly appreciate the invaluable support I received from a variety of people and institutions. Rutgers University was especially generous, providing fellowships, time, space, and an outstanding community of scholars. I was fortunate to present my work during two Institute for Research on Women seminars at which Fran Bartowski offered critical feedback on my notion of *témoignage* in an early version of the introduction, and Marc Matera did the same for chapter 3. It was at the Black Atlantic Seminar under the supervision of Deborah Gray White that I developed chapter 5. The Faculty of Arts and Sciences sabbatical leave program and Rick Lockwood, late chair of the French Department whose sudden death occurred while I was completing this study, were responsible for releasing me from teaching and committee obligations so that I could devote more time to researching and revising the manuscript. I am grateful to the librarians who, over the years, promptly filled my innumerable loan requests. I am also indebted to certain programs and individuals outside Rutgers: chapter 1 took shape at the National Endowment for the Humanities summer seminar, "Roots: African Dimensions of the History and Culture of the Americas (Through the Trans-Atlantic Slave Trade)" at the Virginia Foundation for the Humanities; and colleagues Brinda Mehta, Simone James Alexander, and Janis A. Mayes kindly read draft chapters and offered insightful comments and suggestions for improvement. At the University Press of Florida, I greatly appreciate the assistance of senior acquisitions editor Amy Gorelick and project editor Susan Albury who skillfully guided the project through the publication process; the anonymous readers who made recommendations for strengthening it; and copyeditor Nevil Parker for her meticulous attention to detail. I also thank the editors of *L'Esprit créateur* and the *Journal of Haitian Studies* for permission to reprint in revised and expanded form material that originally appeared under their auspices. *Merci* to Lucien Lemoine, who generously agreed to let me reproduce his poem, "Cannibale, oui!" in its entirety. For their encouragement and unwavering support, I thank and cherish longtime friends Carol Cherry, Signithia Fordham, and Cheryl Wall.

Finally, special recognition goes to my incredible family, my refuge from work: mother Naomi Larrier and sister Diane Collier, each one the epitome of womanhood and whose exquisite needlework (quilts, most recently) has always represented the loving care and craft of *collages textîles*; nephew Matthew Collier and niece Melanie Collier, now successful adults, but who always welcomed me as part of their nuclear family. A source of inspiration, they can indeed dance!

Introduction

Caribbean *Identity* Poetics

Subjectivity, *I-mage*, Collage

*l'aube du troisième millénaire, nous assistons
à l'émergence de populations postnationales.
[At the dawn of the third millenium, we are
witnessing the emergence of postnational populations.]*
Joël Des Rosiers, *Théories caraïbes*

*Martinique is a bewildering place; it is, in my experience,
more French than Paris—just slightly darker.*
Stuart Hall, "Negotiating Caribbean Identities"

Antonio Benitez-Rojo theorizes that the Caribbean novel has "a will to set itself up at all costs as a total performance. This performance ... can be carried out under the roles of several kinds of spectacles: variety shows, circus acts, dramatic works, radio or television programs, concerts, operettas, carnival dances, or any other kind of spectacle that one can imagine" (218). To those major frameworks we can add oral storytelling and traditional dance, for they are also characteristic of the region. While the former has often been cited as the foundation of Caribbean writing, the latter, dance, has been discussed much less often in relation to literature.[1] What Jamaican cultural theorist, dancer, and choreographer Rex Nettleford notes about dance—that it is "'part of a society's ancestral and existential reality ... one of the most effective means of communication, revealing many profound truths about complex social forces operative in a society groping toward both material and spiritual betterment'"—is also applicable to literature in the Caribbean (qtd. in Taylor 1–2). That dance reveals "profound truths about complex social forces" is also comparable to Edouard Glissant's concept of *détour*, a strategy of indirection in a colonial or dominated society. In this study, I combine Benitez-Rojo's statement about Caribbean fiction as performance, Nettleford's privileging of dance's heritage, context, and interaction, and Glissant's *la Relation* and *détour* in order to argue that *danmyé*, a combat dance tradition in Martinique, offers a framework for reading Francophone Caribbean texts.[2] My analysis uses danmyé, also known as *laghia* in the southern part of the island, with all of the tensions inherent in the juxtapositions of combat dance, its articulation of narrative, and its embodiment of Relation and *détour*. Some protagonists utilize the collective ethos, feints, offensive and defensive moves of Martinique's danmyé masters, while others are abandoned alone in the *ronde*.[3]

What exactly is danmyé? It is much more than the sum of its parts: dance, martial art, song, and percussion. Reminiscent of Brazilian capoeira, danmyé is a simulated fight, a competition in which men display their strength and dexterity, although women are said to have been practitioners also. One combatant enters and circles the ronde—the ring formed by the spectators who clap their hands in rhythm—and presents himself to the drummer who he hopes will choose to support him over challengers. A challenger joins the combatant in the ronde as the *tambouyé* hits the drum with the *ti-bwa*, a pair of percussive, wooden sticks, inspiring, supporting, and coordinating the dancers' movements. The dancers relate to each other as well as to the tambouyé. Positioned behind the drummer, the singers—a soloist and *répondés*—alternate vocalizations on a call-and-response model. The dancers "fight" without landing blows. Some of the movements are codified or traditional, while others are improvised. The dancers' steps and the tambouyé's rhythm change in relation to each other. The objective of this simulated combat is not to harm the adversary, but to display power and ability to attack and anticipate, although it is believed that in its earliest incarnation in the slavery period, danmyé involved actual fighting during *swarès danmyé*, gatherings held for that purpose. Here, the combatants were prepared physically (by the oiling of their bodies) and psychologically (through initiation by elders), and the best competitors earned the title of *majò* (meaning major, with military and leadership resonances; *être majò* in French means to be the first). Sometimes during a *laghia de la mort*, two adversaries used razors hidden between their toes to settle a score. Banned by the authorities, the laghia de la mort was driven underground only to resurface as the simulated combat, danmyé. Since the 1950s, however, with the disappearance of the *swarès danmyé*, the combat dance relocated to the performance venues of fairs and the annual carnival. At the same time, the dance aspect superseded the combat element. That the dance/martial art lexicon is represented in the Creole rather than another language reflects race, color, and class stratifications. Considered by certain segments of society as too "African," danmyé, for a long time associated with field workers and the urban poor, was thus stigmatized and largely forgotten as many people tried to distance themselves from the past.[4]

Danmyé can be considered a predominately male activity in that the fighters/dancers, drummers, and instrumentalists are men. The ronde, therefore, serves as an informal space in which masculinity is performed. Linden Lewis reminds us that several factors influence the ways Caribbean men construct their masculinity:

> the cultural milieu within which they operate; the ideological role of the state, that is, the ways in which the state contributes to the formation of social identities; the specific political, economic and historical conditions; the myriad ways in which race, ethnicity, class, sexual orientation, and religion mediate these various practices. The construction of masculinity is a multi-layered phenomenon. No longer can we settle for a one-dimensional view suggesting that men define themselves exclusively through, for example, their work. The process of masculine construction is much more nuanced. (122)

Lewis brings up some excellent points. Given that the region formerly consisted of slave societies, even after abolition men had to negotiate the spaces between patriarchy and masculinity. Gender expectations of autonomy, power, and duty to protect women and children, for example, were not available to black men, who had to construct a masculine identity in other ways.[5]

Because the black male body was read as threatening by the dominant colonial society, many overt expressions of masculinity were suppressed. Along with cockfighting, which also simulated war, for many years, danmyé was one of the few sites available for masculine identity performance.[6] As such, danmyé requires no expensive equipment, costumes, special arenas, or trained animals. Danmyé could certainly be considered an example of "resistant masculinity," a cultural force generated in response to gender oppression, as defined by Darlene Clark Hine and Earnestine Jenkins. The concern with masculinity also emerges in Aimé Césaire's *Cahier d'un retour au pays natal* as the poet invokes "sang viril" (manly blood); "élan viril" (a virility rush); "le coeur mâle du soleil" (the male heart of the sun); "ma prière virile" (my virile prayer); and demands to be transformed: "Faites de moi un homme de terminaison / Faites de moi un homme d'initiation / Faites de moi un homme de recueillement / Mais faites de moi un homme d'ensemencement." [Make me a man of ending / Make me a man of beginning / Make me a man of harvesting / But also make me a man of sowing] (42–58/70–86). Some *négritude* writers' preoccupation with masculinity ended up writing women out of the equation.[7] My utilization of danmyé as metaphor, however, is not gender restricted.

Scholars agree that danmyé has African origins from the slavery era, but differ on whether the practice comes from the west or central region. David Eltis and his team of historians noted that among the more than 138,000 Africans loaded onto French ships—almost 40 percent from the Bight of Benin—116,000 disembarked in Martinique.[8] These figures, however, do not account for smuggling, nor do they take into account that Martinique was a transit point as well as a destination (Harms 409–10). Historian Bernard Moitt argues that not all the one and one half million Africans brought to the French colonies in the Caribbean—more than half to colonial Saint Domingue—arrived on French ships (*Women* 20).[9] Neither raw numbers nor estimates account for the survival and adaptation of certain cultural practices. Nevertheless, because a large number of Africans embarked from the port of Ouidah, dance historian Josy Michalon traveled to Benin to conduct research among the Basantchés people whose annual July yam festival closes with a ceremony called *kadjia*. T. J. Desch-Obi contends on the other hand that a Central African martial art gave rise to danmyé as well as to Brazilian capoeira.[10] Whichever theory of origin one accepts, it is on the plantation that this cultural practice was transformed through creolization, the dynamic process that has an unpredictable outcome according to Edouard Glissant. Enslaved peoples from various ethnic groups utilized danmyé in order to "contourner la loi du silence" (get around the rule of silence) on the plantation (*Poétique* 83/68–69). Over time, danmyé evolved from an aggressive practice of settling a score to a benign sport, entertainment. Reclaimed by some contemporary urbanites, it has reemerged and is performed locally and worldwide.

For a long time, danmyé has aroused the interest of ethnologists, cultural workers, travel writers, novelists, and filmmakers alike. Eighteenth and nineteenth-century visitors to Martinique like Père Labat and Lafcadio Hearn chronicled their impressions in books that were translated into many languages.[11] In 1936, as part of a research trip to the Caribbean, dancer and anthropologist Katherine Dunham filmed demonstrations of danmyé in Martinique.[12] Upon her return to the United States, she penned two articles for *Esquire* magazine and choreographed a ballet called *L'Ag'Ya*, which premiered in Chicago in 1938. In the last section of the thirty-two-minute ballet, Alcide is killed after challenging Julot to a *laghia* over a woman, Loulouse, the character danced by Dunham.[13] More recently, Eric Pagès filmed a documentary entitled *Combat damyé* (2001) that makes the rounds of independent film festivals.

Moreover, on the local level, danmyé is sustained on several fronts. Included at carnival and patronal festivals, it has also found a home at the Service Municipal d'Action Culturelle (SERMAC), a city agency in Fort-de-France that sponsors workshops and demonstrations. Groups like L'AM4 (Mi Mes Manmay Matinik)—an association devoted to the study, practice, and preservation of Martinican music, dance, and martial arts—are exceptionally active in the resurgence and survival of danmyé. Not only offering classes, organizing performances, and publishing an illustrated brochure—*Asou Chimen danmyé: propositions sur le danmyé en Martinique*—L'AM4 is also instrumental in the expansion of danmyé to a global audience. For example, a group of its *danmyétistes* were invited to participate in a conference entitled "Overflow, geste sportif/geste artistique" at L'Université de Paris 8 in December 1999. Looking far beyond the folkloric and tourist-level possibilities of danmyé, L'AM4 is committed to serious research, preservation, and expansion beyond Martinique. Web sites dedicated to danmyé have also increased its international presence.[14]

How is danmyé relevant to fiction? On the most basic level, it appears in twentieth-century Martinican prose. Raphaël Confiant's oeuvre has evolved from including minor characters who are champions of danmyé—in *Eau de café*, *Le Nègre et l'amiral*, and *L'Allée des soupirs*—to centering on the investigation into the murder of a danmyé champion, Romule Beausoleil, the pride of Morne Pichevin, on the eve of a match against a rival from another neighborhood in *Le Meurtre du Samedi-Gloria* (1997). Moreover, while danmyé has resurfaced in recent novels by Confiant, Chamoiseau, and Marcel-François Rapon, Joseph Zobel beat them to the punch, so to speak. The short story "Laghia de la mort," which also provides the title of the 1946 collection, is pertinent to this discussion on both literal and figurative levels. On the one hand, Valère challenges his estranged father Gertal, a champion danmyétiste, to a public match that also narrates their relationship. On the other hand, the ronde becomes the only site of communication between father and son as the combat dance substitutes for dialogue. What the two men cannot express in words, they perform. Although Gertal and Valère manage to connect on a level that heretofore had been impossible, the audience boos because they are unwilling to fight to the death. In another short story entitled "Josephine," from the collection *Le Soleil partagé* (1964), Zobel creates a minor character Témistocle who embodies stereotypical masculinity. He is a seducer, a cockfight fan, and a "vaillant danseur de laghia" (brave dancer of laghia) (95). The combat dance is also resurrected in *La Fête à Paris* (1953), the sequel to *La Rue Cases-Nègres*, republished under the title *Quand la neige aura fondu* in 1979, in which a white man, who taught in Martinique for fourteen years, remarks to the protagonist about an exhibition that he witnessed in Trois-Ilets, "J'ai rarement vu spectacle d'une telle intensité et d'une telle variété d'émotions. Vraiment!" (9). [I have rarely seen a show of such intensity and such a variety of emotions. Really!] This moment of insight, however, is offset by the sojourner's insensitive remark about his ship companion's skin color: "On n'est guère foncé comme vous en Martinique" (8). [Hardly anyone is as dark as you in Martinique.]

My task in this study is not to analyze Martinican novels in which danmyé appears, but to apply the combat dance's principles of narration, initiation, challenge, confrontation, interaction, surprise, anticipation, improvisation, resistance, positionality, displacement, balance, and negotiation to texts from Martinique, Guadeloupe, and Haiti, each of which, along with other Caribbean societies, has its own combat dance tradition.[15] In this endeavor, I limit myself to first-person texts, very common in Francophone Caribbean fiction, which at first glance may appear incompatible with danmyé, which features multiple participants in constant motion. As we shall see, however, in these first-person texts the narrator is positioned, without establishing a fixed center, in relation to someone else inside or outside the story, which mimics the reciprocity of the combat dance. I will analyze danmyé's tropes in works by Joseph Zobel, Maryse Condé, Edwidge Danticat, Patrick Chamoiseau, and Gisèle Pineau.

Caribbean literature is rife with first-person narrators: autobiographical and fictional, autodiegetic and multivoiced, male and female, young and old, rural and urban, literate and unschooled, traumatized and resilient, boastful and modest, observant and unseeing. This privileging of the *I* in Caribbean prose literature is one direct response to particular historical circumstances. The dispossession that resulted from slavery and its legacy of economic exploitation makes challenging the dominant discourse urgent. For one, first-person narratives narrow the gap created since the colonial period during which travelers' diaries, government documents, handbooks for male settlers, and colonial literature constructed an image of the Caribbean that excluded the perspective of the majority population.[16] Caribbean autofiction challenges the authority of travel narratives that for a long time were among the few first-person accounts about the Caribbean. Since the sixteenth century, these chronicles were written by those who encountered societies different from their own. Professing local knowledge, they actually offer a perspective based on sojourn as opposed to settlement, observation by the minority rather than lived experience of the majority; prior to 1800, there were three times as many Africans as Europeans transported to the Americas and four times as many African women as European women.[17] Writings by Lafcadio Hearn and Moreau de Saint-Méry come to mind most readily.

The scarcity of visual and aural evidence challenging the *grand Récit* (the master narrative), makes the need for a Caribbean first-person perspective all the more compelling. Unacknowledged, unrecorded, unpublicized, or suppressed information about slavery led Edouard Glissant to assert that it was a struggle without witnesses: "l'esclavage comme combat sans témoin" (*Discours* 277). Dany Bébel-Gisler and the *créolistes* utilize the metaphor of a buried Caribbean history, while Michel-Rolph Trouillot cites the erasure for more than a century of the defeat of Napoleon's troops by Haitian revolutionaries as one of history's most salient events, as a deliberate "silencing of the past" due to uneven power relations: "Silences enter the process of historical production at four crucial moments: the moment of fact creation (the making of *sources*); the moment of fact assembly (the making of *archives*); the moment of fact retrieval (the making of *narratives*); and the moment of retrospective significance (the making of *history* in the final instance)" (26).[18]

Appropriation of the *I/Eye* inscribes subjectivity, making the previous object of discourse, the subject. It diverts, in part, the dominant gaze exposed in Frantz Fanon's *Peau noire, masques blancs*, which is predicated on curious observation of the colonial subject that results in hypercritical scrutiny, judgments of inferiority, erotic displacements, and scorn as suggested in Mary Louise Pratt's title *Imperial Eyes*. Lafcadio Hearn is one such traveler who demonstrates a voyeuristic, nostalgic, and erotic discourse in *Two Years in the French West Indies* as he gazes at the "dark swordsmen" at work: "the men wield their cutlasses so beautifully that it is a delight to watch them. One cannot often enjoy such a spectacle nowadays; for the introduction of the piece-work system has destroyed the picturesqueness of plantation labor throughout the island, with rare exceptions" (275). Conversely, inscriptions of the *I/Eye* in Caribbean autofiction intersect with danmyé in which the combatant avoids looking his adversary in the eye: "Ne pas regarder dans les yeux permet de ne pas être dominé mentalement, de ne pas subir la force qui se transmet par le regard. Il suffit d'être dominé mentalement pour perdre le combat" (Bertelli 18). [Not looking the opponent in the eye allows you not to be dominated mentally nor undergo the force that is transmitted by the gaze. When you are mentally dominated, you lose the fight.][19] The Caribbean *I/Eye* originates from within the community and thus benefits from insider knowledge, resists the dominating gaze, bears witness (*témoignage*), and transmits ancestral memory; in other words, it is a model for Glissant's notion of *relie, relaie,* and *relate* (link, relay, and relate) as articulated in *Poétique de la*

Relation (183–88). The narrators of these texts are not only concerned with observing without fixing the object of the gaze, but with committing what they see, hear, or experience to memory for later transmission. By controlling their own story or one entrusted to them, they bear witness to the past, a past that denied them voice.

Témoignage overlaps with Trinidadian/Canadian poet M. Nourbese Philip's *i-mage* that she theorizes in her essay "The Absence of Writing or How I Almost Became a Spy." The unconventional spelling of *i-mage* is rooted in the Rastafarian practice of privileging the *I* in many words. The creative writer/*I-mage* maker (she, according to Philip), is in a position of power to broaden and enrich the scope of representation with new metaphorical language (43–49). By extension, subjectivity resonates in the text as the narrator recounts heretofore untold stories from a Caribbean perspective.

As we shall see, the *I* in Caribbean literature assumes an audience (or a reader) and has its roots in cultural practices in which danmyé is a model, but not the only one. A similar pattern of interaction between soloist and *répondeurs* occurs in a storytelling session or *parole de nuit* in which the opening protocol—*krik?*—requires the listeners to respond *krak!* The *conteur* (storyteller) can interject *krik?* at any time during the *séance* to make sure that the audience remains attentive. The call-and-response model also operates during a Haitian *coumbite* (collective labor for the harvest) as the *simidor* paces the work(ers) with his drum and song. Another domain of reciprocity is the Haitian Creole greeting *honè* that anticipates the reply, *respè*. This strategy appears in *Solibo Magnifique*, *Chemin-d'école*, and *Texaco* in which Chamoiseau reproduces the communal experience in spite of the first-person narrator, who is as conscious of his reader as the conteur is of his listener. For example, in *Chemin-d'école* where the primary narrator Oiseau de Cham is complemented by the répondeurs, I believe Chamoiseau strategically offsets Edouard Glissant's critique of the isolation that characterizes reading. This layering of different voices calls to mind a collage. While the créolistes use the images of kaleidoscope and mosaic to describe Caribbean identity, I favor the collage metaphor in talking about literature, because it embodies multiple narrators, different perspectives, fragmented memories, mixing of genres and settings and because it acknowledges the interplay of languages—Creole and French—and of what Chamoiseau labels *sentimenthèque*, that is, the influences of other writers, ancestors, and previous texts on one's work.[20] Moreover, collage appeals to the visual as well as the tactile senses.[21] In some of the texts studied, the first-person narrator is a danmyétiste who challenges, improvises, resists, and negotiates the terrain.

In so doing, he or she offers perceptions of Caribbean people heretofore unexplored, while advocating for those previously excluded.

*I*dentity

Geography, history, and culture converge in defining the Caribbean. Historian Oruno D. Lara argues that the Caribbean includes not only the islands, but the coastal areas of North and South America where Africans were transported during the slave trade. This space is designated by others in ways that are linguistically determined and thus restrictive. The French use "Antilles" to refer to their *départements d'outre-mer* (overseas departments) in the Caribbean Sea—that is, Martinique, Guadeloupe, and also "Guyane," for French Guiana rests on the South American continent. Their affiliation with France also qualifies them as part of the European Union. The French Antilles configuration, however, excludes Haiti, which was also once a French colony—in fact, a *vieille* [old] *colonie* that has been independent since 1804.[22] I agree with Roger Toumson who argues in favor of grouping Haiti along with the French departments because they share a similar cultural and historical heritage (*Transgression* 34–36). *West Indies* usually refers to the English-speaking islands and *Netherlands Antilles* to Dutch-speaking areas, while the Spanish-speaking Dominican Republic and Cuba are subsumed into Latin America. I prefer to use the more inclusive term, *the Caribbean*, because it designates a geographical space that experienced particular, multiple histories of settlement, genocide, colonization, plantation slavery, and indentured servitude under British, French, Spanish, Danish, and Portuguese imperialism. It includes independent nations and dependencies, along with the U.S. Virgin Islands whose regional identity is reflected in gatherings such as the biennial on contemporary Caribbean dance to which Venezuela and Florida also send representatives.

Some writers and scholars combine geography and metaphor in their definitions of the Caribbean. Suzanne Césaire refers to the half-circle formed by the archipelago ("Camouflage" 267), while Eugène Revert calls it a garland (25). Inspired by meteorologists, Raphaël Confiant borrows the phrase *bassin des ouragans* (hurricane basin). Aimé Césaire compares the islands' position in the sea to an umbilical cord, a living, apprehensive protector who nourishes her twins, the American continents: "L'archipel arqué comme le désir inquiet de se nier, on dirait une anxiété maternelle pour protéger la ténuité plus délicate qui sépare l'une de l'autre Amérique." [This archipelago arched with anxiety as though to deny itself, as though she were a mother anxious to protect the tenuous delicacy with which her two Americas are joined] (*Cahier* 24/52). Other creative writers blend geography, topography, and commentary in their description of individual islands. That Guadeloupe resembles a butterfly led Gisèle Pineau to entitle her children's book *Un papillon dans la cité*. Confiant's configuring of Martinique as a fetus harks back to Aimé Césaire, but with an important difference. Suggesting the island's colonial status through metaphor, he accentuates its dependency on France.

Bertène Juminer links location and identity when he poses the following basic questions: "Car ici se situe, pour tout homme de la Caraïbe, une incontournable problématique collective: qui sommes-nous? D'où venons-nous? Où allons-nous et pour quoi faire?" (132). [Because here is a collective and inescapable problem for every Caribbean person: who are we? Where do we come from? Where are we going and to do what?] Juminer declares that the answer lies, in part, in oral stories for children that foster integration into the group, encourage intimacy between the elderly and the young, and transmit collective memory. I would like to extend his argument to say that explorations of identity can be found in all literatures for all ages. As Stuart Hall writes: "it is only through the way in which we represent and imagine ourselves that we come to know how we are constituted and who we are" ("What" 30).

Contemporary cultural theorists agree on the complexity and fluidity of Caribbean identity, rejecting the binaries of colonizer/colonized, black/white, male/female, literate/illiterate, rural/urban, and resident/immigrant. Not always clearly defined, these categories shift and overlap as A. James Arnold observes in the prologue to his *Modernism and Negritude: The Poetry of Aimé Césaire*. The conjunction in the title "Being Black and Being French" signals simultaneously inclusive and exclusive identities, belying the ostensive neatness of the French policy of assimilation that tried to make black Frenchmen out of its colonial subjects. In addition, some sons of European men and enslaved African women in Saint Domingue became slaveholders themselves; peasants migrated to the cities; individuals who cannot read or write French possess historical knowledge that should be recorded in books; large numbers of Haitians voluntarily and involuntarily left the republic, creating a Haitian "dyaspora." Stuart Hall summarizes the forces driving the complexity of Caribbean identity as "Partly because of the dislocations of conquest, of colonization and slavery, partly because of the colonial relationship itself and the distortions of living in a world culturally dependent on and dominated by some centre outside the place where the majority of the people lived" ("Negotiating" 25). The coming together of various cultures is an encounter that Edouard Glissant refers to as a *choc* (shock), a term that also acknowledges the violence accompanying the meeting as well as the ever-changing dynamic that produces a *chaosmonde*.[23]

The Caribbean population is composed of the descendants of Africans, Europeans, Asians, and to a lesser extent Amerindians, all involved in an ongoing, never-static cultural transformation. Moreover, within these foundational groups there was also immense variety, an important fact that Richard Price and Sally Price observe is overlooked by the créolistes (130).[24] Africans, for example, not only hailed from both western and central regions of the continent, but within those locations belonged to various ethnic, cultural, religious, and linguistic groups. Still, so many people of African descent comprised the majority population of the French Caribbean that Michel-Rolph Trouillot can categorically state that "Saint-Domingue and Martinique were not simply societies that had slaves: they were *slave societies*. Slavery defined their economic, social, and cultural organization: it was their raison d'être. The people who lived there, free or not, lived there because there were slaves" (18). Asian Indians were recruited to replace former slave laborers after abolition in 1848. Their presence in the French Caribbean is disproportionate as more of them came to Guadeloupe (42,000) than to Martinique (25,000) during the second half of the nineteenth century (Léti 72). French Guiana, the most multicultural among the French Caribbean territories, has, in addition to its African, European, and Indian descendants, twentieth-century immigrants from Suriname, Indonesia, China, Brazil, and Laos.[25]

Creolization is the operative word, the accepted concept that not only characterizes Caribbean culture, but increasingly the world's populations as well. Oruno D. Lara argues forcefully against the binary European/Other construct operating in French society. In *Caraïbes en construction: espace, colonisation, résistance*, he observes that by excluding people of color, the category *métropolitain* becomes inherently a racial category (19). Although Gisèle Pineau was born in France, for example, she was not considered a *métropolitaine* as a child. She was taunted by her white classmates precisely because she was different from them: "Bamboula! Négresse à plateau! Retourne dans ton pays!" ("Ecrire" 290). [Bamboula! Tray-carrying black woman! Go back to your country!]; these were the race-based insults hurled at her in the neighborhood and in school. Race and color trump birthplace where French identity is concerned.

How the Caribbean is perceived depends upon the way it is represented, upon the promotion of particular images or the imposition of rigid formulas. Edouard Glissant confronts the confounding of his island with Tahiti in the very first sentence of *Le Discours antillais*: "La Martinique n'est pas une île de la

Polynésie. Tant de gens le croient. [Martinique is not a Polynesian island. This is, however, the belief of so many people] (11/1). In fact, Martinique and Guadeloupe are lodged in the Western imaginary as indistinguishable vacation destinations, French Guiana as a former penal colony and site of the space shuttle *Ariane*, and Haiti as a hotbed of poverty and instability. The marketing experts in the Hexagon cultivate images of sun, sand, and sex to encourage tourism in the French Caribbean *départements*, while Haiti resists, unsuccessfully, those imposed on it.

As early as 1931, according to Théodore Baude, the Martinique pavilion at the Exposition Coloniale Internationale de Paris was designed to promote tourism. Reading his 1932 chronicle of the event, one also concludes that the island was marketed to accentuate the wealth it provided the empire. At the pavilion, the colony's most important agricultural products were prominently displayed. A banana tree and sugarcane leaves stationed at the entrance to the building greeted visitors, appealing to their sense of taste. Machinery and materials used in the process of converting sugarcane into sugar and rum for consumption in the metropole and dioramas and photographs of factories and refineries were displayed as signs of French ingenuity. The human dimension of crop cultivation was represented by the photograph "Chargement d'un wagon de cannes à sucre" (Loading a Sugarcane Wagon) (Baude 21). While the title is innocent enough, a reading of the image reveals a more sinister story of power dynamics. Three men, made faceless with their backs to camera, load sugarcane onto wagons. Near them, sporting European-styled dark hats in contrast to the laborers' straw *bakouas*, two other men bear the insignias of authority. One, wearing a jacket and standing on a platform with a stick, appears to give orders by pointing his finger. The other man, though jacketless, wields a rifle. They are clearly in charge.

Not shown, interestingly, were images of women working the cane fields, when, in fact, they performed field labor. Instead, women were represented at the 1931 exhibition as wax-figured, *madras*-wearing domestic workers, a form of display that perhaps invited physical contact, an indication of their vulnerability to unwelcome hands. Visitors could imagine them working in the replica of Josephine Tascher de la Pagerie's lavish bedroom on display inside the pavilion. The wood furniture, a rug, souvenirs, and a picture of the plantation reminded guests that Napoleon Bonaparte's first wife was born in Martinique. Her private space was a microcosm of France's political, social, and economic systems, which were dependent on slave labor.

Some Caribbean countries are like the United States, complicit in selling colonial nostalgia by converting former plantations into tourist sites.[26] In his analysis of the marriage of economics and entertainment in the Bahamas, Ian Gregory Strachan concludes that the official media strategy—brochures with smiling servants and matronly market women—articulates an ideal of service and subordination. In *Paradise and Plantation: Tourism and Culture in the Anglophone Caribbean*, Strachan speculates that the hotel is the new plantation: "Like the plantation, the tourism industry becomes a monopolizer of land, in this case, the shorelines rather than the farmlands" (8–9). To attract vacationers and their leisure dollars, some countries resort to marketing strategies that appear to minimize their autonomy, cultivating images of deferent cultures that, in effect, appeal to an antebellum mentality of supremacy and entitlement.

In the 1950s, Haiti enjoyed a brief period as a favored destination for tourists, a distinction it lost with the changing political climate. Haiti did, however, seize other opportunities to project a favorable national image. At the entrance to its first freestanding pavilion at the 1893 World's Columbian Exposition in Chicago, Haiti asserted its sovereignty, displaying its flag along with engraved insignia of its independent nationhood on the portico. Bearing Haiti's coat-of-arms and the motto "L'union fait la force" (in unity, strength), the portico proclaimed "République haïtienne" in gold letters with the dates commemorating Columbus's first visit, the anniversary of his landing, and the year marking Haiti's independence: 1492, 1892, and 1804. Inside the building, portraits of presidents and pictures of government buildings further defined Haiti's standing. Moreover, that its pavilion was situated between the Canadian and German pavilions, away from the ethnic displays on the midway, cemented its status as an equal partner among Western nations. While Haitian popular culture was conspicuously absent, newspapers and books by local scholars were prominently displayed, while needlework showcased Haitian women's creativity. Samples of mahogany, millet, rice, bananas, and coffee signaled the abundance of Haiti's forests and the variety of its crops. Artifacts were exhibited for their representational power. Toussaint-Louverture's sword, for example, served as a reminder of the successful revolution. President Hyppolite appointed former minister resident and consul general Frederick Douglass to serve as external commissioner. A fervent defender of Haiti in speeches around the country, Douglass was in attendance from the opening of the pavilion in June through October 1893, his presence lending an air of glory and grandeur to the space.[27] Such temporary and transitory moments, however, did not transform Haiti's overall reputation, which differs markedly from that of the other Caribbean islands.

Articulations of Caribbean identity have evolved during the last century, from négritude, an African diasporic construct, to *antillanité* and *guyanité*, which, more narrowly regional, respond to particular historical moments. *Métissage*, an outgrowth of *antillanité*, posits the synthesis of two disparate elements, African and European, which is precisely one of its shortcomings.[28] Relying on an assimilationist, neither/nor paradigm, métissage also tends to ignore the multiple cultural strands—the West and East Indian, for instance—that inform Caribbean identity. Frantz Fanon's theory of lactification (*Peau noire, masques blancs*) and Jean Price-Mars's *bovarysme collectif* consider Caribbean identity in terms of different forms of psychological and cultural alienation wrought by French hegemony. Since the 1980s, Caribbean identity has become less an issue of racial mixing or assimilation, than of creolization. Glissant's theories about Caribbean identity have progressed from métissage to creolisation and finally to Relation, a global phenomenon where identity discovered in "relationship and interaction with other multiracial New World cultures" also provides a model for narrative (Ormerod, "Martinican" 2). The créolistes Patrick Chamoiseau, Raphaël Confiant, and Jean Bernabé formulate a theory of Caribbean identity in *Eloge de la créolité* predicated on Glissant's writings, but take them to the extreme, risking a new essentialism by defining a Creole identity. The importance of identity negotiations to Caribbean cultural experience appears not only among intellectuals but in popular celebrations as well. During the four-day annual carnival, identities are subverted and mocked—without hiding their sexes, men dress as pregnant women, women as men, while classes cross as servants become royalty. Carnival thus provides a space for identity negotiations among the collective populace.

Who, then, is the Francophone Caribbean *I* in the twenty-first century? Joël Des Rosiers says that postnational identities characterize today's world. What distinguishes Martinican from Guadeloupean from Haitian culture? Some scholars argue that they are differentiated by practices such as danmyé, *gwo-ka* (traditional Guadeloupian drumming and music), and *vodou* respectively. How do individuals see their relation to the Hexagon? Musician, Kali (Jean-Marc Monnerville), for one, addresses that question in his "Reggae DOM-TOM," composed with Rémi Bellenchombre. Strumming his banjo, Kali sings, with much irony:

> Ils se sont penchés sur mon berceau
> Et m'ont couvert de leur drapeau
> Me prenant jusqu'à mon destin
> J'aurais dû rester orphelin . . .

[They leaned over my cradle
They covered me with their flag
Even taking over my destiny
I should have remained an orphan . . .]

Kali's lament critiques the *domien*'s (resident of an overseas department) image as a child controlled by smothering parents. Patrick Chamoiseau goes further and questions the ability to write creatively under oppressive psychological conditions, under an invisible power: "comment écrire, dominé?" (*Ecrire* 17).

Migration can further problematize identity. Although the Caribbean population is highly mobile, changing location does not necessarily mean relinquishing local identity. Moving to the Hexagon has often been an option, especially for elite males. During the colonial period, some sons of French *colons* (colonists) and enslaved women were sent to France to complete their educations. *Affranchis* (freed men) and their descendants—Haitians such as Probus Louis Blot, Louis Borno, and Henri Chauvet—attended French universities in the nineteenth century. During both world wars, Martinicans and Guadeloupeans served in the French armed services.[29] At the time of *Légitime Défense* (1932) and *L'Etudiant noir* (1934), literary journals foundational to the négritude movement, Caribbean male students outnumbered their female counterparts in Paris. In his groundbreaking study *The Practice of Diaspora*, Brent Hayes Edwards reinserts Paulette Nardal and other women into the 1930s Paris scene, revealing their roles as much more than salon hosts, but as agents of social and cultural change. After World War II, immigration was institutionalized with the establishment of the Bureau pour le Développement des Migrations des Départements d'Outre-Mer (BUMIDOM). Following the lead of their predecessors, many writers traveled to the metropole after the war, like Martinicans Joseph Zobel and Mayotte Capécia who sailed to France in 1946. Zobel relocated to Senegal in 1957, returning to France in 1977 to retire. Myriam Warner-Vieyra left Guadeloupe at age twelve, lived in France, married, and moved to Senegal. For others, relocation involved only temporary stays abroad: Patrick Chamoiseau spent ten years in the hexagon and Raphaël Confiant, six. At the same time, Antilleans demonstrated their allegiance by voting overwhelmingly for Christiane Taubira, a delegate to the National Assembly from French Guiana, when she ran for the presidency of the republic during the last election. All in all, the large increase in voluntary migration to France in the mid-twentieth century complicated the mix, leading to the creation of new terms—*négropolitain, négzagonal, la troisème île,* and *Euro-black*.[30]

Displacement due to exile has extended Haiti's national boundaries as many of its citizens relocated elsewhere for political or economic reasons. Coups d'état (more than thirty at this writing) and political repression forced many activists, journalists, government opponents, dictators, and ordinary citizens to flee for their safety. At different times in the nineteenth and twentieth centuries, Anténor Firmin and Emeric Bergeaud were exiled in Saint Thomas and President Jean-Bertrand Aristide in South Africa. During the Duvalier regimes, the exodus became especially acute: René Depestre fled to Mexico, Gérard Etienne to Canada, Jean Dominique and Marie Chauvet to New York. Following the first coup that deposed Aristide, thousands of individuals crowded onto boats hoping to reach Florida, but were either turned back by the U.S. Coast Guard or detained at Guantanamo or other sites until their cases for asylum were heard. After her husband Jean Dominique's assassination in 2001 and subsequent attempts on her life, Michèle Montas fled to New York for safety.[31] In the 1960s, other Haitians left the island to provide expertise as engineers and civil servants in the newly independent Francophone West and Central African countries. For one, Raoul Peck's father, an agronomist, moved the family to the Congo. Peck's memories and impressions from his childhood infuse his documentary *Lumumba: la mort d'un Prophète* (1992) and the more recent film *Lumumba* (2002).

Whether exile or migration is responsible for displacement, because so many Haitians have relocated, new terms have been created: *dyaspora*, *half-generation*, *second generation*, and *tenth department*, which extends the nation's nine administrative districts. Large cities like Miami, New York, Montreal, and Paris have sizable Haitian populations able to support their own activities, from Radio Concorde in Boston to the Maison d'Haiti in Paris. The Miss Haiti International pageant brings these communities together every year. Sometimes Haitians abroad are stereotyped by gender and work: cab drivers in Brooklyn, sugarcane workers in the Dominican Republic, women market vendors in Fort-de-France. Sending millions of dollars home, Haitians abroad are too powerful to be ignored. They were formally recognized in the 1987 constitution, which confers citizenship on those whose parents were born in Haiti, taking into consideration the generation born on foreign soil. Circular migration within the Caribbean is also a reality, as I mentioned earlier. Henry Christophe was born in Grenada; Stéphen Alexis was exiled in Venezuela, and Camille Bruno in Jamaica. Temporary exile notwithstanding, historically other young men were routinely sent to France for higher education. Azade Seyhan has coined the phrase "writing outside the nation" and Abdelkébir Khatibi, the "professional traveller," both expressions relevant to this discussion.[32]

Unfixed, multiple or plural identities are the order of the day in postcolonial scholarship in general and Francophone Caribbean studies in particular, seeking to come to terms with the implications of historical and present-day displacements upon constructions of Caribbean identity. René Depestre theorizes *multiples ailleurs* (multiple elsewheres) and *identité banyan* (banyan identity) (42). Joël Des Rosiers calls for a testing of identities, "tester les identités" (182), a process Maryse Condé explores in her fiction as her characters travel far from home. In her novel *Histoire de la femme cannibale* (2004), the Guadeloupean protagonist accompanies her British husband to South Africa where she is mistaken for a Malian and an Ethiopian. In *Desirada* (1997), an extreme example of identity tested appears in Condé's character Ludovic, born in Cuba to a Haitian father who migrated to the United States, Canada, Germany, Mali, Mozambique, Belgium, and France. Arlette Minatchy-Bogat, a fourth generation Indo-Guadeloupean, exposes another layer in the collage of Caribbean identity by tracing Indian migration to the island in her historical novel *Terre d'exil et d'adoption* (2001). Travel, migration, and displacement are strongly implicated in Caribbean identity and resonate in its literature.[33]

Long before the plethora of theoretical writings in the 1980s, Caribbean identity was recognized as a complex issue. Both Anténor Firmin and Jean Price-Mars hinted at a Pan-Caribbean identity based on geography and shared history, and Suzanne Césaire prefigured the notion of creolization in a 1942 *Tropiques* article entitled "Malaise d'une civilisation." For centuries, however, the Caribbean *I* was co-opted and defined by a powerful minority. The 1685 Code Noir defined enslaved people as *meubles*, literally furniture, part of one's personal estate. According to Article 44, slaves were chattel denied human subjectivity and became part of the deceased owner's estate: "Déclarons les esclaves êtres meubles, et comme tels entrer en la communauté." [We declare slaves to be property and as such inheritable.] France boasted that slavery was not allowed on its soil, but what was banned from the metropole was entrenched and flourished in the colonies. In 1998, the 150th anniversary of the abolition of slavery was commemorated in France with great fanfare, but as historians continue to recuperate documents about slaving and slavery in the Atlantic World, what they find typically presents the European male perspective from which the voice of those enslaved is conspicuously absent. In *The Diligent: A Voyage through the Worlds of the Slave Trade*, historian Robert Harms foregrounds the journal of First Lieutenant Robert Durand during his 1731–1732 trip from Vannes, France, to Ouidah in Benin, to Saint Pierre, Martinique, and back to France. Though Durand was clearly an educated man, he was thoroughly indifferent to the humanity of the slaves in which he traded, mentioning them only twice, to tally up deaths, during a Middle Passage journey of more than two months. Similarly, Joseph Crassous de Médeuil's ship log covering the years 1772–1776 evinces the author's considerable blindness about the brutality of his business in human cargo.[34]

During the Caribbean slave centuries, planters also denied the humanity of forced laborers. In a September 12, 1841, journal entry, for example, Pierre Dessalles contrasts his daughter's sadness at the prospect of two burials in one day to "the negroes, on the other hand, [who] looked happy: a funeral is a party for them, and they have been busy getting their clothes ready since yesterday" (Forster and Forster 156).[35] Failing to grasp their meaning, Dessalles devalued the slaves' mourning rituals and misinterpreted their expressions of grief. During the celebratory phase of the *veillée* (wake), mourners tell stories, drink, dance, feast, and mimic the deceased outside his or her house, while inside, the family members somberly keep vigil over the body. Only seemingly antithetical, the emotions expressed by the two groups of mourners are complementary: a grievous loss for the family is simultaneously a joyful escape from slavery for the deceased. The goal of both expressions is to honor the dead. The laying out and wearing of fine clothes was not, as Dessalles misunderstood it, thoughtless frivolity, but an expression of respect for the dead.

Gisèle Pineau and Marie Abraham challenge eighteenth- and nineteenth-century travelers Hearn, Moreau de Saint-Méry, and Dessalles whose journals, travelogues, and papers constitute the Récit. *Femmes des Antilles, traces et voix* (1998), a collage of real and imagined lives, is their attempt to fill some of the gaps in an undeniably one-sided story.[36] In an exemplary case, from facts found in an 1845 report by statesman Victor Schoelcher, Pineau reconstructs a story in which Apolline tells of her suicide by drowning, her way of escaping her owner's wife's threats. Other short narratives recount the capture, Middle Passage journey, rape, sale at auction, and exploitation of Wassia, Bétani, Zanina, Clarisse, Marie-Tyrane, Honorine, and Emeline, reclaiming their stories and recuperating their identities without sparing white women's brutality. Beverly Bell, also mindful of the importance of women's speaking for themselves, interviewed thirty-eight peasant and poor urban women in the mid-1990s for *Walking on Fire: Haitian Women's Stories of Survival and Resistance*. Bell recorded, transcribed, and translated more than one hundred tapes, editing them collaboratively with the women whose full names, photographs, and firsthand testimonies produce gendered récits that stand in stark contrast to the muted voices and buried stories of their anonymous ancestors.

Léon Damas asserts a Caribbean *I* in a line of descent from African captives in the poem "Ils sont venus ce soir." The repetition of the first-person singular disjunctive pronoun "moi" in the line "Combien de / MOI MOI MOI sont morts" (how many / I I Is died) evokes, in its suggestion of an ongoing numeric series, the unknown millions of African ancestors who perished during the slave trade (13). It may also be that the repeated "moi" approximates stuttering, signaling the violent fracturing of the first-person voice that occurs in slavery. "Combien de moi" is also a homophone for "how many months" (mois), a metonymic indicator of the long duration of the slave trade.

Damas's poetic, backward looking *I*, at once plural and relational, prepares the way for Guy Deslauriers's *I*, a male voice-over who narrates the film *Le Passage du milieu* (1999). Dedicated to Africa, to those who were enslaved and their descendants, the film imagines the men and women who experienced the Middle Passage in the hold of the slave ship. As the story opens, the apparent disconnect between the boy who gazes silently out to sea and the adult male voice-over implicitly encompasses both the youngster's presence in the Americas and the hidden horrors the peaceful sea belies. The narrator recounts from memory his capture, sale, and deportation. Most of the film is set on the ship with very few sounds except for the narrator's voice, the noise of the shackles on deck and in the hold, and the ocean waves breaking against the ship. The story proceeds by moans, by mouths agape in horror, by vomiting, rats, and disease, by suicides, rebellions, and rape, by bodies thrown overboard, and darkness. Djimon Hounsou of *Amistad* fame brings a grave resonance to his narration of the English version. This West African actor, who brought Cinque to life, revives the Middle Passage's buried voices. He intones "on the twentieth day," providing a temporal marker of the journey in a phrase reminiscent of Damas's "combien de moi[s]" as he unfolds a perspective radically different from that recorded in Durand's and Crassous's slave ship logs.[37]

With its anaphoric structure, sections of Aimé Césaire's *Discours sur le colonialisme* (1950) also privilege the *I*:

> Moi, je parle de sociétés vidées d'elles-mêmes . . . Moi, je parle de milliers d'hommes sacrifiés au Congo-Océan. Je parle de ceux qui, à l'heure où j'écris, sont en train de creuser à la main le port d'Abidjan. Je parle de millions d'hommes arrachés à leurs dieux, à leur terre, à leurs habitudes, à leur vie, à la vie, à la danse, à la sagesse. Je parle de millions d'hommes à qui on a inculqué savamment la peur, le complexe d'infériorité, le tremblement, l'agenouillement, le désespoir, le larbinisme . . . (19)

[I am talking about societies drained of their essence... I am talking about thousands of men sacrificed to the Congo-Ocean. I am talking about those who, as I write this, are digging the harbor of Abidjan by hand. I am talking about millions of men torn from their gods, their land, their habits, their life, from life, from the dance, from wisdom. I am talking about millions of men in whom fear has been cunningly instilled, who have been taught to have an inferiority complex, to tremble, kneel, despair, and behave like flunkeys...] (22)

Likewise, Césaire's often-quoted mission to speak for the oppressed in *Cahier d'un retour au pays natal* is shouldered by Patrick Lemoine in *Fort-Dimanche, Fort-la-Mort* (1996), in which he documents his kidnapping, arrest, torture, and six-year imprisonment during the Jean-Claude Duvalier dictatorship.[38] Subtitled "témoignage" or "testimony," the récit, dedication, and annexe clearly indicate that the author is bearing witness for his codetainees as well. By keeping an alphabetical list of the names, cities, professions, cell numbers, and sometimes death dates of the prisoners who were freed and the 142 who died or were executed during his three-year incarceration, Lemoine writes them into history and memorializes them.[39]

The testimonial dimension of Haitian literature is one part of a larger advocacy project. Described as a "trophée dressé à la plus grande gloire du pays" (trophy raised to the highest glory of the country) Louis Morpeau's *Anthologie d'un siècle de poésie haïtienne 1816–1925* (1925) is heavily invested in changing perceptions of the nation. Dedicated to his uncle Fénimore Fougère, a Sorbonne student in the 1870s, the anthology boasts—in the new 1925 Paris edition that followed an earlier Port-au-Prince edition—a laudatory preface by a respected Sorbonne professor and complimentary words on individual poets by their acclaimed French counterparts and the Académie Française.[40] Morpeau bolsters these endorsements with scholastic statistics meant to demonstrate the government's commitment to education: he cites 1,000 primary, secondary, and professional schools with a total enrollment of 100,000 students. Similarly, Morpeau's self-portrait as a "sous-inspecteur des écoles" (school administrator) in Port-au-Prince accentuates his professional credentials, and each author profile reveals an accomplished lawyer, journalist, judge, or government worker. Morpeau claims two muses, one Creole, one French, for this autonomous, unique literature by both men and women, locating it within the appropriate historical and geographic contexts in hopes that it will help rehabilitate Haiti's image abroad.

As we have just seen, identity is an issue central to the Francophone Caribbean. As articulated through colonial laws, travelogues, and planters' and sailors' journals, a fixed identity has been imposed on the people, whose humanity was denied and whose culture was misinterpreted. Contemporary texts have attempted to recuperate and rehabilitate coopted and suppressed identities. Writers and filmmakers explore the complexities of identity formation, which is informed by various displacements. These authors transform former "objects" into "subjects" and, in so doing, are involved in a national project with global implications. One particular kind of literature central to Caribbean identity and articulation is autofiction.

Autofiction, the Caribbean *I*, and Testimony

First-person texts have been theorized as autobiography (Philippe Lejeune), autobiographical fiction (Françoise Lionnet), and autofiction (Serge Doubrovsky), which defines particular works that straddle the boundaries between fiction and nonfiction.[41] Although Francophone Caribbean literature has a scant number of autobiographies and no tradition of slave narratives or *testimonios*, its numerous first-person texts are akin to those African American and Latin American genres that articulate resistance and survival. The numerous autofictions by Francophone Caribbean writers range from life stories such as Emile Ollivier's *Mille eaux*, to short stories like Maryse Condé's "La Châtaigne et le fruit à pain," to personal essays like Suzanne Césaire's "Le Grand camouflage," in which the narrator perches over the Caribbean Sea observing the land below. I define Caribbean autofiction as a first-person narrative that may or may not overlap autobiography. I am not concerned with separating fact from fiction or with reading fiction as fact as Frantz Fanon does Mayotte Capécia's *Je suis Martiniquaise*, which led to his personal attack on the author. Neither am I on a quest for authenticity that has led some readers of Chamoiseau's *Texaco* to search for the notebooks purported to be located in the Schoelcher library in Fort-de-France.[42] My task is rather to probe the presence, construction, and the project of *je* in the text.

Autofiction also responds to Chamoiseau's question as to how one writes in a society where there are no traditional signs of oppression, such as barbed wire or strict censorship laws, in an era characterized by silent domination, "une domination devenue silencieuse" (*Ecrire* 18). By appropriating the *I*, his narrator, the *marqueur de paroles* (word marker), asserts his subjectivity, which assumes a *we*: "Le *je* et le *nous* sont indissociables. Le *nous* est indissociable du *je* et le *je* est dans le *nous*.... Ils sont indéfectiblement liés" (qtd. in Perret 251). [The *I* and the *we* are inseparable. The *we* is indissociable from the *I* and the *I* is in the *we*. . . . They are unfailingly linked.] Chamoiseau attests that in *Texaco*, Marie-Sopie's *I* "c'est un *nous*, c'est un *je* qui est relié à un *nous* et qui est constitutif et constructeur du *nous*" (is a *we*, it is an *I*, which is linked to a *we* and which constitutes and constructs a *we*) (qtd. in Perret 253).

First-person texts fall into the category of autofiction, where they are redefined and expanded so that they can accommodate more than one perspective. Raphaël Confiant's *Chimères d'En-Ville* (1997) alternates between two narrators, Homère and Adelise; Edwidge Danticat's *The Dew Breaker* (2004) opens with a first-person and then quickly shifts to a third-person narrator in what may appear to be disconnected short stories, but is actually a sequence of chapters involving a small group of characters whose lives and stories intersect.[43] This plurality of voices reflects the author's already-multilayered perspective. As Gisèle Pineau declares: "Mon univers romanesque est la traduction de ma propre expérience et de mes espérances" (qtd. in Belugue 89). [My fictional universe is the translation of my own experience and of my hopes.] Similarly, responding to those who confuse him with the *je* of his texts, Dany Laferrière conceptualizes his method, which involves imagination: "As for the matter of the percentage of true facts in fiction or fiction in true materials, I have my way of being a writer. When I talk about my books, I always say that they are an autobiography of my feelings. I'm not interested in recounting my life in any traditional way. There are my dreams, my friends' lives, my dream life—so different from my actual life, my lies, my concept of truth, my struggle to become a writer rather than a memoir writer—all of that is a part of my life. And it all comes out in my books. The life I dream is as true as my actual life" (Coates 916). Laferrière thus constructs a blueprint for a *collage text[île]* with *Une autobiographie américaine*—ten books in narrative order:[44]

> Il y a des "je" qui sont simplement une ruse de narration, afin de rendre plus aisée la lecture. Le lecteur est habitué au "je," donnons-lui du "je's." Par contre, il y a un "je," le plus couramment utilisé qui est très juste, très direct, et vraiment naturel: le "je" de *L'Odeur du café*, de même celui du *Charme des après-midi sans fin*, de *Chronique de la dérive douce* et de *Pays sans chapeau*. Il y a le "je" de *Eroshima* (je n'ai pas vécu dans la chambre de cette Japonaise mais cela m'aurait beaucoup plus), c'est un "je" de phantasme, mais c'est aussi important que le "je" authentique. Le "je" contaminé consiste à phagocyter les "je" des autres (se servir d'une histoire qui est arrivée plutôt à un ami). J'aurais pu ajouter un "je" générationnel quand il

s'agit d'un ensemble de personnes qui ont grandi ensemble dans la même époque, sous une même dictature (je tente alors de fondre toutes ces sensibilités dans le "je" du narrateur).... C'est vrai qu'il m'est arrivé de piquer ça et là des moments de vie des autres dans le dessein d'enrichir mon "je." J'ai tendance à dire, afin d'esquiver le problème de la stricte biographie qui ne relate que des faits véridiques relatifs à un individu, que mes romans sont une autobiographie de mes émotions, de ma réalité et de mes phantasmes. Aucun de ces aspects de ma personnalité n'est plus authentique qu'un autre. (Laferrière *J'écris* 161)

[There are *I*s that are simply a ruse of narration, to make reading easier. The reader is used to the *I* so let's give him the *I*s. On the other hand, there is the most frequently used *I* that is very just, very direct, and really natural: the *I* of *L'Odeur du café*, the same as the one from *Charme des après-midi sans fin*, *Chronique de la dérive douce* and *Pays sans chapeau*. There is the *I* of *Eroshima* (I have never lived in the room of this Japanese woman but I would have liked it), it is a fantasy *I* but it is as important as the authentic *I*. The contaminated *I* consists of absorbing the *I* of others (rather using a story that happened to a friend). I could have added a generational *I* when it is a question of a group of people who grew up together during the same era, under the same dictatorship (I try then to melt all of these sensibilities in the *I* of the narrator) ... It is true that I have occasionally stolen, here and there, moments of others' lives with the intention to enrich my *I*. I have a tendency to say, in order to dodge the problem of strict biography that relates only facts relative to an individual, that my novels are an autobiography of my emotions, of my reality and of my fantasies. Not one of these aspects of my personality is more authentic than another.]

First-person texts have a testimonial dimension, which makes them an important tool when they are inserted into a historical context in which individuals testify in open court about atrocities committed against them. Public testimony during the Truth and Reconciliation Commission in South Africa, the Rwanda War Crimes Tribunal, and the National Commission on Truth and Reconciliation in Chile have retrieved suppressed stories about human rights violations perpetrated by governments whose judicial systems have not always favored, and are sometimes hostile to, such investigations. Such testimony is necessary in order to expose the myth of the passive victim, restore voice to muted survivors, excavate the buried history, and in so doing, create an archive. Edouard

Glissant has written that slavery was a "combat sans témoin," a struggle without witnesses. Testimonial autofictions in their own way provide information heretofore unavailable.[45] Caribbean autofiction is invested in remembering and recording history and in challenging society's perception of Caribbean people. Consequently, these texts play an advocacy role as do some of the authors in real life: Maryse Condé ran for elective office, Gisèle Pineau is a psychiatric nurse, Patrick Chamoiseau is a social worker who works with troubled teenagers, and Edwidge Danticat defends the rights of Haitian refugees.

Feminist/womanist discussions hint at the role of women as witnesses, and in Francophone Caribbean literature women characters are often positioned as *témoins*, but seldom in a courtroom. In fact, such characters are most often narrators entrusted with transmitting information: from young, enslaved Lisette, who asks her grandmother Charlotte to repeat the horror story of the Middle Passage in Evelyn Trouillot's *Rosalie L'Infâme* (2003), to old Télumée in Simone Schwarz-Bart's *Pluie et vent sur Télumée Miracle* (1972). However, they are not always publicly recognized as observers, listeners, reporters, curators, or conveyers. In Raoul Peck's film *L'Homme sur les quais*, although the story is filtered through Sarah, the title renders her invisible. This eight-year-old, dark-skinned girl witnesses from a distance the torture of her godfather, a suspected opponent of the Duvalier regime. The moment haunts her, as, throughout the film, that scene is repeated as a nightmare. In omitting Sarah from the title of the film, Peck indirectly makes a strong statement about those witnesses to Duvalier's repression who were silenced by repression, intimidation, and censorship.

I mentioned earlier that témoignage is an operative concept in my analysis. It is the act of bearing witness, that is, declaring what one saw, heard, or perceived that serves to establish truth. Témoignage also denotes testimony as well as evidence, thus it is situated in a space where oral and written discourses intersect. An individual *témoin* is an eyewitness as well as an earwitness—a position that privileges vision and audition. Additionally, the *témoin* reports what he or she purports to be the truth. In a nonjuridical sense, témoignage can refer to an account or an expression, a sign or token, as in a token of friendship or an expression of gratitude. In sports, *passer le témoin* means "pass the baton." Although dictionary definitions of témoignage provide a foundation, they ignore historical, racial, and gender interventions. Article 30 of the 1685 Code Noir, for example, stipulates that enslaved people in the French colonies could not offer testimony at trials: "Ne pourrant les esclaves . . . ni être arbitres, experts ou témoins tant en matière civile que criminelle. Et en cas qu'ils soient ouïs en témoignage, leurs dépositions ne serviront que de mémoires pour aider les juges à s'éclairer ailleurs, sans que l'on en puisse tirer aucune présomption, ni conjecture, ni adminicule de preuve." [Slaves are not allowed to be . . . witnesses in a civil or criminal matter. In cases where they will be heard as witnesses, then their depositions will only serve as memoranda to aid the judge's investigation, without being the source of any presumption, conjecture or proof.]⁴⁶ In France, women were unable to testify in certain court cases until they finally won that right in 1893. Remaining aware of these interventions, I would like to borrow the term *témoignage* as a point of departure for opening other kinds of interrogations.

The model of intergenerational listening and its impact on the future writer provides another useful blueprint in the construction of témoignage. "She-Who-Listens-to-Other-Women in literature and life" is Alice Walker's interpretation of the often-anonymous narratee within a text who herself becomes entrusted with narrating the story of her best friend, for example, Phoeby in Zora Neale Hurston's *Their Eyes Were Watching God* (vii–viii). This kind of adult peer listening is based on, facilitates, and intensifies female bonding. In this study, I explore the roles of the fictional listener, the narrating subject, their interaction, and the text they produce.

My notion of témoignage has particular resonance in Caribbean literature and culture in which women are positioned to see, hear, and report as voyeurs/observers, actors, oral historians, storytellers, or a combination of these. Activist Lita Dahomey, a teacher in Guadeloupe who was dissatisfied with the gap between the rhetoric of gender equality and what was practiced and taught in the home commented in *Femmes des Antilles*: "J'ai accepté de *témoigner* (c'est moi qui souligne) ici, à la demande de Gisèle Pineau pour retracer une période riche en événements et qui a été déterminante dans ma vie et dans mes choix politiques (Pineau and Abraham 152). [I accepted to *bear witness* here, at the request of Gisèle Pineau, in order to trace an eventful period that had a decisive effect both on my life and on my political choices] (emphasis added). The other women in *Femmes des Antilles* represent different races, classes, colors, and age groups. Whether native-born or immigrant, rural or urban, working, unemployed or retired, single, widowed or married, schooled or illiterate, they articulate lives that run the gamut from satisfying to stressful, from ordinary to celebrated.

Femmes haïtiennes, paroles de négresses (1995), composed of twelve interviews with Haitian women between the ages of eighteen and sixty living in Quebec in 1994, *Like the Dew that Waters the Grass: Words from Haitian Women* (1999), interviews conducted between 1993 and 1998, and *Walking on Fire: Haitian Women's Stories of Survival and Resistance* (2001) are best described as conversations with contemporary women. Contributing to our understanding of present-day society, these works, along with the documentary *Tropique Nord* (1994), which examines the issue of racism against immigrants in Canada through the eyes of Haitian journalist Michaelle Jean, make strategic choices about the narrating subject—privileging lived experience over outsider observation—thereby providing distinct perspectives on Caribbean womanhood and society in contrast to stereotypical constructions.

Collages Text[île]s

Narratives from the Francophone Caribbean have been classified in ways that are restrictive and limiting: *roman paysan* [peasant novel] has been applied to certain novels in Haiti, while Richard Burton's *roman marron* [maroon novel] excludes texts by women and Haitian writers. Adlai Murdoch's designation "creole fictions," on the other hand, includes women authors, not just as tokens, but as literary creators equal with male authors. Likewise, my focus on first-person narratives transcends gender, class, and national boundaries, and reinserts Haiti into the Francophone Caribbean paradigm. I argue that collages text[île]s are narratives that assemble diverse fragments, that may unfold in nonchronological time and space, and that privilege the first-person in Relation to others in the past and present, thereby reflecting modern Creole identity, which, while in constant motion, embraces its multiple origins and present-day *errances* (errancies). I borrow the concept from Guadeloupean artist Francelise Dawkins who considers herself a *collagiste textile*. Combining silk and cotton on a hand-painted background, her *Ancient Mother's Visitation* appropriately graces the cover of her compatriot Gisèle Pineau's *L'Espérance-macadam*, a novel where perspective alternates between the first and third-person and where themes intersect in interesting ways with danmyé, the combat dance. Dawkins's juxtaposing of fabrics of different textures, colors, shapes, prices, geographic origins, and class values in relation to other mediums produces a work of art that is a metaphor for the new Caribbean identity, which Dawkins herself embodies in that she was born in Paris of immigrant parents from Guadeloupe and now resides in the United States. The strategy she adopts for her work is also a model for autofiction, most of which is published by large companies located in Paris. To a lesser degree publishers like Jasor, Ibis Rouge, Henri Deschamps, and Desormeaux are implicated in the dissemination of these literatures.

In chapter 1, "To Get Around the Rule of Silence": Performing Masculinity as *Détour*, I apply the trope of danymé to Joseph Zobel's *La Rue Cases-Nègres*, a novel in which two brief récits—M'man Tinc's and Médouze's—are embedded in the principal chronological narrative, suggesting a collage. José Hassam relates his own story of negotiating different terrains in Martinique. Born on a sugarcane plantation where the legacies of slavery—poverty and economic exploitation, for example—are intact, José applies to his own life the lessons of the combat dance, which he witnessed on the plantation, a closed space, according to Glissant. Addressed to those who refuse to acknowledge Martinique's history of oppression, José's récit challenges the silences of the master narrative. In this novel, the seemingly unambiguous *I*, who shares a first name with the author, reclaims his heritage, which helps him land on his feet like a danmyé master.

Chapter 2, "*I* Spy": Observers, Curators, Translators, and In-trust Narrators, examines texts in which a first-person narrator tells someone else's story. These kinds of texts are necessary, for example, when the protagonist does not have access to writing as in Dany Bébel-Gisler's *Léonora: l'histoire enfouie de la Guadeloupe* and Simone Schwarz-Bart's *Pluie et vent sur Télumée Miracle* in which Léonora and Télumée's first-person stories are related anonymously. A typical Patrick Chamoiseau text is narrated by Oiseau de Cham, whose name parodies the author's and who curates the stories in *Chronique des sept misères*, *Antan d'enfance* and *Chemin-d'école* (books 1 and 2 of *Une enfance créole*), *Solibo Magnifique*, and *Texaco*. In the latter Prix Goncourt–winning novel, he interacts with Marie-Sophie Laborieux, who recounts the events entrusted to her by her father Esternome. Supplementing that knowledge with what she witnessed during her lifetime, she relates the founding of the neighborhood, becoming in the process the custodian of Texaco's heritage. Chamoiseau's texts will be the focus of this chapter in which I explore the collective ethos and interaction between author, narrator(s), and protagonist as they negotiate space and voice. In *Chemin d'école*, the répondeurs, who serve an important function in danmyé, have a distinct voice in advancing the narration. In *Solibo Magnifique*, the competing versions of events, the mixture of oral and written discourses and registers, dialogue between narrator and protagonist, and the presence of the sentimenthèque, that is, books that influenced him, make this a true collage text[île].

Gisèle Pineau's autofiction, in which characters resist and escape the latent male violence simulated in and represented by danmyé, is the focus of chapter 3, Secrets and Silence, Displacement and *Délivrance*. In *L'Exil selon Julia*, the narrator, who curates her grandmother Man Ya's story of surviving domestic violence, is initiated by her into Guadeloupean culture. The *I* in *L'Espérance-macadam* is split between two women who are traumatized by incest and denial. The memory of Eliette's childhood rape was effectively erased, and Rosette refuses to believe that her husband abused their teenage daughter Angela. Without support from the ronde, Angela suffers her anguish, shame, and disappointment in silence as her family and neighbors ignore the signs of abuse, another issue that the text explores.

The trauma of displacement is the starting point of chapter 4, Travelers' Trees and Umbilical Cords: Embodying Dyaspora, Renegotiating Home. Here, I interrogate roots and routes, that is, the intersection of migration and identity that Caribbean writers as well as their characters experience. Maryse Condé and Myriam Warner-Vieyra, Edouard Glissant and Joseph Zobel: all are French citizens, who have spent many years abroad, but who consider themselves Guadeloupean and Martinican respectively. Even more than their Martinican and Guadeloupean colleagues, Haitian writers are scattered all over the world, yet retain their Haitian identity. Edwidge Danticat's *The Farming of Bones*, which is the center of this chapter, crystallizes the dilemma of home place. Protagonist Amabelle Désir's first-person narrative about her experiences living on the border between Haiti and the Dominican Republic in fall 1937 when Haitians were targets in the state-sanctioned massacre consists, in part, of recollections, dreams, and mediations typographically set off in bold-face type that, along with the chronological narrative, form a collage. These fragmentary pieces of memory, in the present tense, depict for example Amabelle's first trauma, the drowning of her parents that she witnessed at age eight. In *The Farming of Bones*, testifying about the event is second to remembering it, which "though sometimes painful—can make you strong" (73). Amabelle applies danmyé's principles of resistance, interaction, and balance; builds a supportive ronde on a new site; and negotiates a transnational identity.

Chapter 5, A Roving *I*: Autofiction(s) and Subversions, is devoted to Maryse Condé's work, which epitomizes collages text[île]s and in which the danmyé trope is reflected in the absence of a fixed narrative and a positional, identarian center. Comprised of first-person novels (*Moi, Tituba, sorcière... Noire de Salem, La Vie scélérate*), third-person texts (*Ségou, La Belle Créole*), and multivoiced texts (*Traversée de la mangrove, Histoire de la femme cannibale*), Condé's novels subvert the single narrative perspective and problematize the reliability of eyewitness testimony. At times, her narrators wink at the reader, inviting him or her to be complicit as she borrows excerpts from texts by Jacques Roumain, Aimé Césaire, Nathaniel Hawthorne, and Emily Brontë. *La Migration des coeurs*, a rewriting of *Wuthering Heights*, provides the most blatant example. Dedicated to Emily Brontë "qui, je l'espère, agréera cette lecture de son chef-d'oeuvre. Honneur et respect! (who I hope will approve of this interpretation of her masterpiece. Honour and respect!), it illustrates not only Chamoiseau's notion of the sentimenthèque and Suzanne Césaire's cannibal text, but is composed of récits rather than Récits or master narratives. These stories—told by enslaved people, peasants, women, subalterns, the unschooled, the young, and the voiceless—take into account multiple perspectives, each narrator conscious of the fact that his or her story is not the only authentic one. Condé's texts embody autofiction in the broadest sense.

It should not be surprising that some of these collages text[îles] have also become performance pieces. Condé's *Le Coeur à rire et à pleurer*, Schwarz-Bart's *Pluie et vent sur Télumée Miracle*, and Aimé Césaire's *Cahier d'un retour au pays natal* have all been adapted for the stage by Martine Maximin and Gerty Dambury (*Coeur, Pluie*), and Jacques Martial (*Cahier*).[47] Compagnie Norma Claire, from French Guiana, transformed sections of Pineau's *L'Exil selon Julia* as *Ti Peyi loin, loin*, in which women's intergenerational relations and displacement are figured in a blend of traditional dance and hip-hop. These texts by authors from Martinique, Guadeloupe, and Haiti, whether written or performed, invite readings informed by popular culture expressions such as danmyé, the combat dance, which enriches our understanding of Francophone Caribbean autofiction.

1

"To Get Around the Rule of Silence"

Performing Masculinity as *Détour*

La lecture de Zobel, plus que des discours théoriques, m'a ouvert les yeux.
[Reading Joseph Zobel, more than any other theoretical discourse, opened my eyes.]
Maryse Condé, *Le Coeur à rire et à pleurer*

Le damier n'étant pas affaire de petits garçons.
[Danmyé is not for little boys.]
Raphaël Confiant, *Le Meurtre du Samedi-Gloria*

Guadeloupean writer Maryse Condé asserts in her autobiographical text *Le Coeur à rire et à pleurer: contes vrais de mon enfance* that she was profoundly moved by Joseph Zobel's *La Rue Cases-Nègres*, a book lent to her when she was twelve or thirteen by her older brother Sandrino: "Je pleurai à chaudes larmes en lisant les dernières pages du roman, les plus belles à mon avis que Zobel ait jamais écrites." [I cried my heart out reading the last pages of the book, the finest I believe Zobel ever wrote] (*Le Coeur* 117/109). Centered on sugar plantation workers "que mes parents redoutaient tellement" (that my parents feared so) (117) and on a life she did not know existed, the novel made her feel for the first time the weight of the slave trade, slavery, colonial oppression, color prejudice, and exploitation (118–20, 108–11). Her parents—her father was a banker and her mother a teacher—sheltered her from that past whose legacy was still visible at the time. Set on a cane plantation in 1920s Martinique—a mere decade before Condé's birth—Zobel's novel traces José Hassam's negotiation of the harsh realities of the plantation, where he initially lives with his grandmother, and an educational system where the price for "getting ahead" is cultural alienation. The French school curriculum masks the reality of the islands' beginnings, teaching a chronology-based, metropole-centered *Histoire*—an approach that ignores the enslaved, the masses, and the experiences of women.[1]

In this chapter, I apply the danymé trope to Zobel's *La Rue Cases-Nègres*. The combat dance is an appropriate metaphor for the protagonist's approach to life. Having acquired specialized knowledge and surrounded by a supportive community, he is able to resist the alienation, invisibility, and domination of the French school, which functions to transform students into colonial subjects, *assimilés*, who will, in turn, reproduce the system. José Hassam develops an identity that defies as well as incorporates aspects of this sometimes-hostile environment where local knowledge and the Creole language are banned. Growing up male during a postabolition period in a society that imposes many constraints on black masculinity, José looks to and synthesizes patterns of behavior embodied in elderly cane cutter Médouze, stern schoolteacher Stéphen Roc, and the robust urban stevedores who earn their living hoisting heavy barrels. The unambiguous *I* reclaims his heritage, accepts the support of the ronde, dodges society's blows, and emerges victorious, a majò.

The two direct references to danmyé/laghia in *La Rue Cases-Nègres* illustrate the tension between the entertainment value and violent potential of this performance of masculinity. On the one hand, Monsieur Asselin, Tortilla's favorite adult on the plantation, is the picture of health with his straight white teeth and robust physique. What he lacks in material wealth he makes up in prowess dancing the laghia on Saturday nights to the delight of his neighbors.[2] On the other hand, if the men drink too much *tafia* (an alcoholic beverage made from sugarcane) during the Saturday evening harvest celebration, a card or dice game can degenerate into a laghia de la mort, that is, a fight that ends with someone's death. José does not literally fight or dance in the novel, but he must learn the rhythms and find the correct balance in order to negotiate the landscape. Failure will lead to regression and perhaps a return to a precarious life on the plantation.

That Maryse Condé's political activism began the moment she identified with fictional José Hassam is understandable: prior to the 1940s, most first-person narratives about the Caribbean were written by travelers who for centuries ignored colonialism's power dynamics. A typical example is found in Lafcadio Hearn whose popular *Two Years in the French West Indies* was translated into French and widely circulated. This American who visited Martinique in the late 1880s was mesmerized by the landscape and the laborers' bodies, producing a voyeuristic, nostalgic, and erotic discourse: "the men wield their cutlasses so beautifully that it is a delight to watch them. One cannot often enjoy such a spectacle nowadays; for the introduction of the piece-work system has destroyed the picturesqueness of plantation labor throughout the island, with rare exceptions" (275). According to Hearn, snakes are the greatest danger to these "dark swordsmen" (276). On the other hand, local author Victor Coridun upon viewing a similar scene wrote in 1937, the same era depicted in *La Rue Cases-Nègres* that the men, women, and children labor "sous le soleil meurtrier, courbés du matin au soir sur la 'tâche ingrate' interminable" (under the murderous sun, bent over from morning till night on the thankless, never-ending task) (13). Unfortunately, Hearn's perspective long prevailed as part of the master narrative, while Coridun's remains largely forgotten and unread.

La Rue Cases-Nègres is an example of autofiction. Relating a life under construction, José emphasizes his subjectivity and wrests the *I* from European travel writers. That Zobel chose his own first name as his protagonist's matches a strategy chosen by Mayotte Capécia in *Je suis Martiniquaise*, by Maryse Condé in *Le Coeur à rire et à pleurer*, and by Françoise Ega in *Lettre à une Noire*, in which the protagonist's name, Maméga, is a riff on Man Ega. Emile Ollivier's title *Mille eaux* is also self-referential: *mille eaux* (which sounds like "milo") reproduces his nickname, a diminutive for Emile.

Before writing *La Rue Cases-Nègres*, Zobel published a number of short stories in Martinique and in 1946 produced two novels and a collection of short stories. His first book *Diab'la*, written in 1942, was finally published in Paris by Nouvelles Editions Latines after having been censured as subversive by representatives of the Vichy regime in Martinique. It centers on a fisherman who wants to harvest and sell his own crops, a freedom the agricultural workers, who do not have access to the products of their labor, do not enjoy. Another novel, *Les Jours Immobiles*, and a short story collection, *Laghia de la mort*, appeared in Fort-de-France in 1946 prior to Zobel's leaving Martinique for France. That departure prompted *La Fête à Paris*, the sequel to *La Rue Cases-Nègres*, published by Editions La Table Ronde in 1953 and reissued by Editions Caribéennes in 1979 under the title *Quand la neige aura fondu*. In it the protagonist, no longer the author of his own story, experiences Paris.

La Rue Cases-Nègres emerged at an important moment in Martinican literary history, a particularly productive period for writers that also coincided with departmentalization. In 1947, Aimé Césaire's *Cahier d'un retour au pays natal* appeared in Paris with a preface by André Breton, and the following year, Mayotte Capécia's narrative about an interracial relationship during the interwar period, *Je suis Martiniquaise*, was published. What these texts share with *La Rue Cases-Nègres* is an autobiographical foundation and a critical examination of contemporary society. Raphaël Tardon's novel *La Caldeira* (1948), focusing on the last days of Saint-Pierre, the city destroyed in 1902 by the eruption of

Mount Pelée, and Aimé Césaire's poetry collections, *Soleil cou-coupé* (1948) and *Corps perdu* (1949), also preceded *La Rue Cases-Nègres*. Tardon, in his novel, shows that race, class, and color conflicts, exacerbated by politics, culminate in self-destruction, figured in the annihilation of the city. Césaire's poems balance the local and the diasporic, landscape and spiritual journeys. These works help create a literary crucible in which *La Rue Cases-Nègres* develops. In 1951, Léonard Sainville, a history professor and civil servant stationed in Senegal, wrote *Dominique, nègre esclave* (1951), a historical novel inspired by an uprising in Guadeloupe in 1837 in which the *révoltés* flee to Martinique where they establish a maroon [escaped slave] community. Dominque achieves literacy like José. Although Sainville's novel is set a century before *La Rue*, its themes of agency and freedom resonate in Zobel. Remarkably, the first and second editions of *La Rue Cases-Nègres*, published in 1950 and 1955, coincided with Aimé Césaire's *Discours sur le colonialisme*.[3] Frantz Fanon's *Peau noire, masques blancs* (1952), an essay that addresses the political, social, and psychological effects of colonialism, was published in the interval separating these first and second editions. Both the Césaire and Fanon texts resonate in the subsequently redacted dedication and epigraph to the first edition of *La Rue Cases-Nègres*, as well as in the text itself, with its insights into a period whose history has been suppressed.

Just as *La Rue Cases-Nègres* was among those works first informed by and informing a coming to consciousness of identity constructions among Martinican writers and intellectuals at mid-twentieth century, it also participated in an artistic and ideological revolution unfolding on the other side of the Atlantic—negritude. This revolution is characterized in part by the flowering of a long-nascent black *I* and literary forms precursory and subsequent to Zobel's autofiction in *La Rue*. *Présence Africaine*, the primary instrument of the négritude movement, was founded in 1947, the same year Zobel met one of the movement's founding fathers, the Senegalese poet and politician Léopold Sédar Senghor. That journal's earliest issues serialized Abdoulaye Sadji's *Nini, mulâtresse du Sénégal*. Its theme—the consequences of assimilation for a young person's identity construction—is one Zobel explores later through José Hassam in *La Rue Cases-Nègres*. (With its focus on overcoming the hardships of plantation life, *La Rue Cases-Nègres* also has much in common with two Haitian novels of the period: *Les Semences de la colère* by Anthony Lespes (1949), in which "colonies agricoles" are established to accommodate returning workers who survived the 1937 Dominican Republic massacre, and *Bon Dieu rit* (1952) by Edriss Saint-Amand, in which peasants' daily lives resemble those of their enslaved ancestors.) Also in 1947, Gallimard published the French translation of Richard Wright's *Black Boy*, which enjoyed an enthusiastic reception. Like José, the protagonist was born in poverty on a plantation. In 1953, Guinean writer Camara Laye published the autobiographical novel *L'Enfant noir*, an autofiction whose narrator is initiated into village life by his father before enrolling in school. While Jacques Roumain's posthumously published *Gouverneurs de la rosée* first appeared in Port-au-Prince in 1944, second and third editions were published by the Bibliothèque Française in 1946 and by the Editeurs Français Réunis in 1950. In Roumain's novel, a sugarcane plantation worker in Cuba returns to his home in Haiti, bringing with him knowledge about fighting exploitation. Jacques Stéphen Alexis's *Compère Général Soleil*, appearing at Gallimard in 1955, the same year as the second edition of *La Rue Cases-Nègres*, is set in part in the cane fields of the Dominican Republic. The 1950s also marked the First International Congress of Black Writers and Artists at the Sorbonne, which brought together representatives from several continents in 1956. This conference, sponsored by *Présence Africaine*, facilitated the practice of diaspora, as Brent Edwards would say. The delegates from twenty-four countries attended panels, presented scholarly papers, and discussed and debated topics such as African and African diasporic cultures and their shared condition of colonial oppression. Paris was a literary center for Francophone writers of the late 1940s and 1950s, providing opportunities for interaction as well as publication. Fittingly, at the time when France commemorated the centenary of the abolition of slavery, these authors were writing about the injustices, inequalities, poverty, and exploitation that slavery engendered.

La Rue Cases-Nègres is set less than eighty years after slavery was abolished, during the interwar period when Martinique was still a colony. It was in 1946 that France issued a series of decrees changing Martinique, Guadeloupe, and French Guiana from colonies to overseas departments. However, as Dany Bébel-Gisler observes in *Le Défi culturel guadeloupéen*, these were purely administrative decrees "qui n'ont que peu altéré le système colonial" (that changed the colonial system very little) (97). Zobel's novel omits allusion to actual events, such as the 1935 march of agricultural workers on Fort-de-France or the celebration of the 300th anniversary of the colonies, but their legacy still informs his text.[4] Despite Edouard Glissant's assertion that slavery is a struggle without witnesses (*Discours* 277) and Patrick Chamoiseau's claim that the definitive novel about slavery has not yet been written, Zobel's narrative rises to both occasions. The character Médouze, for example, recounts his father's story of being captured in Africa, separated from his family, and brought to the Americas where he experienced slavery and abolition to José, who is heir to this ancestral memory. Similarly, the novel examines the trajectory of a five-year-old boy, born on a sugarcane plantation, who against tremendous odds, goes on to complete high school and pass the *baccalauréat* despite the challenge of alienating spaces. In addition, Zobel's novel addresses the issues and nuances of class, color, exploitation, prejudice, colonialism, and representation. By tracing the development of a future writer, *La Rue Cases-Nègres* imagines not only Zobel's experience, but that of other boys like him during the 1920s and 1930s, while literary movements—*indigénisme*, the Harlem Renaissance, *negrismo*, and négritude—were being formulated.

Unlike Jean-Robert Cadet in *Restavec: From Haitian Slave Child to Middle-Class American* (1998), for example, Zobel has denied an overt political agenda in *La Rue Cases-Nègres*. Even so, the manuscript was rejected by Juillard, Albin Michel, and La Table Ronde prior to being accepted by Jean Froissard.[5] Dated Fontainebleau, June 17, 1950, it also carries a proud dedication to the women in his family who, ironically, would never read his words: "A Ma Mère—domestique chez les Blancs / A Ma Grand-Mère—travailleuse de plantation, et qui ne sait pas lire"; [To My Mother—a domestic worker in the home of whites / To My Grandmother—a plantation worker, who cannot read]. Zobel suggests that colonialism, racism, and sexism determined their fates. By naming their jobs, which offered little remuneration or opportunity for advancement, he accentuates the women's effort, struggle, and sacrifice so that he could have another kind of life. This heartfelt expression of gratitude is followed by a strong protest against the economic exploitation of the colonial system drawn from the epistle of James: "Voici, le salaire des ouvriers / qui ont moissonné vos champs, / et dont vous les avez frustrés, crie." [Behold, the hire of the labourers / who have reaped down your fields, / which is of you kept back by fraud, crieth.] The verse continues: "and the cries of them which have reaped are entered into the ears of the Lord of sabaoth" (James 5.4). This sentiment is echoed in the last lines of the novel where the narrator situates himself in relation to others for whom he will speak. Unfortunately, the Les Quatre Jeudis edition of *La Rue Cases-Nègres* published in 1955, the definitive Présence Africaine edition of 1974, and the English translation all eliminate Zobel's homage to his family, as well as the passage from James 5. Consequently, the personal context is suppressed and the broader implications of the narrative somewhat diminished.

Negotiating Space

An essential skill of a danmyétiste is the ability to perform, negotiate, and dominate within the confines of the ronde or ring. José Hassam confronts three major spaces in *La Rue Cases-Nègres* that challenge his sense of self, proving that landscape is indeed what Glissant terms a "personnage parlant," a speaking character, in Caribbean literature (*Poétique* 85). As José travels from the countryside to the big city during the 1920s and 1930s, each location is instrumental in the construction of his identity. Relocating from a rural to an urban space—from Petit-Morne to Fort-de-France—is not abrupt; José Hassam's journey includes the transitional factory town of Petit-Bourg. Although he visits the plantation less and less often, his early immersion in that rich culture helps to sustain him. José's physical displacements are often associated with rupture; nevertheless, they contribute to his overall emotional growth.

In each of the novel's three principal landscapes, the structure of colonialism with its resulting discrimination and inequities is paramount. The plantation, the factory town, and the capital city are all divided into separate domestic and work spheres in which race, class, and color differences imposed by the colonial system determine and reflect an individual's economic condition. With blacks the majority on plantations owned by invisible or absentee whites, José is remarkable as the only child from Petit-Morne to make it as far as the prestigious high school in Fort-de-France: "Personne ne me ressemble." [I was the only one of my kind] (221/128). In Fort-de-France, the center of the colonial administration, urban blacks earn more money than their rural counterparts, but are relegated to low-paying service jobs as chauffeurs, gardeners, and domestics. Nevertheless, it is on his initial site—the plantation—that José acquires the knowledge and assistance that will figure in his overcoming the obstacles to upward mobility. José was only an observer of danmyé/laghia on the plantation, but he internalized its strategies, principles, and objectives. More important, with the guidance of individuals dispossessed of material goods and denied access to literacy, José achieves academically. At each site to which he travels, José meets adults and peers with whom he forms temporary or enduring ties instrumental in the construction of his identity.

The sugarcane plantation on which José grows up in Petit-Morne has its own onsite factory and shop run by the administrator's wife, who sells on credit. The plantation is thus self-contained, at least for the poor residents who work in the fields during the day, sleep in their huts on la rue cases-nègres in the evening, and purchase goods in the company store. While Glissant's notion of "l'univers clos de la Plantation" (the closed universe of the Plantation) refers to the fact that the enslaved were required to have passes in order to leave, it also embodies the reality that in postemancipation society workers are still bound in every way to the soil. Beverley Ormerod's description of "the plantation as hell" is also entirely appropriate given the backbreaking work in the fields, child labor (the *petites bandes*), exposure to the sun and inclement weather, women's vulnerability to rape by overseers, poverty wages, and food shortages. Kathleen Balutansky and Marie-Agnès Sourieau assert in the introduction to *Caribbean Creolization* that, more than Paul Gilroy's Middle Passage ship, the plantation is a better signifier for the Caribbean because the "lives and values of Caribbean peoples have been shaped and controlled by this experience, and its resulting injury is still felt deep in the region's psyche" (5).

José is raised in his grandmother's house, a *case-à-nègres*—whose Creole equivalent, *cas-nèg*, is echoed in Zobel's title—a dirt-floored wooden hut that housed plantation families during the slavery and postabolition periods. Lacking electricity, running water, and sanitary facilities, these quarters were used principally for sleeping, as the workers departed before dawn and returned after sundown. Meals were prepared outside over an open fire. In Zobel's novel, the street, *rue*, is actually an unpaved alleyway formed by three dozen wooden *cases* or shacks with sheet-metal roofs built on a hillside at the top of which stands the tile-roofed plantation manager's house. Between his residence and the row of *cases-à-nègres* sits the home of the overseer, Monsieur Gabriel. This housing configuration mimics the economic, social, and class hierarchies intact since the slavery era.[6] The spatial distribution of the vast sugarcane fields, stretched below the cases and also surrounding them, suggests their power to exploit, hinder upward mobility, and stifle dreams of escape.

José and his young friends are unaware of the constraints imposed upon them by the plantation space. For them, the absence of adults in the daytime means freedom to play, even though their parents are performing arduous tasks under the hot sun, forever bound to the plantation for their survival. As Médouze comments, the 1848 abolition required that workers be paid, but they earn so little that they must purchase essentials on credit. With no opportunities for advancement, they remain shackled to the land, and their offspring are doomed to the same fate. Ironically, the young children see themselves as "maîtres de la rue Case" (masters of Shack Alley) (67/38), though their tattered clothes testify to a different reality, one of extreme material poverty. They boast to each other about the food left by their mothers for their lunches—rice with butter, breadfruit and pig's snout, cassava flour and water, dwarf bananas cooked in oil—but are unaware that their parents' meager earnings cannot purchase more copious, nutritious, and varied meals.

In the scene where the children search for the hidden sugar tin, the narrator is more concerned that his grandmother will find the *case* in disarray than he is curious about why M'man Tine hid the container in the first place. Young José does not grasp the irony that field laborers have scant access to the product that they cultivate and harvest, most often for export.[7] Sugar is so costly that his grandmother keeps it hidden from him, and Gesner's mother purchases just a little for coffee on Sundays. The children's glee at the discovery of the hen's eggs, the decision to boil and eat them, and over the purchase of matches at the shop demonstrates that something as seemingly ordinary as eating chicken's eggs is quite rare in this community. In fact, not one of the children has ever eaten one. Their parents raise brood hens to produce more hens that can be bartered for goods at the boutique or sold to the *békés*, descendants of European planters, in the factory. To disrupt this food chain is unthinkable, as it would lead to even more hunger and privation. In recounting the strategy, intrigue, and adventure surrounding the discovery of the eggs, the *I* celebrates not only the children's ingenuity, but their transgression of culinary taboos—especially their claim to the commodities produced by the community in which they live.

Although as a youngster José enjoys playing hide-and-seek among the cane leaves with his friends and delights in sucking the cane stalks until the juice runs down his chin, José's attitude toward the fields begins to shift during his first summer vacation from school. Forced to once again accompany M'man Tine to the fields, he becomes bored in this milieu for the first time. The bell that calls the children back to classes from recess has been temporarily replaced by the bell summoning cane workers back to their jobs: "Il m'était pénible de passer des journées entières sans lire avec d'autres enfants, à haute voix, en choeur. Cela m'était étrange de ne pas entendre la cloche de l'école; et celle de la plantation, à midi, me rendait le coeur gros. J'avais envie de voir et d'entendre la maîtresse." [It was painful to me to spend days on end without reading aloud and in unison with other children. It was strange not hearing the school bell; and the one on the plantation at midday made my heart heavy. I felt like seeing and hearing the mistress] (131/76). The summer vacation marks his transformation from a carefree child to a serious student.

José slowly comes to realize that the cane fields are responsible for killing Médouze. Fatigue, exposure to violent rain storms, and the blistering sun strike down his mentor and, worse still, threaten to take M'man Tine's life as well: "Les champs de canne à sucre m'apparaissaient comme un danger. Ce danger qui avait tué M. Médouze sans que personne n'eût vu comment, et qui pouvait d'un moment à l'autre, surtout un jour d'orage, tuer aussi ma grand-mère sous mes yeux." [The sugar cane fields seemed a danger to me—that danger had killed Mr. Médouze without anyone seeing how and which could at any moment, especially on a stormy day, also kill my grandmother under my very eyes] (133/77).

It is not just his loved ones who are vulnerable to the plantation system. Anyone or anything that traverses the cane fields risks becoming a victim. This landscape has the power to conceal, engulf, and consume. José witnesses such an incident on another plantation. The hen he receives as a gift from his godmother escapes his grip and disappears into the cane fields never to be seen again. It is significant that M'man Tine uses her body to block its route. Although she is unsuccessful, her gesture of protection recalls her efforts to safeguard José's life in other ways, in the cane fields, for example. Later, as a high school student, José briefly considers working on the plantation during the summer vacation in order to buy new shoes for the next academic year. However, understanding the inherent danger, the mechanism of exploitation, and the necessity to distance himself from that life, he decides against it:

> Aucune sympathie pour les champs de cannes à sucre. En dépit de mon plaisir à mordiller et à sucer des bouts de canne à sucre, un champs représentait toujours à mes yeux un endroit maudit où les bourreaux qu'on ne voyait même pas condamnent des nègres, dès l'âge de huit ans, à sarcler, bêcher, sous des orages qui les flétrissent et des soleils qui dévorent comme feraient des chiens enragés.... Je renie la splendeur du soleil.... Il y a trop longtemps que j'assiste, impuissant, à la mort lente de ma grand-mère par les champs de cannes à sucre. (210–11)

> [There was no particular liking for sugar cane fields. Despite all the pleasure I had nibbling on and sucking pieces of sugar cane, a field still represented in my eyes a damnable place where executioners, whom you couldn't even see, condemned black people from as young as eight years old, to weed, to dig, in storms that caused them to shrivel up and in the broiling sun that devoured them like mad dogs.... I wanted no part of the splendor of the sun.... For too long a time I had witnessed, helpless as I was, my grandmother dying a slow death in those fields of sugar cane.] (122)

The narrator has indeed matured. His old ideas about fun and freedom on the plantation in Petit-Morne have been revealed to be deceptive, shortsighted, and erroneous. This *I*-witness comprehends the conditions under which his family and neighbors live and is determined to prepare himself for another kind of life, one that will offer a future unlike the one his friends in the *petite-bande* are doomed to experience.

Not unlike the plantation landscapes romanticized by European travel writers of the 19th and early 20th centuries, the modern plantation landscape has been re-created for Martinique's tourist-conscious economy. Vacation and business travelers or conference attendees like me or Zobel can now punctuate our trips with a visit to a sugar mill and a rue cases-nègres. The Leyritz plantation promotes itself as one of the Caribbean's largest tourist renovations. Originally built in the early eighteenth century for Michel de Leyritz, a resident of Bordeaux, one of France's principal slave ports, it was transformed during the 1970s into a tourist attraction. While many of the buildings have been restored, their use has been altered: the sugar refinery and chapel are now restaurants; the pigeon coop, a discotheque; the sheep pen, a performance space; the *case du commandeur* or driver's home, a welcome area, museum, and boutique. The planter's house, kitchens, and the livery shed are all hotel rooms. Most interestingly, the former guardhouse, administrator's home, and *cases-a-nègres* are now called bungalows, a name that, evoking warmth and intimacy, masks the former violent power structure. The absence of plantation residents, especially field workers, in this restored space erases an essential aspect of the plantation experience, in effect, sanitizing it.

By substituting the more benign word *habitation* or dwelling for plantation, tourists are conveniently distanced from the brutality of plantation life, and the French Caribbean's legacy of slavery and indentured servitude remains hidden. Visitors are instead invited to associate Leyritz plantation and places like it with Tara in Margaret Mitchell's *Gone With the Wind*, an American *lieu de mémoire* [site of memory] whose myth has supplanted history. This mythic transformation complements the well-advertised pristine Caribbean beaches, sites for the docking of slave ships centuries ago. It is understandable that José, a descendant of African captives, has an ambivalent relationship to the sea: "J'avais souvent vu la mer au loin.... La mer c'était pour moi, une chose visible, belle, mais inaccessible comme le ciel, son frère." [I had often seen the sea in the distance.... For me the sea was something visible and beautiful, but inaccessible like its brother, the sky] (207–8/120). Its beauty and serenity cover a loathsome past. Like the adult José, who mentally reconstructs the plantation of his childhood to reveal its hazards, injustices, and tragedies, Zobel mentally reconstructs Leyritz to its original operations during a July 1974 visit to Martinique. He writes in his journal that while strolling on the grounds he imagines the *bois d'ébène* [field hands] toiling under the sun. To commemorate their lives and to defy their erasure from history he appropriates the reading room, the former kitchen of the "big house," as his writing space (*Gertal* 137).

By showing plantation workers in the cane fields in *Rue Cases-Nègres* (1983), her cinematic adaptation of Zobel's novel, Euzhan Palcy makes visible and incontrovertible the abject poverty and exploitation of laborers in 1930s Martinique. Douta Seck, the Senegalese actor known for his many theatrical portrayals of Aimé Césaire's Roi Christophe, lost ten kilos for the role of Monsieur Médouze (Lemoine, *Douta* 78). Skeletal, diminutive, stooped, and white haired, his aged body should have retired long ago, but with no pension to support himself, Médouze must continue working. As Médouze observes, though slavery has officially been over since 1848, the same conditions persist. Darling Legitimus, a fine performer originally from the Caribbean, plays José's no-nonsense grandmother Amantine. Walking slowly, she, too, goes each day to the fields, despite her advanced age. Worn and overworked, both Médouze and M'man Tine contradict the stereotype of the contented slave that was long a staple of Western cinema. Although the title of the American version of the film, *Sugar Cane Alley* elides the race issue, Keith Q. Warner restores it in his 1980 translation *Black Shack Alley*. The cinematic adaptation of the novel, which retains the young man's point of view, ends with the voice-off of José vowing that he will always carry his Rue Cases-Nègres, his origins, with him.[8]

Due to the efforts of his grandmother and their elderly neighbor Médouze, José resists being consumed by the plantation. Amantine, who raises him, has the greatest impact on his life. In the cane fields, she uses her body to protect him from the sun. She refuses to let him join the *petites-bandes* and has no respect for those parents who surrender to the pressure of Monsieur Gabriel. She teaches José manners, how to fish, and instills in him her values and a desire to excel in school. Determined and opinionated, she does not wallow in self-pity, but strives to make a better life for her progeny. At one point, however, she breaks down and exhibits her vulnerability as she tells her life story to an uncomprehending five-year-old José. Her uninterrupted récit reveals for the first time the hardships she has endured: the loss of her family; descent into the cane fields; a brutal rape there as a teenager by the *commandeur* Monsieur Valbrun; and the resulting birth of her daughter Délia. That her grandfather was a white man, a béké, does not afford her any advantages.[9] José is too young to grasp the meaning and implications of her story at this time, but being exposed to workers' protests against their meager wages (one laborer throws his scant coins on the ground in disgust), José gradually begins to question the basis of their brutal poverty. The plantation is at once José's nemesis, home, and classroom without walls.

The second stage of José's journey involves more than a mere change of location. The town of Petit-Bourg, larger than Petit-Morne, is not only a place where poor and working-class people live and work, but also where they gather to worship, play, and go to school. Local activities are therefore not exclusively focused on the production of sugarcane. Though the small wooden houses some residents rent are sturdier than cases, their loose planks nonetheless attest to a precarious existence. The elementary school draws students from the surrounding communities of Fonds Masson and Courbaril. A vehicle for socialization, the school is the site of the students' first contact with French, the language of the dominant society. Their mother tongue, Creole—which until recently was not recognized as a formal language—is devalued. Roger Toumson identifies this situation as "subjugation linguistique" and "répression de la langue maternelle" (linguistic subjugation) and (repression of the mother tongue) (*Transgression* 51–55). Education in this context is not simply a matter of learning a new language, but of mastering the geography and history of the metropole as part of a systematic initiation into the dominant culture. This initiation involves various other prohibitions and marginalizations. Dictation, the standard approach to writing, does not encourage critical thinking, but the reconstitution of sentences and paragraphs based on the application of strict grammar rules. Thus, while José finds at school "un univers nouveau" (a new world) (108/63), it is one that excludes his language from the classroom.[10] That the girls are confined to the veranda during recess while boys play in the yard is a sign of gender-based marginalization.

Petit-Bourg accommodates a mixture of social classes, which exposes José to overt color and class prejudice for the first time. After avoiding entrenchment in the plantation system as part of the *petites-bandes*, José is exploited in Petit-Bourg by individuals who, having achieved a certain measure of financial success, now scorn his humble roots. Although Madame Léonce, a factory worker's wife and an acquaintance of his grandmother, provides him with lunch, she is an obstacle to José's progress, defining him racially as "mon petit nègre" (my little black boy) and insisting that he perform domestic chores, which makes him late for school (118/68). That she asks him to perform tasks usually associated with women makes her resemble a *colonisée* [plantation mistress], who exercises power over the *boy* [domestic worker]. Her house not only functions as a prison, but is compared to a plantation from which he, like a maroon, finally escapes: "Je me suis échappé. Me voilà sauvé!" [I had escaped. I was saved!] (125/72). It is not surprising that when he flees he is drawn to his refuge, the schoolhouse.

Petit-Bourg is also home of José's good friend Georges "Jojo" Roc, whose father Justin represents, like Madame Léonce, the *aliéné* [alienated individual] of Frantz Fanon's *Peau noire, masques blancs*, one who is psychologically attached to the oppressor. The son of an old béké, Justin Roc mimics his father's behavior by having a child with young Gracieuse, who works on the plantation he manages. Straddling class lines, he sets up a household with Gracieuse, only to abandon her to marry a woman of his own social class who resents Jojo's existence, because she regards it a consequence of her husband's "fréquenter des négresses sales et vulgaires" (running around with those dirty, vulgar black girls) (154/89). Promoted to factory foreman, Justin builds a bright-colored house with shutters, buys a car, and hires a servant—all visible markers of his chosen status. Even Mélie, his housekeeper, embraces his class values; she spies on Jojo, reporting to her employers that he is playing with José and speaking Creole, the only language she speaks ironically. That the boys' friendship is relegated and confined to the veranda indicates the degree to which it is considered unacceptable.

In Petit-Bourg, M'man Tine and José reside on Cour Fusil, an inscription indicating a shift in location from plantation alley to court or yard, a domiciliary organizational unit found in Caribbean towns and cities since the beginning of the nineteenth century that housed both enslaved and free people. M'man Tine and José live among factory workers and self-employed vendors, midwives, and performers. Their wooden, tile-roofed houses with loose plank floors that let in roaches and mice stand in parallel lines facing a narrow, paved cul-de-sac. While M'man Tine has a long daily commute to the plantation where she still works as a *sarcleuse* (weeder), residing close to the school is more convenient for José. She is fully invested in his budding literacy knowing it will make him eligible for a better job. His teacher Stéphen Roc even hints at the possibility of a career as a doctor, lawyer, or engineer if he passes the exam for the prestigious high school, Lycée Schoelcher, in Fort-de-France.

Unlike the Petit-Morne plantation, Petit-Bourg is the site of an actual attraction that draws people from surrounding towns to enjoy a leisure activity. The itinerant carousel is mounted on the market square at its temporary home during the annual patronal festival. Accompanying its motions, a live orchestra—composed of instruments like the drum, *ti-bwa* (a pair of percussive wooden sticks), *shasha* or gourd rattle, and clarinet—plays waltzes. The drummer, standing, plays the two-sided *chwoual bwa* drum that is positioned on a stand or attached to a stationary part of the carousel. Using a stick in each hand, he marks the rhythm as men and women sway to the music (Cally 28). José is especially impressed by the strength of the two men who turn the circular floor with their arms. Manually operated by the strength of men, the carousel is the site of the performance of a male ritual, which I discuss in more detail below. Zobel fondly recalls the carousel in the poem "Cours préparatoire" from *Le Soleil partagé* (1964), "où les chevaux de bois / sous leurs peintures usées / tournaient dans la musique / au centre de la place / cinq minutes pour deux sous" (where the wooden horses / under their worn paint / would turn to the music / five minutes for two pennies / in the center square) (193–96).

While the carousel attracts children in general, it also exposes class divisions that exacerbate José's feelings of inadequacy. Customers ride free on Saturday nights and on Sundays after mass, but at other times must pay. Sad because of his lack of money, José watches the "montés d'enfants en robes blanches et à noeuds rouges, d'enfants en costumes neufs, d'enfants à chaussures vernies" (children astride in white dresses with red bows, children in new suits, children in polished shoes) (193–94/112). They provide a marked contrast to the sweaty, barefoot men whose job it is to turn the floor with their hands so that children with money can have fun. At one point, José considers joining the other poor boys, who assist the turners for free in order to jump onto the moving platform: "Ils sautaient dessus et, accroupis ou debout, s'en trouvaient presque aussi bien que sur les plus beaux chevaux du manège." [They would spring on and, crouching or standing, find themselves enjoying the ride as much as if they were on the finest horses of the merry-go-round] (194/112). José's conscience intervenes; he knows his grandmother would disapprove and give him a beating. Luckily, his friend Jojo appears with five francs that one of his parents dropped in the dining room, an amount José cannot imagine finding in his own home.

City(land)scape—Fort-de-France

Located between the plantation and the city, the town of Petit-Bourg is a transitional site from which José emerges proud to have accumulated a wealth of knowledge and experience: "Je deviendrais un enfant du bourg." [I would become a child of the village] (137/79). Fort-de-France's urban landscape, by comparison, has cars, a faster pace of life, and is divided into several distinct neighborhoods. In the poor and squatter communities on the periphery—Bord du Canal, les Terres Sainville, le Pont Démosthène, Desclieux, Morne Pichevin, Sainte-Thérèse, and Petit-Fond—impoverished residents construct homes from discarded materials, such as the cardboard crates used to transport imported cars. The city proper, L'En-ville, with its government buildings, shops, movie theatre, public gardens, and port, employs some of the refugees from a receding sugar economy. With the collapse of the sugarcane industry, many rural Martinicans migrated to the city to find work as chauffeurs, stevedores, and domestics, like Délia, José's mother. José earns the right to enter this urban space by passing a competitive examination that places him in a *lycée* with the most gifted students on the island. Despite his success, he discovers that many of the social barriers erected in Petit-Bourg exist in the city as well.

The city's residential areas are segregated. José and his mother live in Sainte-Thérèse, located east of the city, while she is employed as a maid in the villa of Monsieur Lasseroux, a rich béké, in the Route Didier district.[11] Sainte-Thérèse, according to Michel Laguerre, is the "oldest inner-city slum" whose first inhabitants were dock workers. During the 1930s, its population increased dramatically (31). José's neighbors build homes, carve out streets, open tailor and butcher shops, construct a church, and plant flowers—all of these actions "un témoignage sincère de soin et d'amour" (a sincere token of affection and love) (218/126) that demonstrates their care of their community as what urban anthropologist Philippe Yerro later calls an "urban mangrove," a dynamic rather than a stagnant space. When Délia quits her job as a domestic to take in laundry, they move to Petit-Fond, a neighborhood that, in the shadow of Route Didier, superficially resembles the plantation's rue cases-nègres. While the plantation shacks are free to workers, Petit-Fond rooms and homes must be rented from whites who, like their counterparts in the countryside, own and control the land.

Dotting the landscape of Sainte-Thérèse and Petit-Fond, houses constructed from discarded automobile crates perch on wooden stilts or concrete rubble, symbolic of their residents' precarious situations. Worse, José notices that the tenants of these hovels do not contest their subservience, unlike the Petit-Morne laborers, who not only complained about their meager wages, but protested in front of the middle managers distributing the pay. The chauffeurs and laundresses in Fort-de-France are too concerned about keeping their jobs to challenge their employers: "La circonspection, le conformisme, l'obséquiosité qui marquaient l'attitude et les moindres propos des domestiques... en disaient assez sur la soumission qu'ils vouaient à leurs maîtres et leur respect pour ce lieu qu'ils s'appliquaient à ne troubler aucunement." [The circumspectness, the conformity, the obsequiousness that characterised the attitude and the slightest conversations of the servants ... said enough about the submission they vowed to their masters and their respect for that place that they did their best not to disturb in any way] (253/147). By contrast, José's friends and relatives in Petit-Morne objected to their situations, openly voicing their displeasure: "Ceux de la rue Cases-Nègres et de Petit-Bourg, tels des forçats, trimaient et s'épuisaient au profit de l'espèce des békés; ils les subissaient douloureusement, mais ils ne les portaient pas dans leur coeur. Ils ne se prosternaient pas devant eux. Tandis que ceux de la Route Didier formaient une catégorie dévouée et cultivant avec dévotion la manière de servir les békés." [The people in Black

Shack Alley and in Petit-Bourg toiled and moiled like slaves for the *békés*; they put up with them painfully, but did not bear any malice towards them. They did not prostrate themselves before them. Whereas those in Route Didier formed a devoted category, dutifully cultivating the manner of serving the *békés*] (254/148).

The high school is located far from where José resides. While Lycée Schoelcher, a brick structure situated in the city proper, appears to be an oasis of opportunity, its high walls and enclosed yard represent barriers. It is probably at this site that José is most conscious of his color and class difference: "Je suis le seul de mon espèce." [I was the only one of my kind] (221/128). Not only is he the only student from the school in Petit-Bourg, but his skin color, facial features, hair texture, and even his name accentuate his difference from the other students. Financial problems exacerbate his distress. Though José receives a scholarship, it covers only one quarter of the school fees.[12] Lonely and depressed, he misses class and earns poor grades. In addition, his teacher prejudges him, blind to his gift for writing. Monsieur Jean-Henri has such low expectations of children like José that he accuses him of plagiarizing a heartfelt essay, an elegy to Monsieur Médouze.[13]

The local cinema, which introduces the first sound movies to Martinique, should be a definitive site for relaxation and entertainment. While the carousel does not have a permanent home, but provides a venue for celebrating local culture, the movie theater imports foreign images. Like Monsieur Henri, it harbors and disseminates erroneous perceptions. Purported to reflect the viewers' reality or to expand the audience's horizons, the films shown at the movie house do neither, presenting instead distorted images of black masculinity. José becomes angry and insulted when he sees the rolling, bulging eyes, dumb grins, and grotesque clothes and behavior on screen.

José survives his Fort-de-France experiences with the support of a mother who refuses to be intimidated by challenges, a trait she inherited or learned from M'man Tine. When faced with unexpected school fees beyond her means, she declares firmly: "Tu iras dans *leur* lycée!" [You will go to *their* lycée!] (216/125). José observes his mother without fully grasping her fighting spirit: "Je ne comprenais pas pourquoi, non plus, ma mère ne voulait pas tout simplement abandonner la partie." [I couldn't understand, either, why my mother didn't just give up] (216/125). José does recognize, however, that her quitting her job as a relatively well-paid housekeeper on Route Didier to care for him is a great sacrifice. As he moves further and further away from his rural roots, José also relies on cultural memory for sustenance in his new environment. As friend Carmen whistles and sings plantation songs José goes into a trance, making an imaginative journey across his original landscape from which he returns invigorated. As he matures, this interior landscape becomes a source of José's creative power as well as a place of refuge.

José comes to understand the origins, mechanisms, disparities, and legacies of the colonial system as well as the ways in which it transfers poverty to the city. For example, although Petit-Bourg contains an elementary school serving the surrounding communities, children enmeshed in the plantation system have no access to it. Where one lives in the capital city—divided as it is into neighborhoods separated by race, class, and color—reflects an individual's economic condition. The city is also the center of the colonial administration. Urban blacks earn more money than their rural counterparts, but are relegated to jobs as chauffeurs, gardeners, and domestics. Standing in sharp contrast to impermanent, mobile performance spaces like the plantation shacks outside of which funeral observances and learning take place, brick architectural structures such as the Lycée Schoelcher in Fort-de-France signify solidity and tradition. Nevertheless, it is on the site of his initial life experience—the plantation—that José acquires the knowledge and assistance that will figure in his overcoming the obstacles to upward mobility. At Petit-Morne, José was only an observer of danmyé/laghia on the plantation, but he internalized its strategies, principles, and objectives. More important, with the guidance of individuals dispossessed of material goods and denied access to literacy, José achieves academic success. If he were dancing the danmyé, M'man Tine and Médouze would be supporting him as participants in the ring.

Performing Masculinity

In his article "Emasculation on the Plantation: A Reading of *La Rue Cases-Nègres*," Keith Q. Warner refutes Jacques André's theory that José is homosexual.[14] Warner believes that being the son of unmarried parents and living in two female-governed households would be more apt to make José avoid relationships with women until he could handle the responsibility than determine his sexual orientation (42). While postabolition Martinican society reinforced many traditional constraints on expressions of black masculinity, José has numerous male role models—Monsieur Médouze, Audney's father and his friends, Stéphen Roc, Justin Roc, Carmen, and Jojo—whose examples he is drawn to and either synthesizes or rejects.

Because of the economic system to which his family is subject, José is not raised by a mother and father, but by M'man Tine with financial help from his mother Délia. Having escaped the infernal cycle of plantation life with the help of M'man Tine, Délia sends money from her job as a live-in domestic in Fort-de-France to help cover household expenses. M'man Tine and Délia, then, share the raising and nurturing of José, but not simultaneously. José never meets his father, a coachman, who never returned from World War I. While military service was one sure avenue of employment for black men at the time, it is implied that Eugène was a draftee rather than a volunteer: "On l'a attrapé pour l'envoyer faire la guerre en France." [He was caught to go and fight in France] (44/25). Whether he was killed in battle or abandoned his family back home, Eugène is absent from his young son's life. José, therefore grows up without a male presence in his home. The Martinican rural kinship system, however, furnishes surrogates: M'man Tine and neighbor Médouze act as early primary mentors and teachers, while other elders in the community contribute in other ways. Consequently, José constructs a self in relation to many strong figures: M'man Tine; his spiritual father, Médouze; his mother, Délia; and neighbors, teachers, and friends—people rich in culture and spirit.

As historian Bernard Moitt reminds us, labor in the sugarcane fields was not necessarily divided by gender. The *grand atelier* or first gang was composed of the strongest men and women above age fourteen who performed the most arduous tasks. Weeding was the responsibility of the second gang: "Less robust slaves, newly arrived slaves who had to be acclimatized, pregnant slaves and nursing mothers made up the second gang . . . the third slave gang was made up of children . . . between the ages of eight and thirteen years, who worked under the supervision of an elderly female slave" (*Women and Slavery* 40). All three groups were composed of a mixture of males and females, even the *petites-bandes*. Consequently, the field labor José witnessed was not gender-specific.

Similarly, in *La Rue Cases-Nègres*, José's early-childhood teachers are not selected on the basis of gender, age, class, and color. Although Médouze's advanced years do not spare him labor outdoors, he appropriates the landscape in order to teach José about his surroundings, answering his questions about nature and oppression. Médouze's method contrasts with the rote learning, the memorization and recitation of names of rivers and kings that characterize the French school José will encounter later. In the evenings, Médouze converts the threshold of his shack or the space under the mango tree into a classroom illuminated only by his pipe and a small fire. He uses riddles to stimulate José's imagination and to develop his critical thinking skills. Like a good teacher, when his young pupil cannot identify "letter" as an answer (after all, José would not have received any mail, not yet having learned how to read), Médouze instructs with reference to items from José's immediate and familiar milieu—coconuts, sugarcane, a fingernail. Only then does he proceed to more difficult riddles. José treasures his tutelage with the old man: "Sur la simple intervention de M. Médouze, le monde se dilate, se multiplie, grouille vertigineusement autour de moi." [At the mere intervention of Mr. Médouze, the world expanded, increased, teemed in a swirl around me] (54/30).

Médouze's shack is also the site of the oral account of his own father's family's capture in Africa, their separation and transport to Martinique, and their work on a plantation. This impassioned récit, embedded in José's narrative, explains the African origins of most Martinicans. In addition, it is his first history lesson, one that will not be duplicated in the French school. It is important that José acquire this knowledge as self-defense against the official narrative that pervades and dominates the national curriculum. Médouze delivers this lesson in a manner that conveys his anger to such an extent that his pupil feels the urge to hit the next white man he sees. That this untrained instructor has the power to teach, move, and inspire makes Médouze what Grant Farred calls a "vernacular intellectual," that is, one who challenges injustice outside of the traditional spheres. Without a well-lit space and the conventional teacher's supplies—desk, blackboard, pencils, pens, rulers, maps, and books—Médouze lays the foundation for José's future achievement. In the French system, teaching young children is usually a woman's job; but Médouze, with no materials, is highly effective. He explains that "l'école, c'était un endroit où l'on envoyait des enfants intelligents" (school was a place where intelligent children were sent) (90/51).

Though poor and illiterate, Médouze nevertheless transmits to his pupil a wealth of knowledge about botany and black history—subjects barred from the French curriculum, which instead requires even students in the colonies to master the geography and climate of the metropole. Médouze's ancestral memory, passed down orally to José before he embarks on his physical journey, enables him to understand, survive, and confront various obstacles to academic achievement. Male behavior embodied in Médouze involves not suffering in silence, but articulating opposition to oppression, being a surrogate father, grandfather, teacher, and friend. The rags that clothe his body and his resemblance to a bleeding Christ nailed to the cross symbolize the sacrifices his generation has made on behalf of younger generations. Médouze represents an intellectual masculinity that will be later embodied in Stéphen Roc.

Masculine performances in *La Rue Cases-Nègres* continue to take center stage in José's life, especially when he is eleven. At this time, two events cause a major shift in his development: he makes a new friend and is promoted to a class with his first male schoolteacher. In each case, José observes a new mode of male behavior in a new space. Audney comes into José's life at a crucial time, after he experiences class and color prejudice at a friend's house. Audney, from Haut-Morne, is charged with caring for his father's horse and in that capacity introduces José to an exclusively male ritual. Author Zobel shifts the conventional scene of women bathing and washing clothes in the river to one where men congregate for a similar chore. On Sundays, Audney and José join the male residents of the Poirier plantation who wash the overseers' horses, their own clothes, and themselves in the lake. José marvels at the spectacle: "Et je n'avais jamais rien vu de si simple et d'aussi beau que de grands nègres nus, debout à côté de robustes chevaux." [And I'd never seen anything so simple and so beautiful as big black men in the nude, standing beside stalwart horses] (178/103). Jacques André reads this moment as a homoerotic one in which voyeurism prevails. I believe that it demonstrates José's awakening desire to locate, identify, and honor black male physicality. Unlike Lafcadio Hearn, who, as a privileged, voyeuristic observer, regards the black laborers as emblems of the good-old-days of plantation romance, José, who makes a connection between the men and centaurs pictured on packages of pasta, imagines them as powerful gods in a natural milieu. His experience of the dignified manner of the men astride horses, although transitory, presents possibilities for his own future in which he takes charge of his own destiny.

Intellectual masculinity reemerges as an influence on José's development in Petit-Bourg, where he encounters teacher Stéphen Roc whose presence changes the dynamic of the whole classroom: "On eût dit que la seule présence de notre maître d'école y avait apporté quelque chose de viril." [You might say that the very presence of our school master had made it assume a somewhat manly air] (181/105). Tall and deep voiced, Roc disciplines the students with his bare hands, whereas the women teachers strike with rulers or bamboo canes. Corporal punishment, part of the French teaching method, supports the serious business of learning and preparation for the Certificat d'Etudes Primaires. Stéphen Roc wears pleated, white linen slacks, a jacket, a hat, and shiny black shoes to work—clothing befitting his bourgeois status. The gold watch dangling on a chain from his pocket signals that he controls his own time, in contrast to the plantation workers whose days are regulated by the sun. Roc is a hero not only for accepting the responsibility of educating the local youngsters, but for returning to his own hometown to do so. He is José's first example of a black man in a position of authority whose power does not involve physical exertion.

"To Get Around the Rule of Silence": Performing Masculinity as Détour / 51

José's subconscious search for male models in a society that denies black male authority draws him to the harbor in Fort-de-France without understanding why. In this neighborhood of wholesale stores and garbage-strewn streets, he can view men unloading merchandise from barges, carrying heavy bags, boxes, and barrels on their heads, or passing them from man to man in a human chain. These displays of physical strength in a spirit of cooperation are paced by a silent rhythm. With sweat pouring off their bodies, the dock workers put forth a Herculean effort in a society that denies their humanity. This scene is reminiscent of the one in which workers from the Poirier plantation bathe horses in the lake. In that space and for a short time, they display their autonomy.

José's friend Carmen represents neither a solely muscular nor a solely intellectual masculinity, but he nonetheless occupies an ambiguous position of power in urban Martinique. Carmen enjoys the company of women, mainly dating young housekeepers and market vendors only to end the relationships when they get too close. Calling the shots in these relationships, he cannot, however, refuse the advances of Madame Mayel, his békée employer: "Le regard le pénètre, le brûle, l'attouche, telles les mains de ces femmes qui se sont plu si souvent à le dévêtir et le caresser par tout son corps, comme pour le remodeler à l'ardeur de leur désir." [Her eyes went straight through him, burned him, touched him, like the hands of those women who so often enjoyed taking off his clothes and caressing him all over his body, as if to make him over to suit the ardor of their desire] (302/176). Despite their physical intimacy, Carmen resents Madame Mayel's assumption that she can question him about his private life. That she can order him to return to the house after dropping off her husband illustrates the way that her gender, race, and class combine to give her control over Carmen's body. Her husband is in a similar position; he keeps a black mistress with whom he has children in another part of town. Some of José's working-class neighbors yearn for such a relationship, because they misinterpret it as a source of security. In "polite society," however, Madame Mayel's arrangement with Carmen, which also transgresses race and class lines, would not be tolerated.

Carmen is a chauffeur, another kind of domestic worker who is paid little to serve the middle class by making their lives more comfortable. At first annoyed by having to call this robust man, Carmen, José comes to realize that the name "évoquait ce qu'il y avait de plus mâle, de plus rebelle, de plus bohème" [brought out that which was most masculine in him, that which was most rebellious, that which was most Bohemian] (256/149). Carmen's parents choose this feminine name as a kind of protective talisman; their four sons had all died very young, while their seven daughters survived. This turning of gender identity on its head achieves its goal as Carmen grows to manhood.¹⁵ Carmen migrated to Fort-de-France where he and José become neighbors, but divergent paths brought them there. Born on a plantation, Carmen represents the destiny of the young man to whom military service offers an escape. Although his early life paralleled José's, he lacked advocates and teachers like Médouze, M'man Tine, Stéphen Roc, and Délia to intervene on his behalf. José is protected and spared from bodily harm on the plantation. Carmen, on the other hand, carries the scars from his many close calls with death. As a baby left alone for hours in the shack while his family worked the cane fields and his younger siblings played outside, he crawled toward the light streaming from under the door and caught his head and shoulders in the narrow space, almost strangling to death. At age seven, he is nearly trampled by an ox, and later, a fall shatters one of his shoulder blades. Astoundingly, Carmen survives the plantation, a stint in the army and, luckily, becomes gainfully employed in the capital city. But with his limited ability to read or write French, he is destined to remain a chauffeur.

Carmen's evening visits to José's room recall José's to Médouze's home; though improvised, both are genuine learning environments. Carmen and Jojo represent two options for young men without a secondary education: steady but low-paid service employment as either a chauffeur or a gardener. What binds them is a shared past articulated in Carmen's song, a melody José recognizes from his childhood. They can communicate without words; a whistle is their password. By giving José a lift to school, Carmen invests in and supports his educational advancement. José returns the favor, lending him books from his personal collection.

Books and reading provide the opportunity for serious male bonding. In the confined space of his small bedroom, José introduces his friends to black literature. They especially cherish stories about black men subverting the assimilationist project, such as Claude McKay's *Banjo* (1929), available in French at the time. Brent Hayes Edwards points out that *Banjo* excerpts appeared in the journal *Légitime défense* prior to the complete French translation by Rieder in 1931.¹⁶ The eponymous hero, Lincoln Agrippa Daily, nicknamed for his favorite musical instrument, travels to Marseille where he meets Ray, a Haitian writer. No doubt, the title—the banjo is a popular instrument in Martinique—the setting in a French port city, the interactions among struggling young men discussing relevant issues like race, and the dream of becoming a writer resonate with José, Carmen, and Jojo. They are also moved by René Maran's prize-winning *Batouala* (1921) that, with its preface so boldly critical of colonialism, was banned.¹⁷

Carmen and José are more discerning readers than Jojo, who likes Pierre Loti, the nineteenth-century orientalist author. In any case, evenings *chez* José invoke, on a modest scale, a literary salon like the one hosted by Paulette Nardal in Paris. José's, however, is not made up of Sorbonne students, nor does it have any women members with whom to discuss contemporary transnational Caribbean writers. Zobel has said that he modeled *La Rue Cases-Nègres* after Richard Wright's *Black Boy*, in which the title character also has a passion for books.[18] Unlike the young men in Zobel's text, the Wright protagonist must conceal his literacy and forge a letter from a white colleague in order to borrow books. José, on the other hand, generously teaches, shares, and promotes reading.

Monsieur Médouze, Audney's father's friends, Stéphen Roc, the carousel turners, the stevedores, and Carmen provide various models of male behavior for José. These formal and informal instructors have a major impact on his life. At the same time, these interactions are mutually beneficial. Though Carmen is like an older brother to José, within José's reading group, their roles are reversed. This reversal exemplifies on a local level Chamoiseau's interpretation of Glissant's notion of Relation: "L'Autre me change et je le change. Son contact m'anime et je l'anime" (*Ecrire* 202). [The Other changes me and I change him. His contact animates me and I animate him.] Through José's interventions, Carmen grows to appreciate the intellectual aspect of masculinity.

Zobel's novel belies Raphaël Confiant's remark that "Le damier n'étant pas affaire de petits garçons" or danmyé is not for little boys (14). Confiant implies that danmyé has gender boundaries and age limits, but in *La Rue Cases-Nègres*, women and boys symbolically exhibit the moves of skillful combat dancers. M'man Tine is determined to "*lutter* dans les cannes de M. le béké" (*struggle* in the *béké*'s canes!) (19/10; emphasis added).[19] Délia follows her mother's lead, overcoming mighty obstacles to José's education in Fort-de-France. Initiated at an early age into his natural environment and taught history by Médouze, José is armed with knowledge and supported by the ronde that will assist him in facing opponents throughout his life. He demonstrates exemplary improvisational skills when, unable to attend his grandmother's wake, he pays his respects by re-creating a *veillée* in his small room in Fort-de-France. This resited plantation ritual dictates that a conteur perform for the mourners. Performing that role by narrating himself as acting subject, José's words convey his mission and his power: "Je devrais leur conter une histoire. Mais laquelle? Celle que je sais le mieux et qui me tente le plus en ce moment est tout à fait semblable à la leur. C'est aux aveugles et à ceux qui bouchent les oreilles qu'il me faudrait la crier." [I should, for example, tell them a story. But which one? The one which I knew best and which tempted me most at that time was quite similar to theirs. It is to those who are blind and those who block their ears that I must shout it] (311/182). Autofiction, then, can play an advocacy role. In relating his experience, José performs an ancestral ritual, resists cultural annihilation, and recognizes that he has a broader mission to inform those who disregard lives like his. Profiting from the knowledge and example of his mentors and like a champion danmyétiste, he finds the correct balance and lands on his feet.

2

"I Spy"

Curators, Translators, and In-trust Narrators

> *Notre littérature pourra-t-elle, par exemple, être ce lieu où précisément individualisme et destin collectif ne s'excluent pas?*
> *[Could our literature, for example, be the site where precisely individualism and collective destiny do not exclude each other?]*
>
> Yanick Lahens, *L'Exil entre l'ancrage et la fuite*

After escaping the 1937 massacre in the Dominican Republic, a dying Hilarion Hilarius in Jacques Stéphen Alexis's novel *Compère Général Soleil* articulates the necessity that his wife Claire-Heureuse reproduce his story, which will be forever buried without her assistance.

> J'ai payé cher ce que je sais et voilà que si je ne le donne pas à toi, tout ça s'en ira avec moi sous la terre, tout ça ne deviendra même pas un peu de vent chanteur de musiques, même pas une petite luciole dans les nuits, même pas un peu de douce poussière sous les pieds des pèlerins!" (349)

> [I've paid dearly for what I've learned, and if I can't pass it on to you right now, it will all disappear with me under the earth. It will be nothing more than a bit of musical breath, not even a firefly in the night, not even a bit of soft dust on the feet of pilgrims!] (289)

Hilarion is well aware of the power that his experience—transformed into a first-person récit by his wife—could and would exercise. She, a potential "in-trust narrator," could then bear witness for him and their dead child and thereby be an advocate for the victims, as well as the survivors, of the massacre of Haitians residing in the Dominican Republic in 1937.

Hilarius's entreaty provides a model for the in-trust narrative, for all autofiction does not necessarily relate the narrator's own story. Curated by observers or sister witnesses, who are themselves transformed into surrogate storytellers, translators, and/or scribes, the in-trust narrative is also the heir to the *conte*, whose teller either witnessed the incident or heard the story from a third party and closes it with a stock end line like, "I received a kick in the behind and here I am to tell you the story" or a quick recap of how he or she came into possession of the story in the first place (Laroche 65). These narratives are not reproduced verbatim, but are transformed into a totally new text. Invested with the power to (re)-create, the in-trust narrator may function as the spokesperson for the group or actually relish the opportunity to display his or her storytelling prowess. Nevertheless, the transmission of the material is the paramount objective.

The in-trust narrator appears in various guises, as character, author, scribe, or a combination of these. It is implied that an unseen, unacknowledged, and unobtrusive individual listens to Télumée relate her story while standing in her garden. With only an elementary school education, Télumée would not be expected to write her autobiography. Simone Schwarz-Bart patterned her approach after an interview she conducted with an elderly acquaintance named Stéphanie Priccin, who became the model for Télumée. In *Léonora: l'histoire enfouie de la Guadeloupe*, Dany Bébel-Gisler cedes the *I* to the protagonist until the postface in which the *I* shifts to Bébel-Gisler, who explains the process of transcription, translation, and interpretation. Despite the education gap, anthropologist Bébel-Gisler identifies with her informant because they share the same class and gender: "Jamais, en écoutant Léonora, je me suis sentie étrangère, absente de ses interrogations, de ses doutes, de ses recherches. Une grande part de ce qu'elle me disait répondait en moi, résonnait dans mon corps, faisait resurgir des sensations oubliées." [In listening to Léonora, I never felt myself to be an outsider, removed from her inquiry, her doubts, her searching. Much of what she told me sounded an echo in me, resonated in my body, caused forgotten sensations to surface] (298/233).

Patrick Chamoiseau takes the autofiction genre to new heights, creating a narrator/character whose name is a transparent pun on his own—Oiseau de Cham—and whose *I*, though not the center of the story, nevertheless, plays a crucial role in its production, dissemination, and transmission. H. Adlai Murdoch comments: "This creative conflation of author, narrator, and character produces not simply an additional layer of subjective refraction but a veritable Gordian knot of self-reflexivity" (*Creole* 227). In this chapter, I argue that Oiseau de Cham, an ethnologist and self-defined *marqueur de paroles*, acts as curator in *Chronique des sept misères, Antan d'enfance, Chemin-d'école, A bout d'enfance, Solibo Magnifique, Texaco* and *Biblique des derniers gestes*. Moreover, I explore the collective ethos of danmyé and interaction between author, narrator(s), and protagonist as they negotiate voice and space in Fort-de-France.

In the Prix Goncourt–winning novel, *Texaco*, Oiseau de Cham interacts with Marie-Sophie Laborieux, who recounts the events entrusted to her by her father Esternome. Supplementing that knowledge with what she witnessed during her lifetime, she relates the founding of the Texaco neighborhood to the urban planner and to Oiseau de Cham, who in turn verifies, amplifies, and substantiates the oral story with additional notes and documents archived in the library.[1] In *Chemin-d'école*, the répondeurs, who serve an important function in danmyé, have a distinct voice in commenting on and advancing the narration. In *Solibo Magnifique*, the shifting of the *I* through indirect discourse as the characters testify, the competing versions of events, the mixture of oral and written discourses and registers make this novel a true collage text[île].

Neither a creative writer nor a storyteller like Solibo Magnifique, Oiseau de Cham/Ti-Cham defines himself as a marqueur de paroles, someone who collects and transmits (il recueille et transmet) what the conteur produces (*Solibo* 169–70/115).[2] He trades the conteur's opacity for transparency as he witnesses the telling of the story. While *Texaco*'s translators render marqueur de paroles as "Word Scratcher," the author's original words communicate additional rich possibilities.[3] On the one hand, a marqueur is defined in the French dictionary as a brander, score keeper, and felt-tip pen, therefore, a marqueur de paroles keeps track of words with a writing instrument on a durable surface. In practice, he is an observer, listener, curator, and archivist who facilitates the translation, intelligibility, and transmission of oral and written texts. Martinican Creole also invites a culturally specific interpretation of the marqueur de paroles involving music: a *maké* is the drummer who improvises as he accompanies the conteur or danmyétiste. In that capacity, Chamoiseau's marqueur de paroles can be read as a performer "playing" a supportive role to the protagonist, that is, reorganizing various fragments, but ultimately retelling the story in his own words at his own pace. This strategy allows Oiseau de Cham to distance himself from the story and yet narrow the gap between the protagonist and himself. In addition, Chamoiseau's notion of the writer as a *guerrier de l'imaginaire* (warrior of the imaginary) aligns with the warrior mode of danmyé.

Located in the fluid space between the *oraliturain* (storyteller) and the scribe, the marqueur operates and maneuvers in both oral and written domains. Oiseau de Cham, a researcher, witnesses the performance, translates it from Creole into French, and reproduces a written version for posterity. Aware of the significance of his task, he is attentive to representing intonation, rhythms, and gestures, and yet mindful of the impossibility of duplicating the performance. He puts into practice Maximilien Laroche's idea that the Creole story is a model "pour faire parler le texte écrit comme le récit oral, pour faire réentendre la voix du conteur dans celle du narrateur du texte écrit" (for making the written text speak like the oral narrative, for making the storyteller's voice reheard within that of the narrator of the written text] (64). To achieve that end, the two major divisions of *Chronique des sept misères*—"inhalation" and "exhalation"—mimic the storyteller's breathing pattern.[4] In the very first line of *Chemin-d'école*, the marqueur de paroles warns the reader in rhythmical language reminiscent of a conteur that the protagonist's wish to go to school is a big mistake: "Mes frères O, je voudrais vous dire: le négrillon commit l'erreur de réclamer l'école." [My brothers and sisters O! I have something to tell you: the little black boy made the mistake of begging for school] (17/11). Privileging the marqueur's *I*, this opening establishes an immediate intimacy with the reader, implying a complicit we. In a 1998 interview, Chamoiseau stated: "La formidable écriture, c'est celle qui dit *je* et *nous* et qui fait la circulation permanente entre le *je* et le *nous*, montrant les points d'accord, les séparations, les symbioses, toute la négociation qui s'opère entre individu et collectivité, entre *nous* particuliers et le monde" (qtd. in Perret 252). [Formidable writing is that which says *I* and *we* and which circulates between *I* and *we*, showing points of agreement, separation, symbioses, all the negotiations operating between us individuals and the world.] Lorna Milne notes that in *Texaco* the marqueur: "edits ... admits ... to 'compos(ing),' 'correct(ing)' and 'fix(ing) up' ... [and] therefore, it is explicitly recognized that the character of the 'Marqueur' manipulates testimonies provided by female (and other) characters, thus replicating the activity of the real writer Chamoiseau who more radically fictionalizes material from history" (69). Like a curator, Oiseau de Cham in *Texaco* organizes his notebooks chronologically, numbers the pages, tapes or restitches separated pages and leaves, and covers each notebook with protective plastic. For accuracy, he verifies the material by rereading and consulting these sources before drafting his written text. All of these factors make Oiseau de Cham more than a neighborhood scribe like Ti-Cirique in *Solibo Magnifique*, who, with his impeccable language skills, composes letters and fills out documents for those who do not write French. The marqueur, in *Texaco* especially, brings together different perspectives in his transforming of oral history into written form. In compiling unofficial narratives, he becomes an advocate for documenting and disseminating history. Glissant's idea of *relie*, *relaie*, and *relate* (link, relay, and relate) is useful in this regard.

Ti-Cham positions himself among his subjects while conducting ethnographic research on *djobeurs* in the vegetable market. (In Antillean Creole, a djobeur is one who earns a living pushing fruit- and vegetable-filled wheelbarrows between the market and other public places.) In this way, Ti-Cham recruits informants, careful to minimize the class and linguistic differences between him and them. Inscribing their existence before they vanish, he recuperates their subjectivity in *Solibo Magnifique*.[5] In *Chemin-d'école*, because the marqueur was a student in the same classroom as the *négrillon* (little black boy), admitting to being teased by the other students because his last name is a combination of three animals—*chat, oiseau, chameau* (cat, bird, camel) and *os* (bones)—allows him to empathize with the protagonist, giving the unmediated account an air of authenticity. Creole-speaking djobeurs, conteurs, and *driveurs* (urban nomads or drifters) interact with the marqueur de paroles, who pursues and interviews them, translating and transcribing their experiences for the French-reading public.

The marqueur de paroles also has an intimate relationship with words and books. Heir to several traditions, he is not a blank slate, but is influenced by his predecessors, who comprise:

> Ma vieille Sentimenthèque, sédiments de la présence des écrivains en moi. Ils m'avaient fait don de leurs luttes dans ce pays dominé que chacun porte en soi. Donc, j'ai erré en leur compagnie. Ecrire. Rêver. Percevoir ce qui me restait d'eux. Un mot. Une impression. Un rire. Les sensations accumulées. D'eux, j'ai ramené le sentiment qu'il y a tant d'ombres en nous, tant de forces obscures dans le profond de nos maintiens. (*Ecrire* 314).[6]

> [My old Sentimenthèque, sediments of writers within me. They had given me the gift of their struggles in this dominated land that each one carries within oneself. Therefore, I wandered in their company. Writing. Dreaming. Perceiving what remains of them for me. A word. An impression. A laugh. Accumulated sensations. From them, I draw the feeling that there are so many shadows in us, so many dark forces in the depth of our deportment.]

In other words, Chamoiseau's sentimenthèque, a neologism constructed from the prefix in *sentiment* (feeling) and the suffix *thèque* as in *bibliothèque* (library, bookcase, book collection), is the amalgam of emotions stimulated by more than seventy-five poets, novelists, playwrights, and essayists from all over the world, from medieval French poet François Villon to contemporary Haitian poet, playwright, musician, and painter, Frankétienne.[7] In practice, however, the sentimenthèque also encompasses several purveyors of orature: trumpeter Louis Armstrong, an unnamed Creole storyteller, Amerindians, maroons, and the metonymic hold of the slave ship. While Chamoiseau should be commended for recognizing even these anonymous ancestors who inform his work, he must be chided for his glaring omission of women, with the exception of Toni Morrison. That his sentimenthèque is so severely gender-restricted is most disturbing. After all, it is the négrillon's mother who is responsible for his love of books in *Chemin-d'école*, Man Goul who relates stories in *Chronique des sept misères*, and Marie-Sophie Laborieux who articulates Texaco's history.[8]

Chamoiseau, a child of the 1950s, is witness to tremendous social upheavals and like his literary forefathers—Martinicans Zobel, Césaire, Fanon, and Glissant—is concerned about their impact on masculinity. Departmentalization in 1946, which transformed the existing *vieilles colonies* in the Caribbean into integrated départements did not signal access to economic power for its citizens. The collapse of the sugar industry in the mid-twentieth century, which coincided with Chamoiseau's birth, led to the transformation of the agricultural economy into a consumer one. Many of those displaced rural workers moved to the city in search of employment. Largely unskilled, some workers adapted to the new setting by reinventing themselves to assist the market women as djobeurs. Only a temporary solution to a rapidly changing society, wheelbarrowing soon became obsolete when separate outdoor fish, vegetable, and meat *marchés* providing locally grown fruits and vegetables could not compete with the supermarkets' wide variety of imported goods. Wheelbarrows, dependent on the user's physical strength and balance, were overtaken by indoor grocery carts. Trucks, ships, and airplanes, with their more efficient means of transporting merchandise over long distances, provide a service that djobeurs could not possibly match. At the same time that this increase in modern transport offered consumers greater access to foreign-made products, it also contributed to the destruction of the locally based economy, which drove workers out of rural areas. Through the djobeur in *Chronique des sept misères* and the conteur in *Solibo Magnifique*, Chamoiseau examines the impact of displacement on the poor male population of the city, a microcosm of society. While tackling the issues of *enracinement* (settling), *Texaco* traces the founding of a neighborhood on the city's periphery, by tracing one family's heritage. As Chamoiseau's work shows, adult men are not the only victims of *déracinement*: *Chemin-d'école* explores how the tensions of displacement deleteriously effect boys as well.

Chamoiseau's protagonists are anchored to the island in spite of their local errancy (errance). With no writing tools to inscribe their lives and no photographs to document their existence (like Solibo), some literally disappear. The Creole storyteller—his subversive *parole de nuit* (orature, those stories, proverbs, riddles, and songs in Creole, performed at night, that transmitted cultural memory) once a means of self-identifying while defying the dominant society—is finally marginalized out of society altogether. At the time of Solibo's decline, the French language has displaced Creole in Martinique—a displacement with grave consequences for people's livelihoods and sense of identity. Today in Martinique, as tourism replaces the exportation of sugar and bananas, workers must demonstrate fluency in French if they are to succeed in a changing economy. In addition, as Glissant and the créolistes posit, the low status of the Creole language has taken an even more serious toll on human beings: "L'absence de considération pour la langue créole n'a pas été un simple silence de bouche mais une amputation culturelle." [The absence of interest in the Creole language was not a mere mouth silence, but a cultural amputation] (*Eloge* 44/899).

It is significant that the storytelling sessions in *Solibo Magnifique* are confined to the Savane, an outdoor promenade, the site of the *monument aux morts* (monument to the dead) and the location of Solibo's last performance. This monument is located at the opposite end of the park from the statue of Joséphine Tascher de La Pagerie, Napoleon's wife, who was born in Martinique. A member of a rich béké family, she symbolizes planters' economic and political domination of the island. Her marriage to Napoleon Bonaparte links her to the reinstitution of slavery in the colonies after its initial abolition in 1794. In the 1990s, the statue of Josephine was beheaded and its base defaced with paint, an act that protests against continuing subjugation.

The city center, or l'En-ville, is the site of the investigation into Solibo's death. Fort-de-France, divided into residential, commercial, and administrative areas with bureaus to enforce French hegemony, is not an urban magnet like Paris, to which the Bureau de Migrations des Départements d'Outre-Mer promoted migration to provide manpower for Parisian industries. Fort-de-France has no need of an agency charged with recruiting overseas workers for nonexistent plants: "L'En-ville créole n'est pas la ville occidentale, il ne comble pas l'espoir qui soustend les exodes. C'est un outil militaire et administratif, comptoir gestionnaire aux ordres du Centre lointain. Il n'accueille pas. N'a pas d'usines" (*Ecrire* 190). [The Creole city is not the Western city. It does not fulfill the hope that inspires an exodus. It is a military and administrative tool, a management branch that answers to the far-away Center. It does not welcome. There are no factories.] The island capital is a destination of last resort for displaced rural laborers, providing only limited employment opportunities. Ruled from afar and dependent on the metropole, L'En-ville also thrives on an internal and paradoxical imbalance of power. The survival of the poor depends on their participation in an unofficial economy, the basis of what Katherine Browne calls "creole economics." Echoing and subverting George Bush's notion of "voodoo economics," "creole economics" is the prevailing system in a city that depends in some measure upon the existence of marginalized groups for its own prosperity. Shalini Puri emphasizes the irony operative in this interdependency between city and slum, where the "slum *sustains* the city" and "the margin *reinforces* the center" and where, "by extension ... France is dependent on Martinique" (33).

Urban planners like Philippe Yerro use the urban mangrove metaphor to describe marginalized communities that encircle Fort-de-France because, like the local mangrove swamps, though stigmatized, they produce and sustain life. Crucibles of culture, urban mangroves are rooted in and owe their survival to displacement and poverty.[9] After conducting field work in 1985 in Sainte-Thérèse, a low-income neighborhood to the north of Fort-de-France dating from the postemancipation period, and in Volga Plage, a squatter settlement in the southeast section of the city dating from the late 1950s, Michel S. Laguerre concludes that urban poverty has its roots in the colonial period.

> Throughout the entire colonial era slavery was the main cause of poverty among city blacks. Slavery prevented them from holding positions of power as well as from being able to compete in the free market. In structural terms they were kept at the bottom of colonial society: they were not paid for their labour and were discriminated against in all avenues of power. The colonial system, through its legal apparatus, manufactured and reproduced poverty in the structural, not necessarily the physical, margins of the cities so as to be able to exploit the slave labour force. Poverty had a social function in colonial society. It was the inevitable result of a system of inequality engineered to benefit and maintain the dominant European group. The reproduction of the dominant class was dependent on the reproduction of the slave sector, which was forced, by legal and by physical means, to provide free labour to the white group. The reproduction of the slave group was similarly dependent on the reproduction of the dominant class, which was able to augment and enrich itself through the economic exploitation of the slaves. (2)

With no modification in that basic societal structure after abolition, the transfer of poverty from rural areas to the urban center is not surprising.

Laguerre identifies four phases in the establishment of squatter communities:

invasion, in which migrants appropriate unused public land on which they build small abodes with makeshift and discarded materials; expansion, in which some land is leased legally and roads are delineated; modernization, in which cement-block houses replace the *cases-nègres* and the government introduces electricity, running water, garbage collection, street names, and house numbers, aware that these amenities may bring them new voters; integration, in which people customize their houses—adding floors, for example—which signals a sense of ownership, individuality, and permanence (43–45).

Zobel hints at these kinds of marginalized communities, segregated by race, class, and color, in *La Rue Cases-Nègres*. Individuals travel to jobs in neighborhoods like Route Didier, where they cannot possibly afford to live. Word of mouth, not employment agencies, leads to job opportunities; José's mother Délia, operating in an oral universe, "hears" about an opening as a domestic worker in Monsieur Lasseroux's household. While Zobel does not explicitly indicate the forces that propelled Carmen to become a chauffeur and Jojo, a gardener, Chamoiseau focuses on single, self-supporting adult men in *Chronique des sept misères*, *Solibo Magnifique*, and *Texaco*—driveurs who must negotiate the hostile environment of L'En-ville. ("Driveur" and "la drive" are Martinican Creole words. The first suggests a drifter who works—"working flaneur" is perhaps the most concise definition. The second suggests the drift of driveurs into and around the city for various remunerative and other purposes.) *La drive*, as Chamoiseau explains below, is both a result of urban displacement and a form of resistance to it: "On erre sans fin ... à la sédentarité ou à l'immobilité, ou encore à la déshumanisation enracinée du système plantationnaire resté en place malgré l'abolition[;] ils opposaient la Drive comme une contestation mais aussi comme tentative d'épanouissement de soi" (*Ecrire* 188–191). [One wanders without end ... to sedentarity or immobility, or yet to the dehumanization of the plantation system which remains in place despite abolition[;] they contrast la Drive as a protest, but also as an attempt at self-blossoming].

Local authorities, who wield power in the name of the metropole, are hostile to la drive, which brings workers from their homes on the city periphery to the center of town each day. They pass laws prohibiting loitering, which the police are charged with enforcing, a situation reminiscent of the Code Noir's regulations restricting the movement of slaves off of or between plantations. Nevertheless, la drive can be considered a mode of resistance to legal and societal constraints, an urban form of *marronnage*. Fleeing to the hills to escape slavery has been reversed, replaced by errancy within the city. La drive, then, is a consequence of certain historical and social factors. In order to survive, driveurs maneuver within a confined space and have to be excellent improvisers, like danmyétistes.

With no fixed address, Prosper Bajole, nicknamed Solibo, is a classic driveur. Descending on the downtown area each day from his home in the Tivoli forest, he invents a career from several individual jobs. Charcoal maker and seller, repairman, and philosopher, Solibo is an heir to the enslaved plantation worker who blends in during the day, but who at night transforms himself into a conteur in order to amuse and educate. A paradoxical figure according to the créolistes, he manipulates power and gets around the rule of silence.[10] Elusive and never announcing when or where he will perform, Solibo, as Richard Coeurillon describes him to the police, is like a maroon who hunters and their dogs can never track (196/135). In his daily life, though, he adheres to a routine: traveling between his ovens in Tivoli and the downtown to sell charcoal; wearing a Panama hat; stopping by Chez Chinotte at noon for a drink; repeating the aphorism "La misère dessine toujours de la même manière" (misery draws the same way everywhere) (176/76); visiting Sidonise on Tuesdays and Thursdays until she breaks off the relationship to marry a customs worker; and lighting a candle for his mother Man Florise on All Saint's Day. Within this predictable pattern, however, Solibo still manages to be creative. He improvises by varying his charcoal-selling methods; by entering the bar through different portals, sometimes a door, sometimes a window; by drinking different kinds of rum, white or dark with brown sugar, syrup, or honey; and by modifying the amount of time he spends in the bar. In refusing to surrender to municipal efforts to corral him into participating in folkloric events, Solibo resists domination and embodies resistance.

It is understandable, then, that Zozor Alcide-Victor regards Solibo as a master danmyétiste: "Son équilibre interne le plaçait d'emblée dans un ailleurs." [His spiritual balance set him apart] (171/126). On their first encounter, Zozor is accosted by two drunken men on the Savane. Fearing that Solibo is part of their group (though he is otherwise occupied, urinating under a tamarind tree), Zozor prepares to apply the martial art's defensive moves against him. After observing Solibo up close, however, Zozor perceives that he faces a more experienced danmyétiste than himself. Unlike the two drunks who confront Zozor, Solibo is well dressed, silent, in deep concentration, his head held high, his breathing controlled—"un esprit en état de silence, un corps dénoué parcouru d'énergie libre" (a spirit in a state of silence, a relaxed body flowing with free energy) (172/117). Faced with certain defeat, Zozor follows the unwritten rules of danmyé and immediately concedes without Solibo having made a single offensive move. Solibo engenders danmyé as a state of mind: "L'art martial cesse bien vite d'être une technique pour devenir un éveil de l'esprit, un non-être qui intègre l'univers, une paix." [The martial arts quickly cease to be a weapon and become an awakening of the spirit, a nonbeing that integrates the universe, a peace] (171/117).

Solibo is valued by all of his neighbors, friends, and acquaintances, who understand his worth. City worker Sosthène Versailles considers him a nice guy, a "bougre agréable" (190). Zozor Alcide-Victor shows his respect by referring to Solibo as "sir," the same address he confers on the police inspector to whom he describes the dead conteur as "un nègre important, monsieur l'inspecteur. Sa vie soutenait des dizaines de vies" (a great man, Mr. Inspector. His life was the nourishment for dozens of others) (171/116). Frequenting women from different Caribbean countries, he learns from them and can describe each place and its people without leaving Martinique.[11] Despite his intimate relationships, Solibo does not involve himself in other people's affairs, but offers help only when asked. Such is the case when he comforts lonely Man Gnam after her children are lured to France by the government-sponsored migration plan (BUMIDOM) and later arranges a traditional wake after her death. His most powerful asset is his voice with its many tones. While it can gently advise and caution—as when Solibo warns Pipi always to pose questions—Solibo's voice can also soothe raging animals. When her Christmas dinner pig runs amok, Man Gnam summons Solibo, who calms it "sans mots ni paroles" (without words or stories) (81/48). His mellifluous tones also pacify a *bête-longue* (snake) terrorizing Man Goul. Whispering to it some silent words ("lui souffla des paroles inaudibles"), Solibo turns the snake from its purpose (75/44). In Martinican vernacular lore, the fer-de-lance, a poisonous pit viper, is said to torment maroons hiding in the mountains. In modern-day Martinique, the maroons have become driveurs, displaced to the city but haunted by some of the same terrors that the *bête-longue* represents.[12] In gratitude for saving her life, Man Goul confers on Solibo the title of respect, "Papa."

Solibo has inherited his gift of speech from his father Amédé, one of those workers who migrated to Fort-de-France in search of work after the collapse of the rural economy. Because the military offered a better opportunity, Amédé left to fight the Germans in Europe, after which he returned to Martinique and settled in Morne Pichevin, a poor district in the eastern periphery of the capital. His murder led to a life of abject poverty for young Solibo and hospitalization for depression and alcoholism for his mother. Without an anchor or the guidance of an advocate like M'man Tine, Solibo wanders the margins of the city, surviving on the plants he gathers, the fruit he picks, the bark he strips, and the shrimp he catches, before his descent into what officialdom suggests is a life of vice. Rescued by old market women, Solibo listens to their tales about survival and resistance and recovers, as does his mother. Although not explicitly stated, Solibo's talent for storytelling is the result of the convergence of nature and nurture: his father's genes and the market women's care. It is less important to understand Solibo's words than to be carried away by their rhythm, to open up "au dire, s'y laisser emporter" (to the word, letting it carry you away) (33/13).

Once his storytelling style advances from competence to prowess, Solibo is named "Magnifique" by an expert conteur. Two contradictory words inform his nickname, the first referring to his precipitous fall (Solibo) and the second, (Magnifique), to his capacity for recovery, resurgence, and mastery. As the witnesses attest, Solibo used to perform every night until dawn, but times have changed, and he has fewer opportunities to practice his art. Bête-Longue, one of the suspects questioned by police, notices signs that Solibo has lost his lust for life: "Sa bouche battait silencieusement. Il devait se dire des choses terribles sur la vie d'ici. Sa joie, son allant semblaient éteints. Je découvrais un nègre en souffrance" [His lips moving silently. He must have been telling himself some terrible things about life here. His joy, his swagger seemed gone. I was looking at a man in pain] (187/128). This man-o-words is strangled by his own speech. Having nowhere to go in a world where Creole and *oraliture* (oral literature) are no longer valued, the words literally get caught in his throat: "Un flot de verbe devait lui torturer le ventre." [A stream of words must have been torturing his belly] (224/157). Solibo is killed by *une égorgette de la parole* (having his throat cut by the word). While it is tempting to draw a parallel with tongue swallowing, one way captured Africans resisted enslavement, Solibo does not commit suicide. Instead, he is symbolically excised by Caribbean society. The police search for evidence of crime and conspiracy, but find neither. Solibo dies from neglect, and the community is responsible.

Solibo embodies a changing Martinique, where the government does not bother to retrain a population with skills actually needed in Fort-de-France. At first, displaced laborers turned entrepreneurs respond by creating opportunities for themselves by filling a need. But their resourcefulness will only go so far. One sign of the death of a way of life is the absence of a formal wake to commemorate and celebrate Solibo's life. Instead, an impromptu ceremony on the Savane punctuates the wait while the ambulance recovers the body. The police station is the site of another makeshift wake, where mourners "testify" in front of an audience of one, an unsympathetic interrogator. The traditional group dynamics where reverence and festivity mix in the *veillée* are absent. Far from honoring him, the police show disrespect for Solibo's memory by leaving his body uncovered on the Savane, contaminating the "crime scene," and subjecting his friends to grilling interrogation.

Despite his status as a rebel, Solibo ultimately loses the fight. When the coal piles up in his yard and he disappears from the market, no one notices or inquires about him, making the community complicit in his demise. With no support from the ronde, it is symbolically apt that Solibo succumb at the site of the monument for the dead, his body and his trades (as charcoal maker and seller, repairman, and storyteller) obsolete. Surrounded by tree roots, his body is reclaimed by nature. His death occurs sometime after three a.m., the temporal juncture of night and day symbolizing a transitional moment in Martinican culture. It is only Congo, another character experiencing the process of cultural extinction, who correctly perceives the cause of Solibo's death.

Congo's given name, Bateau Français, signifies the relatively recent arrival of his African-born father, who sailed to Martinique after abolition as part of the colonial government's recruitment of people from central Africa and India to replace formerly enslaved workers.[13] Congo, a first generation Martinican, engenders rebellion and resistance not only on a personal level, like Solibo, but within a collective context as an activist in the struggle for equality. Joining strikers in their quest for better working conditions, he is arrested for setting fire to the sugarcane fields, fined for theft, and taken into custody for public drunkenness. Each of these acts represents his attempt to take possession of the fruit of his labor. Congo's early militancy impedes his later being hired to work on a plantation.

Moving to the city, he makes and sells shredded cassava to a public that now prefers French fries made with wheat flour. Plummeting sales force him to reduce this business activity to once a week, in the market or at the entrance to the bar—locations of his dwindling, loyal clientele. The image of his "silhouette anachronique" (anachronistic silhouette) conveys his status in society (204/142). People think he is wearing a carnival costume. Out of place, he is a throwback to an earlier time. The sound of the drum in the Savane, a reminder of his African heritage, appeals to his cultural memory. A suspect in Solibo's death, he is severely beaten at the police station with a symbolic instrument, a telephone book, which facilitates communication between people at a distance. Solibo's art and Congo's trade, on the other hand, require face-to-face contact. Kicked in the neck and genitals, punched in the liver, his fingers crushed and eyes blinded by his torturer's thumbs, Congo jumps out of the window, an escape suggesting a version of the flying African tale, found throughout the diaspora, in which the protagonist safely returns "home."

Solibo and Congo are not the only displaced male adults whose occupations are resited to the city. Drummers and herbalists migrate, too, bringing their knowledge with them. Neither specialty survives in the new space. Sucette is hit in the head with an enormous notebook, signifying the conquest of his oral domain by French literacy. Those who practice "la science des vieilles herbes" (knowledge of ancient herbs) are replaced by pharmacists (*Chronique* 159/114). The unsuccessful and thus temporary transfer of culture to the urban space is complemented by the invention of new trades: the djobeur and the marqueur de paroles. The djobeurs eventually fade from the market as well as from history: "Nos contours devenant flous: victimes d'une gomme invisible, nous semblions tout bonnement nous effacer de la vie." [Our outlines getting hazy: we seemed quite simply to be fading away, victims of an invisible eraser] (*Chronique* 216/155). The marqueur, proficient in both the oral and the written, requires a specific sensitivity to languages and people in order to interact with his subjects and transmit their utterances. In *Solibo Magnifique*, Chamzibié/Ti-Cham/Oiseau de Cham improvises a discourse characterized by onomatopoeias (flop! cling!) (84); Creole renderings (*souplé* for *s'il vous plaît*) (91); repetitions; asides; and aphorisms—Doudou-Ménar's "gros seins... jamais trops lourds pour une poitrine (huge breasts ... never too heavy for a chest) (47/24)—in order to inscribe Solibo's story and Sucette's drum solo. By contrast, the police report is succinct, dry, and inadequate, carrying no trace of Didon's panic while being questioned by Bouafesse; the official document makes no mention of physical manifestations of fear—Didon trembles, cries, and soils his pants. The deficiencies of writing are further reflected in the sea of discarded paper in the station house: clippings, forms, wrinkled papers, pale carbon paper, and stamps, along with old typewriter ribbons and bottles of wine and rum fill the garbage. The police, in fact, are equally as deficient in the reading of visual and oral signs as they are in communication by written words. They misinterpret evidence at the scene and misunderstand the suspects' status and testimony. The authorities misread the empty bottles they find as signs of poisoning. Ironically, the poison that slaves sometimes used to kill their owners would never be used against a rebel like Solibo.

The fourteen witnesses to Solibo's last performance, collapse, and demise represent various color, class, ethnic, linguistic, gender, national, and regional categories, as well as differing degrees of literacy. The Savane brings together this disparate group whose identities run the gamut; yet they are all part of the

Martinican mosaic. Congo speaks rural Creole; Charlot, urban Creole; Conchita Juanez y Rodriguez from Colombia, a Spanish-accented Creole; and Justin Hamanah, of Indian ancestry, a Guadeloupean-accented Creole. Pierre signs his deposition with two crosses. Their language and intonations give voice to their origins. The gap between the characters' birth names and sobriquets reflects disconnected social domains. The name that appears on government or official documents is rarely used in public, unlike the familiar nickname conferred by friends or kin. That name can point to an individualizing habit, origin, or a physical or psychological trait. What distinguishes drummer Sucette (Eloi Apollon) from his neighbors is that he loves to "sip" (sucer) alcoholic beverages, while Le Syrien (Zozor Alcide-Victor) has one Middle Eastern parent. Created within the realm of orality, however, these nicknames are derided as aliases in Evariste Pilon's police report. The characters' marginal status also resonates in their area of residence. Living in communities on the periphery of Fort-de-France that do not provide jobs—Trénelle, Volga Plage, Texaco, Rive-Droite-Levassor, Terres-Sainville, cité Dillon, Chateau-Boeuf, Pont-Démosthène—they depend and descend on the city for their livelihoods. Not seeing any visible signs of employment, such as a machete for cutting sugarcane, the police assume their suspects are out of work and have committed a violent crime where there is none.

What the suspects have in common is that they are drawn to the Savane. In the manner of *libres de savane* or *libres de fait*, enslaved persons who, as Bernard Moitt explains, "lived in a state of quasi-freedom, having been manumitted by their owners without the authority of the state or the official documents of free status," all the suspects in the police inquiry are positioned somewhere in between, living in the limbo between slavery and freedom ("In the Shadow" 37). These characters suffer the legacy of slavery and do not profit from emancipation's promise of opportunity. According to the state, most have no fixed address or live on unpaved streets in unnumbered houses, except for Justin Hamanah, Charles Gros-Liberté, the shopkeeper Zozor Alcide-Victor, and the marqueur Oiseau de Cham. Experiencing declining demand for their goods and services, Doudou-Ménar sells fewer *fruits confits* (candied fruits), Congo less shredded cassava, and Solibo less charcoal. Though equipped with French literacy, an essential tool for success in L'En-ville, the marqueur does not always control his relationship with Solibo, who operates in the oral domain. The balance of power shifts. Oiseau de Cham, who wants to record Solibo's life, *does* manage to interview the storyteller, but only on his own terms. Because Solibo's schedule is not organized by a watch or a calendar, Ti-Cham must catch up with him in the bar or at the market. Nor can an appointment be made to attend a storytelling session; Oiseau de Cham must wait patiently for three nights in order to witness what turns out to be Solibo's last performance. Neither Ti-Cham's project nor the fact that he dedicates his book to Solibo is important to the conteur. He is indifferent to the written word, conscious that it cannot capture the intricacies and nuances of orality. He dismisses Ti-Cham, who functions as a participant in the production of Solibo's story. Frustrated, the marqueur hesitates, wanting to forget his promise to recount the story, to "porter témoignage" (bear witness).

The marqueur de paroles appears to be more decisively committed to tracing the development of urban boys. In the trilogy *Antan d'enfance*, *Chemin-d'école*, and *A bout d'enfance*, he witnesses, remembers, and narrates the young négrillon's relationships and survival strategies in L'En-ville.[14] *Chemin-d'école*, focusing on the protagonist's first encounter with the French educational system in late 1950s Martinique, is informed not by la drive, but by migration tropes. The négrillon longs to go to school, imagining a paradise in the same way that colonized subjects used to imagine Paris. Once he reaches the new location, however, he becomes bewildered and fearful, experiencing a virtual exile, a paradoxical exile in that it occurs in his own land.[15]

The narrator positions himself at the scene as an observer. Because the main character is designated solely by his racial and gender identities (négrillon), his experience becomes an exemplary one for black boys. Equivalent to a vocal *auditoire* (audience) and the chorus that backs up the soloist in danmyé, the répondeurs from time to time intervene and comment on the action. The narrator, who clearly distances himself from the protagonist négrillon, is not always able to maintain that space throughout the text. For one, the frequent use of free indirect discourse sometimes causes the narrator's voice to be indistinguishable from the négrillon's. This narrative narrowing of the gap between narrator and protagonist reinforces the marqueur's identification with the young student(s).

The *chemin-d'école* (road to school) marks the beginning of a transformative journey for the négrillon. At the Ecole Perrinon, a microcosm of the metropole, Creole-speaking youth interact with Le Maître (the schoolmaster), the intermediary between them and the French state. Although the teacher is a Caribbean male like his students, he has been invested with the power to assimilate them into French culture, illustrating Edouard Glissant's association of French "pédagogie" with "démagogie" (*Discours* 577–89). That Chamoiseau's négrillon undergoes this assimilationist project in *Chemin-d'école* leads one to conclude that his school experience is similar in many ways to a migrant's experience, although the border he crosses is neither to another nation nor to a big city. In this model of intraurban displacement, the host country, embodied by the school, prohibits the Creole language, the mother tongue of the students who live in that community.

Cheikh Hamidou Kane, whose classic novel *L'Aventure ambiguë* is also centered on a young boy's encounter with the French school in Senegal, provides us with a lens and language through which to read that experience.[16] Kane posits that the real colonial power resided not in the first cannons, those that accompanied the soldiers in their invasion and conquest of Africa, but rather in what came afterwards, the French colonial school, which Kane likens to a cannon and a magnet. It is La Grande Royale who foresees the hegemonic consequences of the new order, but still encourages her brother to enroll Samba Diallo:

> L'école nouvelle participait de la nature du canon et de l'aimant à la fois. Du canon, elle tient son efficacité d'arme combattante. Mieux que le canon, elle pérennise la conquête. Le canon contraint les corps, l'école fascine les âmes. Où le canon a fait un trou de cendre et de mort et, avant que, moisissure tenace, l'homme parmi les ruines n'ait rejailli, l'école nouvelle installe sa paix. (60)

> [The new school shares at the same time the characteristics of cannon and of magnet. From the cannon it draws its efficacy as an arm of combat. Better than the cannon, it makes conquest permanent. The cannon compels the body, the school bewitches the soul. Where the cannon has made a pit of ashes and of death, in the sticky mold of which men would not have rebounded from the ruins, the new school establishes peace.] (45–46)[17]

To Kane's cannon trope I would like to add its homonym "canon" as in prescribed texts by French authors. Both can[n]ons have the overwhelming impact of weapons of mass destruction, one physical, one psychological. School is also a location where Ngugi wa Thiong'o's "cultural bomb" explodes. In *Decolonising the Mind*, Ngugi writes that a cultural bomb is designed to

> annihilate a people's belief in their names, in their languages, in their environment, in their heritage of struggle, in their unity, in their capacities and ultimately in themselves. It makes them see their past as one wasteland of nonachievement and it makes them want to distance themselves from that wasteland. It makes them want to identify with that which is furthest removed from themselves, for instance, with other peoples' languages rather than their own (3).

Just as it is for Samba Diallo in Kane's narrative, the school experience is a similarly ambiguous adventure for José and the négrillon.[18] José's love of reading in *La Rue Cases-Nègres* is initiated and nurtured in part by Christian Bussi, who lends him books that his parents purchase. During a school vacation in Petit-Bourg, José cultivates this new hobby by reading for hours outside. The books that he finds, borrows, and begs for pile up in M'man Tine's home, distinguishing her residence from all of the others on Cour Fusil. While José's books awaken his imagination to worlds previously unknown, they do not elucidate Martinican history.

Admittedly, school is a place where learning how to read and write French opens up new opportunities, but it is also the place where students are denied the right to speak their own language, an issue that remains somewhat muted in *L'Aventure ambiguë* and *La Rue Cases-Nègres*.[19] In *Chemin-d'école*, the young students at the Ecole Perrinon are taught French using a total immersion methodology characterized by humiliation and violence. Learning another language is not the source of controversy, but the fact that French has been elevated to an exclusive position of superiority along with the national culture it supports. Subject to ridicule by Le Maître, the students become frustrated and demoralized, robbed of a healthy sense of self. The can[n]ons and cultural bombs explode in the classroom with all manner of destructive psychological repercussions as articulated by Fanon.

Dedicating *Chemin-d'école* to *students* from the Caribbean, French Guiana, New Caledonia, Reunion, Mauritius, Corsica, Brittany, and Africa, Chamoiseau shows empathy for young people from former French colonies and provinces who had to endure the prohibition of their mother tongue from school. By writing "dites en votre nom" (told in your name), he assumes the responsibility of linking, relaying, and relating (*relie, relaie, relate*) to others, paying homage to Aimé Césaire, whose poem *Cahier d'un retour au pays natal* had a tremendous impact on him. The often-quoted line of this poem resonates in the dedication: "Ma bouche sera la bouche des malheurs qui n'ont point de bouche." [My mouth shall be the mouth of misfortunes that have no mouth] (22/50).

The tension between French and Creole and between oral and written cultures is figured in two characters who share a bench in the classroom: the négrillon, who adores learning to read and write, and Gros-Lombric for whom literacy is a genuine struggle. The négrillon has a ronde that nurtures his curiosity, assists in his instruction, and acts as his advocate. His oldest sister, La Baronne, supervises homework around the dining table. He imitates his teacher and his mother's fetishizing of the book. Although he does not understand the French words, le négrillon experiences vicariously the pleasure Le Maître derives from reading aloud. When his mother, for whom books are "tabernacles des sciences" (tabernacles of the sciences), discovers his fascination, she brings home discarded print material from the market—old newspapers, almanacs, comic books, crime novels—to supplement the books she stores in a potato crate under a shroud in a closet. Even though he doesn't yet know how to read, he consumes these treasures, making up his own stories in relation to his sense of pages and print.

By contrast, Gros-Lombric, a muscular and fidgety boy whose family lives in a one-room shack, does not have a network of support. He must rise before dawn to do a whole host of chores before leaving for school, located two or three kilometers away. One of eleven children who share the feeble light from an oil lamp to do their homework, he is deemed unintelligent by the Maître, who singles him out for ridicule. Gros-Lombric's strengths are not appreciated in a formal French school setting. He excels at calculating numbers in his head and is an expert marbles player. Moreover, he recites proverbs and is an adroit storyteller—a future Solibo or Médouze, if you will, in a world that has no need for his talents. In short, Gros-Lombric is "attached" as his nickname suggests— "Lombric echoes *nombril* or navel—to the Creole oral tradition. Unsuccessful in school, Gros-Lombric gradually loses interest and is pushed out, while the négrillon adapts, achieves, and flourishes. Nevertheless, Gros-Lombric remains a hero to the adult narrator who now appreciates the extent of his rebellion.

> Je te sais gré, Gros-Lombric, de ta parole souterraine, tu t'enfuyais par là, tu te réfugiais là, tu résistais là, tu l'habitais d'une minutie immodérée, et cette greffe-en-terre lui conférait une force latente—je n'en percevrai la déflagration qu'une charge d'années plus tard malgré l'oubli de ta figure et du son de ta voix. (Tu n'étais pas conteur, tu étais toutes-mémoires.) (181)

> [I'm grateful to you, Big Bellybutton, for your underground language. You fled through it, took refuge in it, resisted with it, inhabited it with infinite familiarity, and this fierce deep-rootedness endowed your language with a latent strength whose combustive power I would realize only many years later, when your face and the sound of your voice were already forgotten (You were not a storyteller—you were a repository of memories).] (128–29)

Gros-Lombric represents boys who fail in traditional schools. There is a disconnect between their talents and mainstream academic expectations. Nonconformists and experts in the realm of orality, their numbers are increasing dramatically. In his professional life, Chamoiseau works with such teens, some of whom become disruptive, fail, drop out of school, and get into trouble. The question is how to integrate them into society.

Chemin-d'école is divided into two unequal parts, "envie" (longing) and "survie" (survival)—a juxtaposition that reproduces the way in which the protagonist's desire to go to school is quickly transformed into a need to survive the experience. In fact, this shift in perspective occurs on his very first day. In the short "envie" section, the négrillon pesters his mother Man Ninotte to allow him to go to school. Envious of his older siblings and the other neighborhood children who leave each morning and disappear in the distance unaccompanied by their parents, he muses: "'Je veux aller avec les Grands là où ils vont.'" [I want to go with the Big Kids to where they go] (22/14). So far, his independent travel has been limited to running errands at the local shop. Therefore, his desire for independence coincides with a craving for power: "Le départ matinal vers ce lieu inconnu, relevaient à ses yeux d'un rite de pouvoir auquel il voulait s'initier." [The morning departure toward this unknown place seemed linked to a ritual of power into which he longed to be initiated] (32/22). The naïve boy longs to be assimilated into this space. His dream to conquer new worlds is partially realized when his mother enrolls him in Man Salinière's preschool, where he learns to sing the ABC's and write the letters of the alphabet. At this point in his young life, "l'école était douce" (school was fun) (41/28). He impresses his mother with his new knowledge of the Eiffel Tower, broom-flying witches, the four seasons, and his ability to draw snowflakes and apple trees. But his learning about French landmarks, orature, and climate, all embodied in the repetition of the phrase "my ancestors the Gauls," has nothing to do with his reality in Martinique.

Contrary to the nurturing atmosphere of Man Salinière's home, where students vie for the teacher's attention, public, or "real" school, as the négrillon's brother Paul calls it, proves to be a nightmare where the students deliberately avoid the teacher's gaze. Bad omens—rain and a cold wind—abound the first day. The négrillon feels abandoned, overwhelmed, and anonymous in the huge classroom with its menacing blackboard. His knees shake as Le Maître calls the roll. The négrillon concludes that this school is a hostile, frightening place where the students are held captive like fish in a net. Unfortunately, the kind of net he needs is a metaphorical one, a ronde or support network that eases the newcomer's transition. Instead, his brothers are located in a classroom on an upper floor. Moreover, this new space welcomes neither his Creole language nor his Creole culture. In fact, the fence that keeps the sweets vendors outside the school yard functions to exclude the "contaminating" presence of local cuisine. School, an arm of France's assimilation policy, consumes the students instead.[20] Wanting no part of creolization, French culture insists on assimilation.

The largest portion of *Chemin-d'école*, the "survie" or survival section, is dominated by the Creole-speaking students' encounter with the French language, a metaphor of the dominant system. This encounter opens in the early afternoon as the négrillon returns to the Ecole Perrinon after the lunch break. The *chemin* (road) is dusty, the balconies deserted, the asphalt hot. Inside the classroom once again, the air is still; there is silence, dust, and sun. There is no scheduled nap as there was at Man Salinière's preschool. This milieu where students are made to feel ashamed of their language and their culture resembles a prison or a desert. Creole as a language, Creole as Caribbean culture are forbidden in the strictly French space:[21] "On allait à l'école pour perdre de mauvaises moeurs: moeurs d'énergumène, moeurs nègres ou moeurs créoles—c'étaient les mêmes." [We went to school to shed bad manners: rowdy manners, nigger manners, Creole manners—all the same thing] (169/120). *Civiliser* (to civilize) is Le Maître's mission—to transform students into French subjects. Heir to the plantation *commandeur* or slave driver, Le Maître enforces the policy of assimilation. Using violence and intimidation, he denigrates his students when they mispronounce French words. He responds with "horreur," "agonie," "hoquet" (hiccup), "rage," "indignation," "pitié" (pity), and "sa voix tremble" (his voice trembles). The consequences of Le Maître's making his students use French words *fée* (fairy) *elf*, and *gnome* instead of their more familiar Creole *zombi* and *casserole* (pot) instead of Creole *canari* are more complex and insidious than a process of word substitution implies. This erasure of cultural codes revisits the colonial conquest in which new names and identities were imposed on people and places.

The road to school, reassures Le Maître, leads to places far from the cane fields. In the meantime, his adopted language and culture distances him from his own students. It is a gap that is reflected in his speech peppered with allusions to Napoleon, Racine, and Cyrano de Bergerac that the young students do not comprehend: "Mais là, avec le Maître, parler n'avait qu'un seul et vaste chemin. Et ce chemin français se faisait étranger." [But now, with the Teacher, speaking traveled far and wide along a single road. And this French road became strangely foreign] (68/47). The négrillon's father articulates what appears to be ambivalence about the school experience when he comments: "On entrait mouton pour en sortir cabri." [You went in a sheep only to come out a goat] (45/30). In the multicultural Martinican context, which includes Indian among many other strands, this aphorism can also be read as a *strong* condemnation of the educational system, as goats are sacrificed in Hindu religious practice.

The alphabet lesson scene crystallizes the clash between French and Creole language and culture, which represent the dominant and the dominated in *Chemin-d'école*. Announcing that they will study the sound "A," Le Maître tries to elicit a response from the young students by showing them a pineapple. "Comment s'appelle ce fruit?" (What is this fruit called?), he asks. "Un zannana, mèssié!" (A pineapple, sir), the students reply proudly in unison. The teacher is horrified, indignant: "Une agonie déforma son visage. Ses yeux devinrent des duretés étincelantes." [His face was contorted with anguish. His eyes became glittering stones] (85/61). This pivotal confrontation is at once amusing and tragic. On the one hand, desiring to finally prove their intelligence to a teacher who calls them stupid, the students, upon seeing the fruit, think that they will be rewarded with the teacher's praise. But in this classroom their mother tongue is banned, rendering their correct answer in Creole, *zannana*, unacceptable. Banning the Creole language in school is tantamount to denying Martinicans' identity and access to their own history. As Dany Bébel-Gisler asserts in *Le Défi culturel guadeloupéen*, Creole is "une archive matérielle et symbolique des peuples de la Caraïbe" (a material and symbolic archive of the Caribbean people) (323). Nevertheless, suppressing the Creole language is the teacher's principal mission:

> Plus que jamais le Maître abominait le créole. Il y voyait la source de ses maux et l'irrémédiable boulet qui maintiendrait les enfants dans les bagnes de l'ignorance. Il sommait les parents de soustraire leur engeance aux infections de ce sabir de champs-de-cannes en exigeant d'eux le français du savoir, de l'esprit et de l'intelligence. (90)

> [Now the Teacher hated Creole more than ever, seeing it in the root of these evils, the ball and chain that would keep the children prisoners of ignorance. He called upon our parents to protect their progeny from the contamination of this cane-fields pidgin by demanding that we speak French, the language of wisdom, wit, and intelligence.] (64)

The business of imposing a language and culture is figured in the text in terms of a battle or, more appropriately, a conquest. Le Maître's weapons are any one of his named switches—Durandal, Excalibur, Attila, Apocalypse, La Guerre-14, Hiroshima, Jeanne d'Arc, DuGueslin, Electrique, Robespierre—that he uses whenever a student mispronounces a word. One switch is called "liane-bois-volcan (qu'il appelait liane-allemand, car elle envahissait) qu'il savait faire claquer comme un coup de *canon* au-dessus de nos affres" (volcano-wood switch [he called it German vine, because it was invasive] that he could snap above our anguished labor like a gunshot) (96 emphasis added/68). The names Le Maître chooses for his switches are associated with Europe and war, making the refrain "Le Maître était armé" entirely appropriate: "Le Maître était armé. Au fil de nos bêtises, il dévoila son arsenal. Il y avait bien entendu la liane-tamarin-verte qui séchait redoutable au-dessus du tableau et qu'il renouvelait de semaine en semaine pour cause d'effritement ou de disparition rétive à toute enquête." [The teacher was armed. As we blundered along, he unveiled his arsenal. Of course there was the green tamarind switch drying up over the blackboard and renewed from week to week when it wore out or simply vanished, no one knew how] (95/68). But these battlefield or plantation weapons are used against defenseless children in an elementary school classroom. On the other hand, instruction in Man Salinière's dining room was characterized by encouragement and praise. Far from being his students' champion like Stéphen Roc in *La Rue Cases-Nègres*, the anonymous Le Maître embodies the kind of alienation described by Fanon in *Peau noire, masques blancs*.

The *chemin-d'école* can be fraught with identarian peril in that it leads to a site reserved for the mission of imposing French hegemony. Represented as a battleground, the classroom is a microcosm of colonial society. The négrillon learns to read and write there, but he subverts the school's assimilationist project by honoring those who maintain the oral tradition despite the superior weapons of his formidable opponent and his own love of books. Punctuating his text with remarks from the répondeurs, the narrator generates a text that intersects with danmyé.

Overall, in his work, Chamoiseau choreographs the interplay among author, narrators, protagonists, characters, and marqueurs de paroles, who negotiate voice and space in contemporary Fort-de-France. The collage of oral and written discourses in *Solibo Magnifique* is comprised of Solibo's *dit* (oral performance), Sucette's drumming, official police reports, and witnesses' testimonies mediated by the marqueur de paroles. At various stages in *Texaco*, Marie-Sophie Laborieux, Oiseau de Cham, Esternome, and the urban planner take charge of the story, relate it, and relay it. Each *I* is, at some point, witness, custodian, and transmitter. Marie-Sophie's "sermon," with its religious and oral resonances, is complemented by the urban planner's notes to the marqueur, the ultimate curator, who reconstructs the story by recuperating other sister witnesses' accounts, thereby restoring their subjectivity. In *Chronique des sept misères*, although the *I* circulates while Man Goul, Elmire, and Afoukal relate stories in turn, the main narrator is a djobeur/handyman.[22]

Chamoiseau's professional life informs his autofiction. Acutely aware of delinquent boys' struggle to find their place in society, he examines their plight as well as that of displaced adult males. He is their advocate, situating their dilemma within Martinican history. In the next chapter, I turn from local masculinity and le drive to analyze, among other issues, women's positionality and the implications of their transatlantic migration.

3

Secrets and Silence, Displacement and *Délivrance*

> *Elle était toujours restée à l'abri dans la paix de sa case,*
> *complice de tous les complots, témoin sans paroles.*
> *[She'd always remained safe within the peace of her cabin,*
> *consenting to all conspiracies, wordless witness.]*
> Gisèle Pineau, *L'Espérance-macadam*

Gisèle Pineau from Guadeloupe, a psychiatric nurse by profession, explicitly assumes the role of advocate in her writings: "J'ai le sentiment de construire une oeuvre cohérente où je délivre le message qui est le mien, celui d'un plaidoyer pour l'humanité, les humanités" ("Entre ombre" 84). [I want to create a coherent work in which I deliver the message that is mine, that of a plea for humanity, for all people.] Pineau links this stance to a personal gendered mission: "Ecrire en tant que femme noire créole, c'est apporter ma voix aux autres voix des femmes d'ici et d'ailleurs qui *témoignent* (c'est moi qui souligne) pour demain" ("Ecrire" 295). [Writing as a black Creole woman is to bring my voice to those of other women from here and elsewhere who *bear witness* for tomorrow] (emphasis added). Her novels, *L'Exil selon Julia, La Grande drive des esprits, Un papillon dans la cité, L'Ame prêtée aux oiseaux,* and *Chair piment* as well as the anthology *Femmes des Antilles, traces et voix* that she coedited with Marie Abraham, privilege women first-person narrators. From young Félicité in *Un papillon dans la cité*, to adults Eliette and Rosette who share the task in *L'Espérance-macadam*, her narrators model Glissant's idea of *relie, relaie,* and *relate* (link, relay, and relate) as explicated in his *Poétique de la Relation*. While Pineau has often talked about the autobiographical aspects of her novels, she makes it clear that they are not strict autobiographies: "Mon univers romanesque est la traduction de ma propre expérience et de mes espérances" (Belugue 89). [My fictional universe is the translation of my own experience and hopes.] In this way, she resembles Dany Laferrière who claims that his books are an autobiography of his feelings (Coates 916). However, while Laferrière disparages *engagé* (politically committed) writing, Pineau explicitly embraces it. Autofiction, women's subjectivity in exile, and advocacy converge in her texts. The fact that Pineau's work is also informed by her medical training relates her perspective to Fanon's.

I argue in this chapter that Pineau's autofiction focuses on women, gender relations, secrets, and silence and that characters in her oeuvre are profoundly marked by the rupture and alienation brought on by displacement. *Un papillon dans la cité*, *L'Exil selon Julia*, *L'Ame prêtée aux oiseaux*, and *Chair piment* involve immigrants and take place, for the most part, in France, while *La Grande drive des esprits*, whose title suggests wandering, is anchored, paradoxically, in Guadeloupe. Geographical displacement or errance is replaced by psychological trauma in *L'Espérance-macadam* where domestic violence disrupts, distracts, and destroys. Some of Pineau's characters suffer, suppress, or escape the latent male aggression simulated in and represented by danmyé. In *L'Exil selon Julia*, for example, the protagonist of the title, whose story is curated by her granddaughter, endures her husband's blows to the narrator's disbelief.[1] The *I* in *L'Espérance-macadam* is split between two women whose lives are jolted by incest and denial. Eliette's memory of childhood rape is effectively erased, and Rosette refuses to believe that her husband has abused their teenage daughter, Angela. Without support from the ronde, Angela suffers in silence her anguish, shame, and disappointment, while her family and neighbors ignore the signs of abuse, another issue that the text explores.

Pineau's advocacy project extends to *Femmes des Antilles, traces et voix*, an assemblage of first-person narratives by historical and contemporary women that she coedited with journalist Marie Abraham. This collage of real and imagined lives, published in commemoration of the 150th anniversary of the abolition of slavery, seeks to recover voices silenced by history. Because conventional sources are unavailable, Pineau assumes the task of restoring subjectivity to enslaved women in particular, their only historical trace often no more than a name on a bill of sale or auction notice. Reconstructing the stories of Wassia, Bétani, Zanina, Clarisse, Marie-Tyrane, Honorine, and Emeline, Pineau imagines their capture, march to the coast, and horrific Middle Passage journey, events made subsequently more traumatic by rape, sale, and vulnerability to violence on the plantation. In one story, based on an 1845 report by Victor Schoelcher, Apolline relates her suicide by drowning, a fate she prefers to repeated whippings. Some French women are guilty of the most heinous abuse: Emeline recounts being tortured with hot pepper by her "madame," who then banishes her to work in the fields after learning that her husband is sleeping with the young woman. *Femmes des Antilles* balances these kinds of imaginary self-portraits with narratives by contemporary women—a teacher, singer, prisoner, scientist, cashier, and lawyer, along with migrant workers from Haiti and Dominica—who experience color prejudice, confront single motherhood, struggle with mental illness, face violence, but also foster healthy relationships, raise children, and work. That they meet with varying degrees of success provides a more balanced portrait of Caribbean women's lives.[2]

Born in the mid-1950s, Pineau, Chamoiseau, and Confiant all belong to the same generation, though gender and geographical position differentiate them and their novels. Chamoiseau grew up in the urban milieu of Fort-de-France where his narratives of childhood are set. Confiant hails from one of Martinique's rural areas, though some of his novels explore city life. Pineau, on the other hand, was born in a Paris suburb and spent her young girlhood there. As young adults, both Chamoiseau and Confiant spent many years in France and returned to Martinique, while Pineau, after living many years in Guadeloupe, returned to France. Pineau's father, a World War II veteran, migrated to the metropole as part of a movement that gained so much momentum—with the establishment of the Bureau pour le Développement des Migrations des Départements d'Outre-Mer (BUMIDOM) in 1963—that Paris earned the name *troisième île* (third island).[3] It is estimated that one-third of French Antilleans reside there, giving rise to a film like *Antilles sur Seine*, and labels such as *négropolitain* and *négzagonal*, which are derisive. Travel or migration to the Hexagon, which was considered advantageous, can have a profound effect on identity as Frantz Fanon and Alain Anselin have written.[4]

If in-betweenness is experienced in the overseas departments, the pressure of being both Caribbean and French becomes even more acute in the metropole. Helpful here is Shalini Puri's summary of Homi Bhabha's theory of culture, which focuses on "the tension between the heterogeneous people and the homogenizing nation" (19). No longer part of the racial or ethnic majority, some new migrants accept the myth of assimilation while others hold steadfast in their allegiance to their home culture. The former as policy is not only perceived by the migrant, but encouraged, advanced, and imposed by the host country that disparages the alternative as *dépaysement* (disorientation). In truth, as Glissant reminds us, adherence to *le Même* (the Same or the status quo), as represented by French culture, is hegemonic, impractical, and unrealistic, because all cultures are becoming more creolized (*Introduction* 15). By choosing to migrate, the Pineau family demonstrated a willingness to assimilate, distancing themselves from their island heritage. Nevertheless, they found comfort living among other Caribbean families wherever they settled.

It was not until her rural, non-French-speaking grandmother joined the family that Pineau was consciously immersed in several essential elements of Guadeloupean culture. Ironically, in 1950s Paris, négritude was at its height: the First International Congress of Black Writers and Artists was held at the Sorbonne, and the second edition of *La Rue Cases-Nègres* and *Discours sur le colonialisme* appeared. At a time when a Pan-African identity was claimed by some black intellectuals in response to racism and colonialism and when Algeria was fighting for independence from France, Pineau's parents believed in the promise of assimilation and put its agenda into practice. The very language and culture that they claimed and helped propagate in the colonies, however, was used against Gisèle. In her neighborhood and at school race-based insults often assailed her: "Bamboula! Négresse à plateau! Retourne dans ton pays!" ("Ecrire" 290) [Bamboula! Tray-carrying black woman! Go back to your country.] These slurs imply unbridled wildness (*bamboula*) and facial features unattractive by European standards. Such representations of black women are consistent with the Western imaginary, which does not allow for multiple models of beauty. Ironically, of course, by obeying the command to "go home," Gisèle would have ended up right back in her family's Paris apartment. These binaries of French/non-French, black/white are indisputably shortsighted.

That Pineau is taunted precisely because of her race and gender proves Oruno Lara's claim in *Caraïbes en construction: espace, colonisation, résistance* that the category *métropolitain* excludes people of color (19). In the words of H. Adlai Murdoch, the family is "stigmatized by a society that refuses to recognize [its] Frenchness" ("Negotiating" 136). Although Caribbean overseas colonies were transformed into *départements d'outre-mer* in 1946, legislating equality did not necessarily change attitudes or behavior. School, a site of learning, is also an instrument of French domination; reflecting society's attitudes, it is not necessarily a center of tolerance. While Zobel and Chamoiseau's school experiences were marked by class, linguistic, and color differences, Pineau's in France was constrained by race and gender. Intellectually as able as the other students, she demonstrates strength in language arts. Nevertheless, she is marginalized in a classroom where the curriculum has evolved little since Zobel's time. Race and color trump birthplace where French identity and home are concerned.

Pineau's grandmother Man Ya gives her a Guadeloupean identity that might be interpreted as fixed, in that her Creole language defies the challenges of an inhospitable environment, breaking through its concrete-hard surface like a wild plant: "Man Ya m'a consolée en me conférant—un temps—l'illusion d'une identité à laquelle j'agrippais, trésor de l'exil. Le créole de ma grand-mère poussait comme de la mauvaise herbe, rebelle, entre les murs gris, les trottoirs de l'exil, les fissures de la sacro-sainte langue française suçotée par mes parents et les injures racistes des enfants de mon âge" ("Identité" 220). [Man Ya consoled me by giving me—for a time—the illusion of an identity that I clung to, a treasure of exile. My grandmother's Creole language grew like a weed, rebellious, between the gray walls, the sidewalks of exile, the fissures of the sacrosanct French language sucked by my parents and the racist insults of the children my age.] Creole is Pineau's second language, a language of choice and necessity that allows her to access Man Ya's culture. Paraphrasing Frantz Fanon, assuming a language assumes a culture, and Pineau embraces and cherishes her "langue grand-maternelle" (grandmother tongue) ("Identité" 222).[5] At the same time, however, the language tension is eased, because Pineau does not denounce her mother tongue, but proudly claims it. Her assertion of her own language is one reason why, though challenging, her transition to school is not difficult for the same reasons it is for Zobel's José and Chamoiseau's négrillon.

If we were to assume that because Grandmother Julia does not speak French, she is completely out of place in Paris, we would be mistaken. As Glissant reminds us, Creole is a product of cultural contact (*Discours* 241).[6] Anchored in the Caribbean as she is, Julia still enjoys listening to Edith Piaf's music, which transcends linguistic boundaries. Open to further Relation, she does not fear negotiating the unfamiliar streets of Paris and transforms her grandchildren in the process. Pineau positions herself as an heir to her grandmother Man Ya, whose tales teach lessons about Guadeloupean culture and history ("Ecrire" 290). This informal education supplements what she learns from her parents and at school. Pineau's arsenal of stories, then, is informed by oral as well as written traditions from a wide variety of sources. She draws knowledge from orature and readings of authors in her sentimenthèque: Emile Zola, Richard Wright, Paule Marshall, and Camara Laye. Zola's blending of determinism and naturalism is evident in *L'Espérance-macadam* in which the marginalized characters cannot escape the curse of their slave past.

Among the many books important to her, Pineau specifically identifies *Native Son* (1940), *Black Boy* (1945), *Brown Girl, Brownstones* (1959), and *L'Enfant noir* (1953)—texts in which the protagonist confronts the white world ("Ecrire" 291). It is significant that these African and African American novels focus on poor and working-class children's formative years and the ways in which the characters face challenges in a new environment. Wright provides a model for

Pineau in his depiction of young protagonists and their dislocation from the rural South—where they were in the numerical majority—to the urban North where they were part of the minority.[7] I believe that Pineau finds Paule Marshall's life and work even more relevant: both daughters of migrants, *íliens* (islanders) who relocate from a one-story island house to a multi-leveled host-city apartment, they develop a special relationship to space. Born in Brooklyn to parents from Barbados, Marshall, had to construct an identity—as does her heroine in *Brown Girl, Brownstones*—in relation to relatives and friends, as well as older women who operate within the oral tradition, a situation that resonates in Pineau's *L'Exil selon Julia*. Selina Boyce is caught between two opposing views of settling in America, one represented by her mother, the other by her father. Marshall and Pineau offer a third option—a both/and rather than an either/or positioning—once again demonstrating that binaries are no longer viable. The fourth text Pineau mentions, Camara Laye's autobiographical novel *L'Enfant noir*, also situates its protagonist in a nurturing domestic and rural milieu seemingly untouched by colonialism, until Laye's Guinean protagonist encounters the French school. The text closes on the youth's imminent departure for the Hexagon armed with a map of the Paris subway to aid in his exploration of and integration into the city. It is easy to see why Pineau identifies with these four texts published in the 1940s and the 1950s because they resonate in her life. She is careful, however, to articulate the specificity of the Guadeloupean experience in her oeuvre.

Pineau enjoys multiple positionalities as a French, Guadeloupian, black, Creole, female, and migrant author. In the tradition of women prose writers from the Francophone Caribbean–Martinicans, Mayotte Capécia and Françoise Ega; Haitians, Cléante Valcin, Annie Desroy, Marie Chauvet, and J. J. Dominique; Guadeloupeans, Simone Schwarz-Bart, Michèle Lacrosil, Myriam Warner-Vieyra, Dany Bébel-Gisler, Lucie Julia, and Maryse Condé—Pineau articulates women's subjectivity. As it is for Capécia, Ega, Lacrosil, Warner-Vieyra, Bébel-Gisler, Chauvet, Dominique, and Condé, displacement is an integral part of her personal experience that resonates in her autofiction to counterbalance errance.[8] At the same time, due to her postmodern narrative strategies, critics place Pineau among the créolistes as well as the Afro-Parisian writers Alain Mabanckou and Daniel Biyaoula from the Congo and Calixthe Beyala from Cameroon, members of the generation that came into prominence in the 1990s with their discussions of displacement-driven alienation.

Carole Boyce Davies argues that black women's writing "should be read as a series of boundary crossings, and not as a fixed, geographical, ethnically or nationally bound category of writing" (4). As I mentioned briefly above, Francophone Caribbean women authors and their characters are especially mobile. Davies's "migratory subject" provides a useful framework through which to read Pineau. In *Black Women, Writing and Identity: Migrations of the Subject*, she interrogates the idea of home: "Migration creates a desire for home, which in turn produces the rewriting of home. Homesickness or homelessness, the rejection of home or the longing for home become motivating factors in this rewriting. Home can only have meaning once one experiences a level of displacement from it. Still home is contradictory, contested space, a locus for misrecognition and alienation" (113). As a result, Pineau's migratory subjects have to renegotiate their identity.

The construction of identity is embedded in *L'Exil selon Julia* (1996), a first-person text with an unnamed narrator reminiscent of José in *La Rue Cases-Nègres*. Like Chamoiseau's novels *Chronique des sept misères, Antan d'enfance, Chemin-d'école, Solibo Magnifique, Texaco,* and *A bout d'enfance*, the récit is curated. Although the title gives the impression that the novel recounts a life "according to Julia," it actually foregrounds the impact of Julia's experiences on her granddaughter, the narrator, whose development from girl to young woman is traced in her relationship to the island through her grandmother. The text enacts la Relation as it explores subjectivity, mutually fostered growth, and reciprocity. The narrator, exiled like her grandmother, is initiated into Guadeloupean culture through her grandmother's tales, oral history lessons, and example. The home depicted in Ya's stories is no island paradise, but a site where flying creatures, jealousies, and cruelty, even among women, reign. Yet it is also the location of her garden, a refuge of peace that provides sustenance and ingredients for healing.

Combining the prefix *ex* with *île* (island), the title word *l'Exil* compresses the meaning "away from the island." While the narrator's récit purports to articulate exile from Ya's perspective, *L'Exil selon Julia* actually examines the displacement, *délivrance,* and reconnection of the extended family. The family is doubly exiled, both physically and metaphorically, from Guadeloupe and Ile-de-France, the host "city" that refuses to completely accept them. In fact, the narrator wonders if her parents are still Guadeloupean because their ties to the metropole are so tenuous. The text exposes the contradictions between French ideals of equality and actual practice. Birthplace, citizenship, military service, and devotion notwithstanding, the family is displaced and estranged from Guadeloupe and France. Their voluntary exile should require them to renegotiate their identity, but they sometimes refuse to participate in Relation. Wherever they settle, they create an oasis, isolating themselves from other people and from their surroundings. In Africa, for example, instead of venturing outside the army base to explore the vicinity or to form relationships with the members of the community, the adults frighten the children with stories about wild animals and give them picture books that reinforce the stereotypes about the continent. The family, therefore, distances itself from any idea of kinship with Africa and is complicit in its conventional representation.

While her parents' eleven-year absence from the island is interrupted by a four-month visit in 1961, their estrangement begins long before their initial departure. Like some young Guadeloupeans, they are mesmerized by superficial signs of upward mobility. Daisy, from Goyave, is the daughter of an independent businessman and shopkeeper firmly entrenched in the middle-class until a friend's fraud and betrayal drive him to financial ruin. Light-skinned, with long silky hair, Daisy is initially attracted to Maréchal, the dark-skinned son of peasants, because of his military uniform, ability to speak French, and promises of "toute la magie d'Afrique, la France, des siècles de lumières" (all the magic of Africa, France, centuries of enlightenment) (26/15). Under normal circumstances, because of his color and class, Maréchal would have been an unacceptable suitor.

The day they meet by chance on the street, he is on leave from a tour in Senegal. As he regales her with tales of his adventures, Daisy imagines him warding off bullets with his bare hands beside General Charles De Gaulle. Literally blinded by the sun, she decides to cross class and color lines to quickly marry this grandson of field workers who, like José Hassam, has used school as a vehicle for upward mobility. An avid reader, Maréchal excels in his studies and earns a scholarship, but his academic advancement is derailed by the outbreak of war. Encouraged by his mother to enlist in order to see the world, he joins the Dissidence, the Caribbean wing of the French Resistance, to channel his rage against his father for physically abusing Julia.

Maréchal stands to profit handsomely from marrying Daisy. This decorated sergeant, for whom an advanced degree would have guaranteed entry into the middle-class, assumes her status instead. This arrangement is comparable to a mutually beneficial business transaction: "Ils ont couru ensemble, jeunesse dans l'espérance, désirs partagés." [They both rushed into it together, young people filled with expectations, with shared desires] (27/16). The narrator, however, is perplexed by their decision to leave the island: "Pourquoi ont-ils emmêlé leurs destins dans l'idée d'un exil?" [Why did they link their destinies to the idea of exile?] (28/16).

Daisy and Maréchal's relocation to France in 1950 coincides with an era of fervent literary and artistic activity centered in Paris. Not only were political manifestos (*Discours sur le colonialisme*), psychological studies of alienation (*Peau noire, masques blancs*), and autobiographical novels (*La Rue Cases-Nègres*) written by Martinicans during this period, but African American intellectuals, veterans, writers, musicians, and artists flocked to the Left Bank in the postwar decade.[9] Paradoxically, these expatriates fleeing racism relocated to a country where French (Caribbean) citizens were subject to discrimination.

Maréchal is a curious figure. As a member of the French military, he may have participated in suppressing anticolonial struggles. In the decade following the end of the Algerian War, the establishment of self-governing nations in Francophone West Africa, and independence movements in the French Antilles, Maréchal decides to return to Guadeloupe in 1970 with the five youngest children. (Paul is engaged and chooses to remain in France.) This decision is not prompted by homesickness, but rather by Maréchal's unwavering loyalty to President De Gaulle and anger against those who are disillusioned by his policies. Maréchal's departure is tantamount to a death sentence, a defeat: "Il part en guerrier vaincu." [He is leaving like a conquered warrior] (165/124). Daisy and the children, on the other hand, are eager to reunite with relatives and friends and visit imagined places. Transferred to Martinique, which serves as a transitional site before their total reimmersion into Guadeloupean culture, the family travels to Fort-de-France by plane. This trip stands in stark contrast to their 1960 return journey by ship with its echoes of the Middle Passage.[10] The sister island so resembles Guadeloupe that when the narrator finally arrives there she feels at home.

School in Martinique, a prism through which young people encounter French culture, is a critical site where race, color, gender, and class divisions merge and shift in ways that cause the narrator to question her place in the world once again. As the child of a career soldier, she has the privilege of attending a parochial high school along with the daughters of other military men and *coopérants* (young men who work abroad in lieu of military service). These girls form a distinct minority on Martinican soil as do the békées, descendants of French colonists, who disavow racial kinship with the white girls among the group in order to preserve their inherited power. During recess the békées speak Creole like their island-born black, Indian, and mixed-race classmates, with whom they also share certain cultural traits such as ways of walking and talking, but they do not socialize with them. Despite the homogenizing effect of the girls' uniforms, divisions persist and displace, reflecting the fluidity of identity. The thirteen-year-old brown-skinned narrator is positioned in several camps at the same time. Like the soldiers' daughters, she grew up in the metropole, is a native French speaker, and an immigrant. Even so, some of her fellow pupils are precisely the kind who badgered her with insults in Paris. Unlike the Martinicans of African and Indian descent, she struggles with the Creole language, and her accent sets her apart from them. Her close friends, blacks and *chabines*, whose skin color most closely resembles hers "se moquent de mon ignorance quant à des choses élémentaires essentielles à ma survie ici" (laugh at my ignorance about things basic to my survival here) (188/142). Nevertheless, they enthusiastically share their locally acquired cultural codes with her. Other girls, the older sexually active ones who wear makeup and high heels and secretly date married white men, make assumptions about the narrator based on her birthplace. They are surprised to learn that a teenage Parisian girl has not already had an intimate relationship. All in all, rigid perceptions of identity prove to be restrictive and often incorrect.

The narrator's school experience in Fort-de-France, along with Man Ya's teachings, prepare her for a reunion with Guadeloupe sight unseen. From a distance, she imagines it as a vast land, though many adults characterize it as a place of evil, poverty, and witchcraft: "Il n'y a rien de bon pour vous au Pays." [There is nothing, absolutely nothing good for you Back Home] (28/16). They stress France's numerous advantages—material goods, job opportunities, philosophical ideas, legendary writers—but do not mention that it is also a haven for criminals, like Daisy's father's former business partner, a fugitive who escapes prosecution and reinvents himself in the metropole as a prosperous entrepreneur. Julia is not duped—perhaps, in part, because she did not attend school and thus avoided the colonial educational system's indoctrination. Having to contribute to the family income at a young age, she was never forced to recite or believe "nos ancêtres les Gaulois" (our ancestors the Gauls). While the migrants in *L'Exil selon Julia* harbor ambivalent feelings about their homeland, Julia accepts Guadeloupe for what it is, shortcomings and all. Her out-of-placeness in Paris despite the presence of her son, daughter-in-law, and grandchildren translates into a deep depression and a yearning to return to Routhiers. The care packages filled with "treasures" and "riches"—vanilla, nutmeg, cinnamon, and rum—sent by Daisy's mother Man Bouboule are not enough. Valued by the narrator's family, these local spices with a strong distinctive odor provide sustenance, bind them to Guadeloupe, and must be used sparingly so that they last a long time.[11] Even the newspaper in which the ingredients are wrapped is a precious commodity. Carefully unwrinkled, it furnishes news of a distant homeland.

The school in France is a more alienating space for Pineau's narrator than it is for Chamoiseau's négrillon in the Martinique of *Chemin-d'école*, even though the condescending Le Maître humiliates the students into submission, loath to hear their Creole words. In *L'Exil selon Julia*, Madame Baron is so outraged by the hypervisibility of a black body in her classroom that she orders the narrator to sit underneath her desk. Myriam Warner-Vieyra experienced a similar kind of exclusion in her 1940s parochial school in Guadeloupe where the students were assigned seats according to the shade of their skin: black students in the back, light-skinned in the middle, and whites, the majority, in the front nearest the instructor ("Depuis" 54). Imposing conformity, the elementary school teacher in *L'Exil selon Julia* raps the naturally left-handed narrator's knuckles with a ruler to force her to use her right hand. Convinced of her own self-worth, however, she resists exclusion and confides in her mother Daisy, who confronts the teacher. The narrator next resists the teacher's retaliatory indifference by acquiring literacy and devouring the classics: Madame de Lafayette's *La Princesse de Clèves*, Choderlos de Laclos's *Les Liaisons dangereuses*, and Charles Baudelaire's *Les Fleurs du mal*. Nor does the narrator's consumption of the French canon distance her from Man Ya, with whom, instead, she shares her newly acquired literacy, teaching her grandmother to write, much as José did Carmen.

The enticing, tropical Guadeloupe of tourist brochures is, in fact, a place of adamant patriarchy where gender relations have not evolved much for centuries. In that context, Julia experiences the family as what Carole Boyce Davies calls "a site of oppression for women" (21). Astrubal, a philanderer and a former overseer, is attracted to Julia precisely because he can easily control her. The two marry, and domination escalates to physical abuse, which Julia is convinced is the result of psychological damage connected to his participation in World War I. Citing her religious convictions, she ultimately stays in the marriage. It is significant that Astrubal returns from overseas in 1928, the year of the hurricane. (The association of weather with aggressive male behavior is a trope that Pineau will develop more fully in *L'Espérance-macadam*.) Astrubal's brutality, however, cannot be blamed entirely on his experience in the military, for he is violent toward his wife prior to his enlistment. Nevertheless, Ya's remark is both sympathetic and astute: "Il est plus égaré que moi, Astrubal." [He is more lost than I am, Astrubal is] (99/72). She senses his displaced loyalty.

Julia is the instrument of reconnection to the family's Caribbean heritage. That she is unable to tell time in France is consistent with Glissant's perspective that Caribbean time is not a linear dimension as it is in the West, where list-driven history also prevails. Nevertheless, familiar with the temperate cycling of wet and dry seasons, she adapts to a four-seasonal pattern, enduring freezing cold, snow, and dim sun. Innocently donning her son's *képi* (military cap with a visor) and army coat to protect herself from the rain, she is accused of impersonating a French soldier. While as military men her husband and son participate in colonial projects, but do not always enjoy the fruits of that sacrifice, Julia's temporary appropriation of this identity attracts the attention of the police, whose escort she misreads as a rescue mission launched by her husband. The intersection of her race and gender contributes to her hypervisibility. Julia is, in fact, a veritable *guerrière de l'imaginaire* (warrior of the imaginary), who, operating in an oral universe, embodies ancestral memory like Médouze, Solibo, Toussine, and Man Cia and transmits her repository of lore to the next generation. As Dany Bébel-Gisler explains: "Le passé des sociétés antillaises, pour une part [est] archivé dans la langue créole, les contes, les proverbes, la musique, les pratiques magico-religieuses, dans les rêves, l'imaginaire social, la tête" (*Le Défi* 119). [Antillean societies' past, [is] partly archived in the Creole language, oral stories, proverbs, music, magico-religious practices, in dreams, in the social imaginary, in the mind.] At the same time, Julia promotes the children's formal French education by accompanying them to school and supervising the writing of letters to their father serving in the Pacific.

Two chapters in *L'Exil selon Julia* are entitled "délivrance," a word that denotes relief from death, release from prison, or a country's liberation. In Pineau's text, "délivrance" pertains explicitly to Julia, who is set free, first from her husband's abuse in Guadeloupe and later from exile in France. Each time, emancipation is involuntary, for it is her son who takes the initiative. Maréchal misinterprets her wishes, convinced that he is saving his mother from a brutal husband when, in fact, she is committed to him because of her religious beliefs. Paradoxically, her first délivrance is an abduction, albeit by a well-meaning son who believes he has her best interests at heart. The second délivrance is spurred by Julia's depression, its source more complex than simple nostalgia for Guadeloupe in a dark and cold France. Her *return* from exile signals a release from prison, not vice-versa. Synonymous with her garden with its fruit and healing herbs, home is unambiguous to Julia. She is overjoyed at the prospect of seeing her son's in-laws, that is, her daughter-in-law's parents, Papa Emile and Man Bouboule, again. Having been prepared so well, her grandchildren share her enthusiasm for the space that is not entirely unfamiliar to them. Observing

Man Ya in her accustomed milieu in Guadeloupe, they come to appreciate her knowledge: "Nous étions à son école." [We were at her school] (219/166). It is fitting that the narrative ends with the narrator's reunion with Man Ya in her privileged space.

The narrator comes to better understand displacement, exclusion, and confinement by way of extracurricular material. Ironically, it is Julia, *l'analphabète* (the unlettered), who explains slavery to her (as does Médouze to José and Man Cia to Télumée), suggesting that literacy is not obligatory in accessing specific historical knowledge and that collective memory is transmitted through the oral tradition. Anne Frank's diary, which the narrator reads during an Easter vacation, provides a more contemporary story with which the narrator can easily identify: "Comment vivre dans un pays qui vous rejette à cause de la race, de la religion ou de la couleur de peau? Enfermée, toujours enfermée! Porter une étoile jaune sur son manteau. Porter sa peau noire matin, midi et soir sous les regards des Blancs" [How do you live in a country that rejects you because of race, religion, or skin color? Locked up, always locked up! Wearing a yellow star on her coat. Wearing your black skin, morning, noon, and night under the eyes of whites] (153/114). A function of the hegemon, the dominant gaze delimits, confines, and discriminates. It assigns identities based on stereotypes and clichés and bans from the media all but denigrating images of blacks as subordinates, servants, porters, and slaves—the kinds of images that so anger José in *La Rue Cases-Nègres*. (Consider, for example, television announcer Sylvette Cabrisseau's being driven off the air in France by disgruntled viewers, who protested the presence of a black woman on screen.)

In *L'Exil selon Julia*, migration, abduction, and alienation are various forms of displacement. Man Ya's journeys function to accentuate the whole family's identity construction and fluid positionality. Until her arrival in France, a virtual silence surrounds Guadeloupe and the family heritage. Pineau explores their shifting relation to each other as well as to the larger society. By comparison, displacement results not from transatlantic travel in *L'Espérance-macadam*, but from trauma, the internal dynamic operating in a claustrophobic space, a small, poor, isolated community in Guadeloupe, a model for any one of the Caribbean. Turning its energy on itself and catapulted by external forces, Savane Mulet, figured in the body of a woman, self-destructs, but not without the hope of rebuilding. Pineau explores the physical and psychological scars of survivors of rape, victims of murder, as well as those of the perpetrators, whose inherited or learned behaviors make them dangerous predators in the manner of "the Executioner" in *L'Exil selon Julia*. It is significant that the crime of incest in *L'Espérance-macadam* is evoked in the image of a hurricane. Both operate on an imbalance of power, are physically and psychologically destructive, unpredictable, and doomed to recur like trauma. In the novel, the silence of family members and neighbors who decline to act as witnesses exacerbates the situation.

Pineau explains in an interview the genesis, rationale, and mission of *L'Espérance-macadam*: "I wanted to bring to life the forces of nature, their violence, and the violence of human beings. I wanted to evoke the whirling winds of the cyclones through a circular construction that grows denser and denser until you see the father commit this act of violence.... I wrote *L'Espérance* to show the human being in this violence, bounced around like a canoe at sea, wounded by the hurricanes, like an island, like Guadeloupe.... I told myself that Guadeloupe had been raped" (Veldwachter 181). Pineau accomplishes her narrative mission by making the cyclone a protagonist, a strategy also adopted by Maryse Condé in *Hugo le terrible* (1990) and Daniel Maximin in *L'île et une nuit* (1995).[12]

Hurricane Hugo frames the novel, situating it in time and space and fostering autofiction's tenor of authenticity.[13] Between September 16th and 18th, 1989, Hugo's strong rain and winds passed through the Virgin Islands, Puerto Rico, Saint Kitts, Nevis, Guadeloupe, and Montserrat before hitting Charleston and North Carolina, and leaving devastation in its wake. Originating as a thunderstorm off the coast of West Africa, it traveled west, gaining momentum and developing into a tropical storm. Reaching hurricane status, it struck Guadeloupe after midnight on Sunday, September 17, its 140 miles per hour winds disrupting electrical power, toppling the airport control tower, downing trees, and leaving roads blocked, ten thousand people homeless, eighty injured, and five dead. Much of the damage occurred in Basse Terre before the storm moved on to the island of Montserrat.

In the aftermath of natural disasters, property damage is routinely surveyed, and statistics impersonally record the loss of life. Missing are the individual testimonies in the form of récits by those who experienced events firsthand and whose voices are rarely solicited. It is fitting then that Pineau, Maximin, and Condé recruit women and children as narrators, whose récits in no way resemble sojourners' travelogues extolling the island's beauty.[14] On a symbolic level, the fact that Hugo crossed the Atlantic Ocean and indiscriminately struck former French, Spanish, and British plantation societies suggests that it retraced the path of the Middle Passage. Descendants of those captured Africans and indentured Indians, potential migrants to the metropole, are reminded of their powerlessness on their own soil and that, with the closing of the BUMIDOM in 1981, their mobility will be somewhat curtailed.

As I suggested above, a hurricane can be a traumatic event. Cathy Caruth's definition of trauma is instructive:

> Trauma is described as the response to an unexpected or overwhelming violent event or events that are not fully grasped as they occur, but return later in repeated flashbacks, nightmares, and other repetitive phenomena. Traumatic experience, beyond the psychological dimension of suffering it involves, suggests a certain paradox: that the most direct seeing of a violent event may occur as an absolute inability to know it; that immediacy, paradoxically, may take the form of belatedness. The repetitions of the traumatic event—which remain unavailable to consciousness but intrude repeatedly on sight—thus suggest a larger relation to the event that extends beyond what can simply be seen or what can be known, and is inextricably tied up with the belatedness and incomprehensibility that remain at the heart of this repetitive seeing. (91–92)

Eliette Florentine embodies the repetitiveness of trauma as delayed response, discussed at length below.

Though the action of *L'Espérance-macadam* unfolds in one week's time, the events of one particular Sunday precipitate an emotional eruption of regret that motivates Eliette to shoulder responsibility and achieve agency. Returning from church in Ravine-Guinée, she notices her next-door neighbor, Rosan, sitting in a police car in town. Later that evening, she hears his sixteen-year-old daughter Angela screaming while her mother beats her. As Angela flees, Eliette coaxes her into her home. Upon hearing Angela's story, the memory of her own violation by her father sixty years earlier resurfaces for the first time.

The text opens with a description of the calm that follows Hurricane Hugo on September 17, 1989: garbage, ruined houses, leafless trees with broken, twisted branches, and a lone mattress clinging to a pole. Angela's notebooks, in which she has recorded oral stories dictated by her mother, are rinsed of her script and carried away by the wind, symbolizing her invisibility, her silencing by intimidation and fear, and the inexpressibility of incest. Eliette, too, survived similar abuse when she was eight years old, the memory of which she has suppressed.[15] Her mother Séraphine fled town and went mad, but not before cutting off her husband's ear, a deformity that distinguishes him. While Eliette's physical wounds heal, the visible evidence of Séraphine's retaliation on Ti-Cyclone remains. Incest is a crime that society too often refuses to discuss. Young victims like Angela are coerced into silence with threats: they are made to feel ashamed, fear being labeled traitors, and risk not being believed by those closest to them. She breaks the cycle by denouncing Rosan to the police in order to protect her seven-year-old sister, Rita. Others, like Eliette, repress the memory, which can erupt from the subconscious at any moment. Eliette's permanent wound is the inability to give birth; she displaces her desire for a child onto caring for her newly discovered niece Angela.

The confluence of narrative and metaphor structures *L'Espérance-macadam*. The "whirling wind of the cyclone through a circular construction" is achieved textually through the repetition of individual lines ("Rosan dans la voiture de police" [Rosan sitting in the police car]); through stories, flashbacks, and memories; and through sudden shifts in time, space, and narration, from first-person—either Eliette or Rosette—to third-person, without transition. The resulting jerky, spasmodic rhythm approximates the anxiety, volatility, and unpredictability of memory, its fragmented language—the language of shattered souls—and Savane-Mulet's continually shifting atmosphere as it changes from safe to hazardous space, altogether creating a collage text[île]. The hurricane and the crime become one as Ti-Cyclone, who as a young boy earns the nickname because of his destructive tendencies, eventually sexually abuses his daughter Eliette. What Séraphine calls "le Passage de la Bête" (passage of the beast) in 1928 refers to Ti-Cyclone as well as to the hurricane, which caused floods, uprooted trees, killed two thousand people, and left many others missing.

L'Espérance-macadam traces the resurgence of involuntary memory figured in the resurfacing of Eliette's own trauma through listening to Angela's account. Her previous attempts to recall the incident have been unsuccessful. Eliette realizes that her only memory from that time is of her mother later telling her about the "passing storm," a rafter piercing her abdomen, and treatment by Ethéna, a midwife/healer who put "tes chairs en place et déposé l'oubli comme un onguent sur tes brûlures" (your body back together and laid forgetting over you like an unguent on your burns) (274/196). Eliette never questioned the circumstances of her wounds nor her mother's rendition. With this recovered knowledge, she ventures into Pointe-à-Pitre to seek more information from her godmother Anoncia, Ti-Cyclone's sister, who mistakenly thinks she is free of the weight of the secret, "délivrée à jamais du rongement intérieur" (deliver[ed] . . . at last from the inner gnawing) (289/207). Eliette's délivrance is her rescue of Angela, whom she frees from the prison and psychological death of incest. By extension, Pineau implies that Guadeloupe's inner turmoil can also be relieved.

These two perspectives on father-daughter incest display male domination, aggression, and extreme alienation. The perpetrators are not necessarily members of the ruling class, nor does their brutality take place on the plantation as it does in *Femmes des Antilles: traces et voix* or in *La Rue Cases-Nègres*. Rosan, a construction worker, feels compelled to dominate, convincing himself that he is not hurting Angela, though he completely disempowers her. Unloved, he had been abandoned by his parents and raised by his maternal grandmother, who beats him unmercifully with a switch. Rosan, however, is capable of compassion: he cradles the dead body of Glawdys's baby when she throws it off the Nèfles Bridge. In this novel, violence abounds as men batter their companions (Régis beats Hortense and Brother Delroy strikes Edith); a husband murders his wife in a jealous rage (Régis stabs Hortense); a man and a woman conspire to execute her husband in order to possess his promised wealth (Christophe and Eusbelle hang Marius and claim it is suicide); and a mother wounds her daughter with a belt (Rosette leaves welts on Angela's body in addition to a swollen eye and a skinned leg). These episodes and acts are traumatic symptoms themselves. As exemplified by bus driver Renélien, however, they can be traced, explained, and conquered. In accepting responsibility for kicking his first wife because of a burned dinner, Renélien realizes that his behavior is much more complex than it seems. It is the memory and fear of hunger that lead to his anger: "Oui, c'était sa faute, ce jour-là, il avait faim, et un Nègre qui a faim est comme un animal: son ventre se souvient du vieux temps d'esclavage, du manque de pain et la rage se lève du mitan de son âme." [Yes, it was his fault, he'd been hungry that day, and a hungry black man is like an animal: his belly remembers the old slavery days, the lack of bread, and rage wells up from the pit of his stomach] (148/105).

There are warning signs of the impending danger. For one, Julia has the ability to read changes in nature that announce inclement weather. Rosan, the son of Ti-Cyclone, inherits his father's curse, an aggressive, depraved power that erupts within the family. Carrying the weight of history, Rosan, unaware of Ti-Cyclone's assault on Eliette, repeats his aberrant behavior. (This curse of repetition is suggested by the circular winds of the *cyclone*, the French word for hurricane, embedded in his name.) His physical interaction with Angela escalates from tickling to fondling to constructing an extension on the house for a private room, but Rosette, an enabler, does not intervene.

Eliette's narrative serves as an outlet for her to relate her trauma. In so doing, she makes a private violation a public story. While in *La Rue Cases-Nègres*, Amantine recounts her assault to her uncomprehending five-year-old grandson, Angela tells her story three times: to the police, who respond by arresting Rosan; to her mother, who reacts inappropriately by beating her; and to Eliette, who offers consolation and a safe haven. The written word seems to give oral testimony more credibility; the police take Angela seriously only when she threatens to inform the district attorney in writing.

It is not only the victim whose voice seeks utterance. "Rien vu, rien entendu" (nothing seen, nothing heard) is the oft-repeated refrain as witnesses decline to assume responsibility. Eliette shields her eyes and covers her ears to the violence in Savane Mulet. She has seen Glawdys tethered to a post by her stepmother, but turns up the radio to drown out her cries; she has seen the bruises on Hortense's body when she passes in front of her house; and she has heard Rosan's footsteps in the courtyard and the sheet metal squeak as he enters Angela's room at night. Profoundly regretting her inaction, Eliette's performance of agency begins the moment she hears Angela's screaming to her mother that Rosan is molesting her. In fact, Eliette's decision is triggered by the sight of Rosan in the police car earlier that day. Traumatic memories of other events that she has ignored reemerge: "J'aurais pas rappelé ce temps—Glawdys, avec ses belles couleurs accordées—si j'avais pas vu les yeux de Rosan ce dimanche-là." [I wouldn't have recollected those days—Glawdys and her lovely matching colors—if I hadn't seen Rosan's eyes that Sunday] (72/48). What happens to a nightmare suppressed, to echo a few lines from the Langston Hughes's poem? In the case of *L'Espérance macadam*, it explodes. Eliette's memory of her rape by her own father resurfaces when she encounters Angela's story.

According to Cathy Caruth, in addition to trauma's "unconscious act of the infliction of the injury and its inadvertent and unwished-for repetition" is "the moving and sorrowful *voice* that cries out, a voice that is paradoxically released *through the wound*" (2). Caruth continues: "trauma seems to be much more than a pathology, or the simple illness of a wounded psyche; it is always the story of a wound that cries out, that addresses us in the attempt to tell us of a reality or truth that is not otherwise available" (4). Pineau foregrounds the long-term effects of sexual abuse in her novel. Though potential witnesses can corroborate the survivor's story, they become accomplices like Anoncia, whose forty-year silence functions to shield her brother. She lies about Ti-Cyclone's whereabouts and squanders two opportunities to reveal the "poisonous secret." Once, when Renélien declares his love for Eliette, Anoncia "cloua ses lèvres et remisa ses confidences" (buttoned her lip and stowed her secret back away) (273/195). Then, celebrating Rosan's death with champagne, she wants to reveal the secret, but still "les mots s'agglutinaient au tréfonds de sa gorge. La honte la possédait" (the words stuck at the back of her throat. She was consumed with shame) (291/208). Consequently, Anoncia becomes "complice des actes de La Bête. Secret qui entachait son âme et marcottait en elle de sombres réminiscences. . . . avait assuré la prophétesse, il y aurait toujours en dedans même de son corps une [*sic*] rongement dû à une peine infinie qui ne s'éteindrait qu'avec la décharge du secret" (a party to the acts of the Beast. A secret that tarnished her soul and rekindled dark recollections [;] . . . the prophetess had assured she would always feel something gnawing inside of her, due to an incalculable sorrow that could only be assuaged by unburdening herself of the secret) (272/194).

Pineau questions the idealization of family relations in *L'Espérance-macadam* and *L'Exil selon Julia*. It is precisely kinfolk who are responsible for much of their families' sufferings in the form of domestic abuse, molestation, and abandonment—legacies, in part, of the slave trade, slavery, and colonialism with their fragmentation of the family structure. Some adults fail their children. Rosan repeatedly rapes Angela, and Rosette is an accomplice by whipping her daughter when she confides in her.[16] That Rosan and Rosette share responsibility for Angela's pain is reflected in their names. While the parents' names are derived from the same root, the beautiful red flower with thorns, they are differentiated by the imbalance of power and gender: "an" is an augmentative, "ette," a diminutive.[17] Only Moïse and Eddy survive their parents' disastrous journey to the hills where the Rastafarian community drowns in a flood. Orphaned and homeless, they return to Savane Mulet. As articulated by Ludovic in Condé's *Desirada*: "Nos mythes ont la vie dure. Nous croyons que les liens de parenté sont les plus solides. Le sang n'est pas de l'eau, ressassent les voix sorties d'Afrique. Tous les enfants torturés, maltraités, dépecés, tous ces foétus jetés dans les poubelles, mis à pourrir dans les grands bois ne les ont pas réduites au silence et nous sommes là à répéter, après elles, des choses que la réalité contredit." [Our myths are hard to dispel. We believe the ties of parenthood to be the strongest. Blood is thicker than water, repeat over and over again the voices out of Africa. All those tortured, dismembered, and abused children, all those fetuses thrown out as garbage, left to rot in the depths of the forest, have not silenced these fables, and here we are still repeating things that reality contradicts] (277/255). Both Condé and Pineau examine the dynamic of kinship, the self-destruction of a community, and the damage wrought by internecine conflict on a broad scale.

Savane Mulet is the site of upheaval, but also of refuge. Séraphine flees with Eliette to the burgeoning squatter community on the periphery of Ravine-Guinée, founded by Joab who is responsible for Eliette recovering her speech at age eleven. It is similar to Chamoiseau's Texaco or to the peripheral Fort-de-France neighborhoods in Zobel's *La Rue Cases-Nègres*—Bord du Canal, les Terres Sainville, le Pont Démosthène, Desclieux, Morne Pichevin, Sainte-Thérèse, Petit-Fond. Similarly, in Pineau's novels, the poor migrate from the countryside and construct homes from discarded materials. The peripheral status of such neighborhoods is reflected in the fact that the bus goes only as far as the town of Ravine-Guinée; from there, one must walk the two kilometers to Savane Mulet. This kind of isolation reproduces the condition of living on an island where there is little economic activity. Glawdys participates in the informal, "creole economy" by selling "christophines" (a tropical, pear-shaped squash), but her inability to support herself and her baby leads her to kill her own child. The title word *macadam*, a spicy cod and rice dish, a staple of Guadeloupean cuisine among the poor because it is filling, suggests resilience.[18] The hard surface of macadam contrasts with the flimsy, make-shift houses that are vulnerable to and carried away by high winds. (The community *does* come together to protect itself from the hurricane.) But the surface tranquility can hide hurt and quickly transform into rage. The poverty in Savane Mulet can breed violence, and that violence can lead to madness.

With its focus on women in the wake of slavery and colonialism, *L'Espérance-macadam* is indebted to Toni Morrison as sentimenthèque. Rastafarian Beloved, née Edith, carries the name of the Morrison title character; however, it is Glawdys who commits infanticide by throwing her baby off the Nèfles Bridge, an act reminiscent of Sethe, who kills her infant Beloved in order to spare her a life in slavery. More intriguing is that, like Morrison, Pineau tackles the trauma of enslavement manifest in and as urban violence. J. Brooks Bouson remarks in *Quiet As It's Kept: Shame, Trauma, and Race in the Novels of Toni Morrison* that Morrison depicts "defective or abusive parenting or relationships" that result in child abuse, incest, infanticide, self-mutilation, suicide, and murder and that her characters are haunted by "'rememories,' that is, spontaneous recurrences of the past" (3). As I discussed above, Pineau explores similar concerns in *L'Espérance-macadam*.

In any case, memory is called upon to reconstitute the past, a task Emile Ollivier finds difficult as he articulates in *Mille eaux*:

> J'ai toutes les peines du monde à ordonner mes souvenirs d'enfance. Ma mémoire clignotante, pleine de trous, ne parvient pas à reconstituer de façon quelque peu exacte une séquence d'événements dans sa cohésion et sa logique interne. Elle me joue des tours, oblitérant le passé ici, gommant là certains aspects, plaçant d'autres en relief, faisant parfois l'impasse sur des pans entiers d'une existence qui, loin d'être un fleuve tranquille, se transforme, trop souvent à mon gré, en un torrent impétueux. Faire revivre ces souvenirs enfouis, rien de plus simple en apparence. Il suffirait d'interroger quelques témoins encore en vie. (48–49)

> [I have all the trouble in the world trying to put my childhood memories in order. My flickering memory, full of holes, cannot manage anymore to put together in a somewhat accurate way a sequence of events cohesively and logically. It plays tricks on me, obliterating the past here, erasing certain aspects there, highlighting others, sometimes making a dead end out of entire sections of an existence that, far from being a tranquil river, is too often to my liking transformed into a raging flood. Nothing seems more simple than reviving these buried memories. You only have to interrogate some witnesses who are still alive.]

Reconstituting memory is rendered even more complicated when trauma is involved, when no one steps forward to perform in the ronde or to testify as depicted in *L'Espérance-macadam*.

Women's displacement, secrets, silence, and relationships are central to Pineau's autofiction. In *L'Exil selon Julia*, Man Ya's relocation permits her to impart the buried history of Guadeloupe to her grandchildren in France, one of whom relates her own journey while curating her grandmother's. One life depends on the other for its telling, one depends on the other for knowledge, growth, and reconnection. This embodiment of Glissant's notion of *relie*, *relaie*, and *relate* (link, relay, and relate) from *Poétique de la Relation* echoes in Chamoiseau's declaration: "L'Autre me change et je le change. Son contact m'anime et je l'anime" (*Ecrire* 202). [The Other changes me and I change him. His contact animates me and I animate him.] Pineau's work hints at a former extreme form of danmyé in which blows land and cause serious injury. However, with the proper foresight, attention, and agency, délivrance is possible for these women whose bodies are exploited, abused, and scarred in their own homes.

Pineau's overall mission of testifying makes her a committed advocate like Danticat, whose autofiction is the focus of the next chapter. The first-person narrator in *The Farming of Bones*, displaced twice by traumatic events, reconstitutes in detail a perspective absent from the official historical record, interrogates the idea of home, and reproduces the transnationalism of the author.

4

Travelers' Trees and Umbilical Cords

Embodying Dyaspora, Renegotiating Home

> *My nation lives in the waters between spiritual and physical homes.*
> Miriam Neptune, "Hat Tricks," from *Butterfly's Way*

> *Soy un testigo mudo. Un testigo cómplice. Estoy acusado por mi consciencia.*
> *Cual es mi deber? . . . Acusar!*
> *[I am a mute witness. A complicit witness. I am accused by my conscience.*
> *What is my duty? . . . To accuse!]*
> Freddy Prestol Castillo, *El Másacre se pasa a pie*

As we saw in the previous chapter, no one claims the torment of incest nor testifies about its trauma in Pineau's *L'Espérance-macadam*. One *I* suppresses the memory, remains mute for three years, and as an adult ignores the violence around her. The resulting silence surrounding this heinous crime and the repressed memories of its victims perpetuate the anguish and prevent its cessation. The alternating first and third-person narrators in the text mirror the shattered self, which sometimes speaks on its own behalf and at other times relies on someone else to tell the story. On the contrary, Amabelle Désir, the protagonist in Edwidge Danticat's *The Farming of Bones* (1998), retains control of the narration and makes every effort to testify about her flight from the state-sponsored massacre of Haitians in the Dominican Republic in the fall of 1937. While Eliette's voice in *L'Espérance-macadam* is sometimes still, Amabelle's chronological récit alternates with her own personal memories, dreams, nightmares, and meditations set off in bold-faced type, forming a collage. Ultimately unsuccessful in giving testimony to the authorities about her ordeal, she can only offer her written text as a worthy substitute for an affidavit or proceedings from a jury trial. In order to survive and land on her feet, like José in *La Rue Cases-Nègres*, Amabelle applies danmyé's principles of resistance, interaction, balance, and displacement.

The Farming of Bones is set in Haitian and Dominican border towns, dangerous intersections that also symbolize their respective nations, adversaries negotiating the same space, the island of Hispaniola. Characters such as Amabelle search for a safe haven, a place to belong. In this chapter, I offer a close reading of *The Farming of Bones* in which the protagonist, after being stranded in another country as a child, is forced to return home as an adult. Seeking landmarks in Cap Haitien with special national or cultural resonance, she attempts to reconnect to a place she barely remembers. Renegotiating her identity, she embodies the borderless Haitian nation.

The traveler's tree and the umbilical cord are appropriate tropes for the Haitian experience.[1] Native to Madagascar, the former was transported to the Americas centuries ago. Known for its fan-like leaves that spread out, the tree gets its name from the fact that water accumulates in its folds, providing refreshment for the thirsty traveler. In the Caribbean it is believed that the tree has the power to draw an individual back to his or her native land. In *The Farming of Bones*, Man Rapadou plants one in her yard when her son Yves migrates to the Dominican Republic, and he does indeed find his way back to her. The tradition of burying placenta in one's courtyard is another way of assuring a return home; the umbilical cord is said to tie that individual to a specific place. For Aimé Césaire, the Caribbean archipelago is an umbilical cord connecting the North and South American continents. This image of interdependence serves as a model for a world in which Relation is the norm. In discussing the relationship between Haitians abroad and the *pays natal* (native land), Edwidge Danticat cites the trope of the umbilical cord: "We of the Haitian dyaspora maintain a very long umbilical cord with our homeland" ("AHA" 42).

Cultural beliefs and practices embodied by the traveler's tree and umbilical cord are retained, inscribed, and problematized by many of the younger generation of Haitian writers who left the island as children and grew up elsewhere. Although Haiti remains a spiritual home for many, others address important issues emanating from migration or exile. For some, exile is no longer the central issue it was for their parents, many of whom fled the oppression of the Duvalier regimes and planned to return to their homeland later. Instead, the "in-betweenness" that Martinicans and Guadelopeans feel as French citizens whose *pays natal* is yoked to the metropole is experienced by some Haitians who are also American, Canadian, Spanish, German, or Senegalese. As essays collected in *The Butterfly's Way: Voices from the Haitian Dyaspora in the United States* attest, Haiti has become remote for some members of the younger generation. Joanne Hyppolite, a resident of Boston, questions her authenticity because she does not enjoy rice and beans, a staple of Haitian cuisine (8). Brooklyn-born Sandy Alexandre rebels against her parents' expectation that she preserve, respect, and conform to customs in the new space. As punishment for disrespecting familial norms—being rude to her mother—she is sent to live with relatives in rural "Hades," a double punishment. She comes to realize, however, that she must reconcile her multiple identities (*Butterfly's* 184). The practice and terms of relocation can be nuanced by a dominating culture that imposes its own conditions for acceptance. While Myriam J. A. Chancy asserts that "I stand between two cultures," she perceives that "Canada did not demand that I strip myself of my identity to remain on her shores as I believe America does" (*Butterfly's* 228–29).

In *Writing Outside the Nation* Azade Seyhan poses questions relevant to the transnationalism of Haitian writers: "How is national identity transformed in the modern world that exists in a state of perpetual geopolitical shifts? When origins and heritages become recollections and merge into other histories, who guards and guarantees our national histories and the specificity of our past? Who claims that past and to what ends?" (20). Seyhan locates transnational literature as a particular genre of writing "that operates outside the national canon, addresses issues facing deterritorialized cultures, and speaks for those in what I call 'paranational' communities and alliances. These are communities that exist within national borders alongside the citizens of the host country but remain culturally or linguistically distanced from them and, in some instances, are estranged from both the home and the host culture" (10). While I agree in principal with Seyhan's theory, the Haitian example presents certain specificities that must be taken into consideration. For one, its writers must challenge the hegemonic essentialism that associates the island nation with poverty, AIDS, illiteracy, and instability. In addition, the Haitian literary community is concentrated in different linguistic sites that produce texts in French, Creole, English, German, and Spanish. What then are the consequences of that dispersal in so far as creating a unified school or movement? In other words, how are national tendencies generated when a group is spread around the globe? What is the relationship between literature being produced by "écrivains du dehors et écrivains du dedans" (writers of the outside and writers of the inside), a distinction articulated by Yanick Lahens (*L'Exil* 74)? Joël Des Rosiers, the self-defined Quebec Haitian poet who is also a surgeon, speaks of an "archipelago of writers," suggesting intimate connections between them despite the physical distances separating them from the homeland. Carole Boyce Davies's notion of "migrating subjects," which she uses in another context, is relevant here in a literal sense. How, then, is the *I* positioned and articulated when the author and/or narrator claim more than one home? In a metaphorical sense, like a danmyétiste, he or she chooses mobility over establishing a rigid center.

Edwidge Danticat embodies the young, contemporary transnational writer. Born in Haiti, she joined her parents in Brooklyn at age twelve and is thus considered "half-generation." Educated in Port-au-Prince and New York, she is fluent in Creole, French, and English, which distances her from most native-born Americans. Nevertheless, since the success of her first novel *Breath, Eyes, Memory* (1994), she has become firmly ensconced in the African American canon. Although she claims Paule Marshall, Maya Angelou, and Toni Morrison as literary predecessors, it is clear that her sentimenthèque includes Haitian writers Marie Vieux Chauvet and Jacques Stéphen Alexis, whom she quotes in *The Dew Breaker*.[2] While I believe that Alexis's collection of stories *Romancéro aux étoiles* served as an inspiration for *Krik? Krak!*, his *Compère Général Soleil* resonates in *The Farming of Bones*. Amabelle's last name, Désir, is reminiscent of Désiré, the name Alexis's Hilarion and Claire-Heureuse give to their newborn son. Alegría, the fictional Dominican town featured in Danticat's novel, is a Spanish dance mentioned in *Compère Général Soleil*. The transnational thrust of Danticat's work is reflected in the fact that it was translated promptly so that it could quickly reach the French-reading Haitian public. Danticat herself participates in making her work accessible to Creole-speaking Haitians by reading stories from *Krik? Krak!* over the radio, a small, but integral part of her advocacy and activism.

Danticat explores the ruptures of displacement in *Breath, Eyes, Memory*, *Krik? Krak!*, *The Farming of Bones*, and *The Dew Breaker*: the ambiguity of the location of home; the desire to stay connected through the resiting of cultural practices; the impact on intergenerational relations; the trauma of forced migration; the past's haunting of the present despite attempts to forget it; and the urgency of renegotiating identity, especially among girls and young women. Autofiction figures prominently in her oeuvre. *Behind the Mountain* depicts migration for an adolescent audience. It is the diary of thirteen-year-old Céliane Espérance, who records her experiences in rural Haiti during the 2000 elections before joining her father in New York where she adjusts to the new environment and circumstances. By contrast, in *The Farming of Bones*, Amabelle Désir experiences two traumatic episodes that involve involuntary uprooting accompanied by violence. At age eight, she watches her parents drown in the swelling Massacre River as they attempt to cross back into Haiti following a shopping trip to Dajabón to purchase cooking pots. Orphaned and alone in the Dominican

Republic, whose language she does not speak, she is rescued by a group of boys and brought to Don Ignacio, who takes her in as his eleven-year-old daughter Valencia's companion and servant. The second traumatic event occurs years later when, as a young adult, Amabelle is caught up in the massacre that took place in 1937 and forced to flee back to Haiti, where again she is rescued near the river shore. Centered on the terror of the slaughter, Amabelle's escape, her search for loved ones, and her new life in Cap Haitien, the city of her birth that she now barely recognizes, the novel also addresses issues of exile, class, racism, and the exploitation of foreign workers. That the novel is set in border towns during this explosive period enhances its exploration of positionality, a pivotal dimension of danmyé.

Haitian/Dominican relations have ranged from civil and cordial to troubled and antagonistic. Tensions date from 1822 when Haiti annexed its eastern neighbor, a move that engendered feelings of resentment among Dominicans. A century later, the massacre took place in an atmosphere of nationalistic and racist rhetoric. To counter the visibility of "alien" black bodies, that is, the massive numbers of Haitian migrant workers in the Dominican Republic, President Rafaël Leonidas Trujillo y Molina encouraged the immigration of white Europeans. Constructing and imposing essentialist and distinctly separate Haitian and Dominican identities despite the creolized character of the island, Trujillo, a partisan of the *racine unique* (single root) philosophy, made claim to a pure European heritage for his country that excluded "Africa-descended" Haitians.

In late September through early October 1937, Trujillo gave speeches on the radio demonizing Haitians and giving orders to arrest, beat, and kill them. Because skin color could not always distinguish Dominicans from Haitians, people were asked to pronounce the word *parsley* in Spanish: *perejil*. A Haitian accent betrayed one's ancestry. Thousands of small farmers, cane cutters, mill workers, domestics, landowners, men, women, and children, in more than sixty towns all over the country, some who had lived on Dominican soil for generations, became the victims of soldiers as well as civilians who took part in what is now euphemistically termed *ethnic cleansing*. Haitians were dragged from their homes, rounded up, shackled, beaten, shot, hanged, hacked with machetes, and their bodies piled high along the river bank or dumped into mass graves. Those who were able to flee across the border escaped with their lives. The wounded were treated in hospitals in Cap Haitien and Hinche. Some survivors were interviewed and depositions were taken, but there was no serious investigation nor was anyone ever prosecuted. It is suspected that presidents Vincent and Trujillo entered into a secret agreement.[3]

The location of the exact boundary between the two republics has shifted as a result of government negotiations over the years. This contested site mirrors the relations between the two nations. Delineating the northern border, the Massacre River earned its name in the eighteenth century when Spanish troops killed French pirates in retaliation for stealing their bounty (Hicks 103). This notorious site, therefore, had its share of violence before the mass killings in 1937. In the novel, the shores of the Massacre River figure prominently as a symbol of disruption, separation, and attachment. It is the bridge at Dajabón–connecting the Dominican Republic to the Haitian town Ouanaminthe (Juana Mendez in Spanish) and located just one kilometer across the bay—that the Dominican soldiers patrol, while their Haitian counterparts are stationed further away at the customs house on the other side.

Alegría, where Amabelle lives with Valencia's family, is a fictional border town par excellence. Made up of estates, small plantations, and sugar mills with compounds on which Haitian workers or *braceros* live, it incorporates different ethnicities, colors, classes, languages, and genders that sometimes share the same space. Don Ignacio's household is not the only one in which nationals of both countries interact. Their contact does not involve equal social, economic, and class status. Mimi "Micheline" Onius works as a domestic for widowed Doña Eva, mother of Dr. Javier and Beatriz. Don Gilbert and Doña Sabine employ ten Dominican guards on their estate.

The tensions between the two countries sharing Hispaniola are made manifest, in part, through language. For Valencia, the situation is an antagonistic one with a transparent boundary: "On this island, you walk too far and people speak a different language. Their own words reveal who belongs to what side" (304). However, the line of demarcation is in reality fluid, blurred, and ambiguous like the more complex border space. Diglossia and bilingualism are an unquestioned necessity for the Haitian characters in the novel. They must be multilingual. Among themselves, they converse in Creole, but speak to their employers in Spanish. Where the 1937 massacre is concerned, because most Haitians were phenotypically indistinguishable from certain Dominicans, the pronunciation of a single word—*perejil*—was used to target people for death. The Dominicans in the novel, however, are with few exceptions monolingual.[4] Occupying positions of political power exempts them from having to learn the language of their "foreign" employees. On the other hand, so dire is the matter of the massacre that immediate access to news about it requires the use of every language of communication in Alegría. Tellingly, the Creole and Spanish names for the massacre reflect different subject positions. The slaughter in Creole is called *kout kouto*—words that name the killing method (*kout* = cutting) and its instrument (*kouto* = knife). Without the syllabic repetition and alliteration of the two Creole words, which suggest stabbing, the Spanish term *El Corte* (the cut), used by Señora Valencia, a sympathetic Dominican, remains semantically distant from the massacre victims.

The Haitian characters communicate in different languages out of necessity. Sylvie is one whose language skills are typical among the occupants of border spaces. She speaks Creole-accented Spanish. Sebastien code-mixes when pigeons' sounds cause him to reminisce about his mother back home. "Pobrecita manman mwen" (my poor little mama) he utters nostalgically as Spanish and Creole intersect to reflect his present and past locations (25). Dr. Javier, Valencia's doctor, is the only Dominican who speaks Creole, which he does like a Haitian with only a slight accent. Showing his respect for Vodun beliefs, he wears conspicuously on his shirt collar a small wooden carving of cane leaves that resembles "the amulets the cane cutters here in Alegría wore around their necks to protect them from evil spells" (36). That parsley leaves get caught in his hair as he walks through the living room is another sign of his solidarity with the Haitian workers. In addition, his name, Javier, is almost identical to the month, *janvier*, in which Haiti celebrates both its independence and heros' day—January 1st and 2nd. Dr. Javier, a Dominican national, performs Glissant's Relation.

Hispaniola's languages and geography and the potential reconciliation of the two republics that share it are embedded, yet explicit, in the name *Amabelle*. Three syllables meet to form a border: the first two, *ama*, mean "he or she loves" in Spanish, while the last syllable, *belle*, translates as "beautiful" in French and Creole. Amabelle's last name is Désir, meaning the desired or the ideal. The ideal relationship between the two nations—reconciled and peaceful—is not yet attained in the Hispaniola of *The Farming of Bones*. Amabelle is an ambiguous figure in that she represents both republics. Her position as intermediary is reflected in her training as a midwife, a skill she learned from her parents, who were trained in the art of healing. That the border remains an ambiguous site is illustrated by the fact that while Amabelle's knowledge of midwifery is instrumental in delivering Valencia's twins, as an intermediary, she is powerless to intercede in other areas.

Valencia's womb is another trope of the island Hispaniola, accommodating, sheltering, and nourishing fraternal twins. The brown-skinned Rosalinda, whose compound name—*pretty rose*—reproduces, in part, the themes apparent in Amabelle's name, will also choose healing as a profession. Rosalinda becomes a doctor. Because of her skin color she can represent Haiti, the eastern part of the island, or the dark-skinned Dominicans, a fact that troubles Valencia at her birth. She is keenly aware of the stigma of dark skin in Dominican society. She articulates that fear to Amabelle, blindly unaware of the stinging affront: "My poor love, what if she's mistaken for one of your people?" (12). The boy twin Rafaël, named after the dictator, is his father's favorite because he is male and white skinned. However, it is the girl, born with several additional strikes against her—a caul and the umbilical cord wrapped dangerously around her neck—whose smaller body conceals an inner strength that will guarantee her survival. Rosalinda Teresa will eventually marry and enroll in medical school, while her seemingly stronger and healthier twin brother dies shortly after birth. These children are born into a world of privilege, material comfort, overt racism, and fanaticism that end in a massacre. Dr. Javier's observation that sometimes twins strangle each other (while it does not occur in this case) presents another metaphor for the hostile and sometimes deadly relations between the two republics.

Characters in the novel all inhabit the border, travel back and forth across it, or are forced to return to Haiti. Nonetheless, whether it is the cookpot maker Moy, *vwayajè* (wayfarers) like the cane workers, or *nonvwyajè* (settlers) like Unèl, their Haitian identity is immutable, their status precarious. The skilled workers—stonemasons, seamstresses, farmers, shoemakers, teachers—some with Dominican spouses,[5] live in wood or cement houses, signs of permanence, yet are still considered foreigners even though many were born in the Dominican Republic: "My mother too pushed me out of her body here. Not me, not my son, not one of us has ever seen the other side of the border. Still they don't put our birth papers in our palms so my son can have knowledge placed into his head by a proper educator in a proper school" (69). Such workers are denied the rights and privileges that come with full citizenship, such as the vote and access to free public education. The cane workers are also held hostage, because their documents remain in the possession of their employers: "Papers are everything. You have no papers in your hands, they do with you what they want" (70). Without their citizenship papers, they are people without a country.

Why are these people located in the Dominican Republic? Displacement follows the search for employment and business opportunities. The *vwayajè* are migrant workers who have left Haiti because of violent weather and the promise of a better life in the Dominican Republic. The devastating hurricane of 1930 drives Sebastien, Yves, Mimi, Joël, and Kongo to look for work on the other side of the border. Moy is a businesswoman, a pot maker whose reputation and superior products draw Haitians from across the river. Amabelle's parents are seeking her wares on the one-day shopping trip that leaves her orphaned and stranded. For Amabelle and other longtime residents of the Dominican Republic, the exact location of home remains an open question. The *nonvoyajè* are settled, with few ties to Haiti. Most return only when there is an emergency or when their lives are threatened.

Not fully integrated into Dominican society, Yves, Sebastien, Mimi, and Amabelle are, in fact, marginalized from it. In very strong terms David Howard characterizes the status of migrant workers in the following way: "The Haitian experience is one of internal colonialism as a core element of Dominican economy, yet peripheral to polity. Haitians exist as an internal colony, marginalized individuals in a society that demands their labor, but refuses to accept their presence beyond that as units of labor. Haitian settlements in the sugar fields are effectively ethnic ghettoes, segregated physically and socially from Dominican society" (30). Father Romain, who was born in Cap Haitien like the migrants, encourages the formation of kinship ties. They usually gather to celebrate Haitian national holidays, but the massacre forces them to form new alliances in order to survive. Traditional class divisions become irrelevant and erode, offering new possibilities for interaction. Rich Haitian landowners Don Gilbert and Doña Sabine open their estate, otherwise surrounded by high walls, as a refuge to their poor compatriots as the massacre begins. Don Gilbert and Doña Sabine straddle the border in other ways. Their class status is modeled in the Spanish titles *don* and *doña*, earned by their long-time residence in Alegría. In fact, they have not changed location; it is the boundary separating the countries that has shifted by official decree negotiated by the two nations. Their national identity was negotiated without their participation. Nevertheless, their French first names, Gilbert and Sabine will always convey their Haitian origins.

Some characters manage to transgress the imposed social and economic barriers through close relationships. Father Vargas and Father Romain, brought together by their common Christian faith, collaborate and build a school. Doloritas has a Haitian boyfriend Ilestbien, whom she accompanies on his flight to freedom. Don Ignacio makes a similar gesture of crossing racial, national, and class lines to pay a condolence call on Kongo, the father of the Haitian cane worker killed by Pico Duarte's car. He and Kongo bond over their lost sons. Papi's died in childbirth along with his wife: "We spoke like men. I told him what troubled me, and he told me what troubled him. I feel perhaps I understood him a trace and he understood me" (145). Being a Spanish national living far away from his native land, Don Ignacio grasps the meaning of loss and exile. Growing up without a mother unites Amabelle and Valencia despite race, class, and national differences. Although the island of Hispaniola is divided, practically at war, some of its citizens build bridges by practicing good will and building mutual understanding.

On a broader scale, Amabelle embodies the new Haitian nation in that she represents those who migrate and must, therefore, renegotiate their identities.[6] Born in Cap Haitien, orphaned and stranded in Dajabón at age eight, Amabelle grows up in Alegría and would thus be considered "half generation." Forced to reconstruct home within a space where, ironically, she is practically a *restavec* or child-slave who wears clothes that her employer discards. Her only contact with her *pays natal*, other than her memories of her parents, is through the other Haitian workers who are displaced like she is. Amabelle Désir has no papers attesting to her Haitian citizenship or to her residence in the Dominican Republic. In her twenties, she experiences the horror of the massacre and flees across the border back to her natal Cap Haitien, which has become unfamiliar to her. Again, with no one in the city with whom to reconnect, Amabelle must start anew. She renegotiates her relationship with Yves, becoming his companion and lover and forming kinship ties with his and Sebastien's mothers. After the death of Trujillo years later, she crosses back to the Dominican Republic looking for the waterfall near the cave where she and Sébastien first made love. That she fails to locate these landmarks represents the intensity of her errance and the ambiguity of home.

Fittingly, two other Caribbean writer/critics have commented that the current era is characterized by the loss of landmarks. Joël Des Rosiers states: "L'homme du XXe siècle, qui a perdu ses repères, se trouve abandonné sur le chemin d'une errance sans fin." [Twentieth-century man, who has lost his references, finds himself abandoned on the road to an endless odyssey] (166). Edouard Glissant posits: "Dans la rencontre planétaire des cultures, que vous vivons comme un chaos, il semble que nous n'ayons plus de repères" (*Introduction* 71). [In the planetary meeting of cultures that we live like a chaos, it seems that we don't have landmarks anymore.] This loss is illustrated in *The Farming of Bones* by the curious absence of mothers, who are not only associated with a motherland, but traditionally with providing protection and identity: Amabelle's mother drowns; Valencia's dies after giving birth to a boy; Sebastien and Mimi's resides far away; Man Ramapou is separated from her children; and Juana miscarries. Danticat locates three principal landmarks in the novel that reflect the characters' desire for an anchor, security, and the stability of home. Each landmark proves to be elusive, however: the Citadelle; the traveler's tree planted by Yves's mother in Cap Haitien; and the waterfall in Alegría, Amabelle and Sebastien's secret place.

Begun under Dessalines and completed in 1816 under Henri I, the Citadelle was originally constructed to accommodate thousands of soldiers who would defend the nation against French troops sent to reenslave them. Still standing majestically on the top of a hill overlooking the city of Cap Haitien in the north, with a view as far east as the Dominican Republic, this iconic stone monument, a *lieu de mémoire* (site of memory) symbolizes the origins and struggle of the young Haitian nation (historian Elizabeth B. Bethel considers Haiti an African-American *lieu de mémoire*). Henri Christophe is buried at this UNESCO-designated cultural heritage site. A center of remembrance and pride, it also represents failure and disappointment. With its canons still aimed at the sea, the Citadelle is a reminder of Haiti's unfulfilled potential as a leader of the black world that could not protect Amabelle and her compatriots from Trujillo's wrath. It is ironic that the 20,000 people who died during its construction approximate the number of lives lost during the 1937 slaughter (Wilson 852). The 200,000 men who helped build the Citadelle are as anonymous as those who toil in the cane fields in the adjoining eastern republic.

Aimé Césaire's Roi Christophe, often played by Douta Seck, the Senegalese actor celebrated for his performance as Médouze in Euzhan Palcy's *Rue Cases-Nègres*, insists in the play that the Haitian people participate in the construction of the monument after his engineer, Martial Besse, suggests that he build a patrimony for them. Hallucinating, the king imagines a memorial to which he attributes human qualities: "Il vit. Il corne dans le brouillard. Il s'allume dans la nuit. Annulation du négrier!" [It's alive. Sounding its horn in the fog. Lighting up in the night. Canceling out the slave ship] (63/45). Christophe explains to Besse what they need: "Je dis la Citadelle, la liberté de tout un peuple. Bâtie par le peuple tout entier, hommes et femmes, enfants et vieillards, bâtie pour le peuple tout entier! Voyez, sa tête est dans les nuages, ses pieds creusent l'abîme ... c'est une ville, une forteresse, un lourd cuirassé de pierre ... Inexpugnable." [The citadel, the freedom, of a whole people. Built by the whole people, men and women, young and old, and for the whole people. Look, its head is in the clouds, its feet dig into the valleys. It's a city, a fortress, a battleship of stone. Impregnable] (62–63/44–45). This forceful scene ends the first act of the play.

In times of stress, Amabelle, too, conjures up the fortress. She associates it with her blissful childhood and her parents' house on the road leading to the Citadelle. Not only did her father spend all year lovingly constructing paper

Christmas lanterns shaped like the monument as a gift for her, but she delighted as well in rehearing him tell her about King Henry's place in history. She had played in the Citadelle's courtyards and visualized the splendor of centuries past. In her room in Alegría, to calm her fears as she waits for Sebastien to come to her room as the novel opens, Amabelle temporarily escapes to that more innocent time: "I closed my eyes and imagined the giant citadel that loomed over my parents' house in Haiti, the fortress rising out of the miter-shaped mountain chain, like two joined fists battling the sky" (45–46). After having sufficiently recovered from her wounds to leave the border clinic, as she approaches Cap Haitien along with Yves, she searches the sky for the familiar sight. That night, to avoid thinking about the loss of her family and friends, Amabelle again conjures up the Citadelle: "its closeness to the sky, its distance from the river. With my childhood visions of being inside of it, protected, I fell asleep" (227). More than twenty years later, she is again drawn to the Citadelle. This time she wanders among the rooms, following a group of young Spanish-speaking tourists and their guide. The experience serves as a reminder that despite its historic origins, the Citadelle has been reduced to a regular stop on sightseers' itineraries. They will not spend much time learning about its significance. These day trekkers cross the Dominican border to engage in a tourist activity diametrically opposed to the experience of the Haitian wayfarers (*vwayajè*) who spend many years laboring anonymously in the cane fields.

That Amabelle searches for these landmarks but fails to locate her family home in Cap Haitien and the stream and waterfall in Alegría reinforces their tenuousness. By contrast, as their individual names suggest, the couple who employs her is firmly anchored: Valencia is a port city on the eastern shore of Spain, and Pico Duarte is a mountain in the Dominican Republic. Collective memory endows Amabelle's markers: one natural (a waterfall), two planted (a tree, an umbilical cord); and one constructed from stone (the Citadelle). Associated with life, longevity, permanence, and pilgrimage, they are not only visible, but conspicuous, and draw an individual back to the *pays natal*. Conversely, without official papers there is no proof of whether the victims of the 1937 slaughter lived or died. No obituaries were published in the press; no lists of the dead were broadcast on the radio; no rituals of commemoration took place, no monuments were constructed. Neither collective despair nor individual pain and suffering were publicly acknowledged, although Haiti has a strong tradition of commemorations.

The statue *Nègre Marron*, sculpted by Albert Mangonès and positioned for many years opposite the National Palace in Port-au-Prince, symbolized resistance to slavery. Breaking the shackles that bound him, with a conch shell to his lips summoning his compatriots to battle, the *Nègre Marron* embodied the revolutionary spirit and honored those who dared to choose freedom. But because it was commissioned during the Duvalier regime, it was toppled by the dictator's opponents. The Citadelle in Milot, completed not long after independence, stands on a hill challenging foreign invaders. Ironically, these symbols of defiance are juxtaposed to the reality of the nation's powerlessness in the face of danger, particularly in 1937. The massacre victims are as anonymous in death as they were in life. The survivors, struggling to have their testimony heard, acknowledged, and recorded, "[look] for someone to write their names in a book, and take their story to President Vincent. They wanted a civilian face to concede that what they had witnessed and lived through did truly happen" (236).

Michel-Rolph Troulliot offers another blueprint for reading *The Farming of Bones*. In *Silencing the Past: The Power and Production of History* he accounts for certain gaps in the discourse about the Haitian past. Silencing in the production of history, according to Trouillot, is a practice and process in which power determines what gets collected, recorded, and thus remembered. He cites the striking example of the way the Haitian Revolution is typically narrated in Western discourse. The defeat of the French is credited to disease rather than to the agency and superior military prowess of the Haitian troops (21).[7] In other words, presumed objectivity in the production of history is a myth: "Silences enter the process of historical production at four crucial moments: the moment of fact creation (the making of *sources*); the moment of fact assembly (the making of *archives*); the moment of fact retrieval (the making of *narratives*); and the moment of retrospective significance (the making of *history* in the final instance)" (26).

Amabelle Désir's attempts to collect information about the massacre correspond to what Trouillot calls fact assembly or "the making of archives." This step in the production of history "is not limited to a more or less passive act of collecting. Rather, it is an active set of production that prepares facts for historical intelligibility. Archives set up both the substantive and formal elements of the narrative. They are the institutionalized sites of mediation between the socio-historical process and the narrative about that process" (52). *The Farming of Bones*, one book in that fictional archive, recuperates a long-neglected story, one that Dany Bébel-Gisler, in the case of Guadeloupe, equates with a buried history. Silenced or buried, Caribbean history deserves attention.

Making available and disseminating material is an important step in the recuperation of buried history. *The Farming of Bones* incorporates oral testimony into history, thereby giving voice to those who are usually excluded from history production due to class, language, gender, or censorship. Although it is clearly labeled a novel, *The Farming of Bones* flirts with authenticity. The end pages reproduce an actual five-page letter from President Sténio Vincent to Georges Léger, the secretary of state for foreign relations. Dated October 27, 1937, it voices the president's fear that the number of people killed is much higher than that reported by the Dominican authorities. In addition, he is apprehensive that the perpetrator of the crime in the Dominican Republic is conducting the investigation. Juxtaposed with this "effet du réel" (realistic effect) is the book's dedication—"In confidence to you, Metrès Dlo, Mother of the Rivers," signed Amabelle Désir–a dedication issuing from a fictional narrator who entrusts her story to a Vodun spirit rather than to a government representative or an official institution. Metrès Dlo will not only keep her story, but assure its repetition and remembrance. The slippage between actual and fictional discourse—one characteristic of autofiction–reflects the author's confidence about the insertion of oral testimony into official history and suggests the permeable boundary between the two countries that share the island.

The Farming of Bones represents a document that should have been and still has not been made public. The circumstances of the massacre are known to those who experienced it, to those who listened to and recorded testimony, and to the scholars who dedicated studies to it. A few non-Haitian authors have treated the event. Rita Dove's poem "Parsley" speaks the fatal password. Julia Alvarez's *In the Time of the Butterflies* and Mario Vargas Llosa's *The Feast of the Goat* are set during or make mention of the massacre. *The Farming of Bones* is the longest creative work by a Haitian to treat the slaughter and still rival the popularity of Freddy Prestol Castillo's *El Másacre se pasa a pie* (1973), already in its eleventh printing. Prestol Castillo's novel is told from the first-person perspective of a Dominican child of privilege, an observer, not a victim or a participant. While the narrator goes to Dajabón to investigate the tragedy, the récit is centered on his anguish. The Haitian characters are relegated to the background.

Other Haitian writers have dealt with the 1937 massacre. Jacques Stéphen Alexis devotes part three, the last section, of *Compère Général Soleil* (1955) to Hilarion Hilarius's escape from the Dominican Republic with his wife Claire-Heureuse and baby. Anthony Lespès's *Les Semences de la colère* (1949) focuses on the aftermath, that is, the establishment of government-sponsored "colonies agricoles." René Philoctète's *Le Peuple des terres mêlées* (1989) presents the story of "mixed" couples in the small Dominican border town of Elias Piña who experience the massacre: Pablo Nuñez and Antonine; Celio Marquez and his wife Sanite; Victoria and her husband, Monnuma St-Hilaire; Alberto Rava and pregnant Marcelle; Emmanuelle, mistress of Don Agustin de Cortoba—all "gens d'une même terre" (people from the same land) (22).[8] The use of free indirect discourse allows Philoctète to alternate between an omniscient narration and the first-person perspective of Adele Benjamin and her husband Pedro Alvarez Brito, a sugarcane factory worker and activist. Through them, Philoctète poses a fundamental identity question about the refugees who flee across the border to Haitian soil: "Sont-ils Haïtiens? Sont-ils Dominicains? . . . Ils sont venus coupler leur vie, d'ici à l'autre bord, avec le rêve de créer le peuple des terres mêlées" [Are they Haitians? Are they Dominicans? . . . They came to join their lives, one side to the other, with the dream of creating one people from two lands mixed together.] (147/213–14). That they share the same island renders the slaughter all the more tragic.

With two prose works on the subject herself, Danticat addresses the silences surrounding the massacre. Prior to publishing *The Farming of Bones*, she wrote the short story "Nineteen Thirty-Seven," which appears in the collection *Krik? Krak!* (1996). Set many years after the massacre, it invites the reader to make comparisons between the targeting and killing of Haitians in the Dominican Republic and the arrest and execution of suspected witches in Haiti under the Duvalier dictatorship. "Nineteen Thirty-Seven" foregrounds three generations of women jolted by the massacre, each one suffering a virtual sentence of silence. Narrator Josephine's pregnant mother witnessed the killing of her own mother on the Dominican side as she leapt into the Massacre River to freedom, giving birth to Josephine on Haitian soil. Josephine has long suppressed that knowledge until her mother's death in prison: "The story came back to me as my mother had often told it" (49). She remembers her mother's account of annual pilgrimages made with other female survivors to dip their fingers in the Massacre River. Later denounced by neighbors for sorcery, Josephine's mother is imprisoned in Port-au-Prince.

"Nineteen Thirty-Seven" forecasts features that Danticat will revisit and develop in *The Farming of Bones*. Tropes of silence abound in the story, reflecting the suppression of evidence that the characters will struggle to voice in the novel. Josephine's mother forbids her to utter the name of the place where the horror occurred, and Josephine is rendered mute in the prison yard. The mother figure, whose absence signals loss of home and security, asserts her presence powerfully in the story. The statue of the Madonna, in Josephine's family for six generations, represents a legacy of survival despite tremendous odds. Défilée, a heroic figure in Haitian history because she retrieved Dessalines's body after he was assassinated, is Josephine's ancestor. "Nineteen Thirty-Seven" represents Danticat's first attempt at recuperating the 1937 tragedy for an English-reading audience. In *The Farming of Bones*, she goes on to heed Trouillot's mandate by restoring that which has been ignored, buried, or suppressed and by privileging the acts of witnessing, of collecting testimony, of remembering, and of producing archives.

The novel opens on August 30, 1937, the night Amabelle helps deliver Valencia's twins and at the same time Valencia's husband, Pico Duarte, kills a Haitian man with his car in his rush home. In the midst of circulating rumors about the impending danger and Dr. Javier's suggestion that she return immediately to Haiti, Amabelle weighs her options. Deciding to flee, she convinces her lover, Sebastien Onius, to meet her at the church where a group plans to escape. She arrives there late and never sees Sebastien again. She learns later than the fugitives, along with Dr. Javier, were herded into a truck by Dominican soldiers and taken away.

The Farming of Bones occupies an important historical moment where first-person accounts are increasingly sought after as measures of "what really happened." Testimony was very much in the public consciousness in 2004, when Rwandans commemorated the tenth anniversary of the massacre of 800,000 Tutsis and moderate Hutus by Hutu extremists and the Rwandan army. The United Nations' establishment of the International Criminal Tribunals for Yugoslavia (1993) and Rwanda (1995), which continue to hear hosts of testimonies, is just one step in the healing process. In a similar way, some survivors of the terrorist attacks on September 11, 2001, felt compelled to write down their experiences and circulate them via email. When those who survive *cannot* write, they must depend on others to transcribe their stories. In *The Farming of Bones*, Amabelle depends on government officials and priests, not realizing, however, that what they hear and write down will not necessarily reach the public.

After she is released from the clinic, she travels to the police precinct in Cap Haitien for sixteen days in the row (except Sundays) and waits her turn in the hot sun to appear before the justice of the peace. Among the more than one thousand people on line, some share their stories with one another, as if rehearsing. Generous Amabelle contemplates shortening her story so that more people will have a chance to speak. Before her turn comes, however, it is announced that no more testimony will be heard because all of the money set aside to compensate the victims' families has been distributed. The officials, however, have misinterpreted the survivors' purpose. The angry crowd charges the building. They do not seek payment but are, rather, "looking for someone to write their names in a book, and take their story to President Vincent. They wanted a civilian face to concede that what they had witnessed and lived through did truly happen" (236). Written documents that record oral testimony are perceived to have more authority than the oral testimony alone.

At another site in Cap Haitien, priests collect testimony in Creole for local newspapers and radio. They are deemed more trustworthy than the corrupt state officials, who are suspected of keeping the money paid to the Haitian government by Dominican President Trujillo to compensate the victims and their families. No one questions Father Emil's motives when he decides to stop listening to the "terrible stories" about the slaughter. He realizes that offering prayers for dead relatives takes time away from ministering to the living: "To all those who tell us of lost relations, we can offer nothing, save for our prayers and perhaps a piece of bread. So we have stopped letting them tell us these terrible stories. It was taking all our time, and there was so much other work to be done" (254).

Many survivors, then, have to be content with listening to each other, so great is their need to speak: "Taking turns, they exchanged tales quickly, the haste in their voices sometimes blurring the words, for greater than their desire to be heard was the hunger to tell" (209). This chain of witnesses—each member alternating between listening and speaking—functions like a supportive ronde. Although Amabelle fails to convey her personal ordeal to the officials, she still imagines testifying to those who need to hear ("I dream all the time of returning to give my testimony to the river, the waterfall, the justice of the peace, even to the Generalissimo himself" [264]), and *for* her lover Sebastien Onius, whose story is incomplete since he disappeared ("his story is like a fish with no tail, a dress with no hem, a drop with no fall, a body in the sunlight with no shadow" [281]). Finally, given the chance to speak to Father Emil, she asks for information about Sebastien and his sister Mimi.

Testimony is inscribed on human flesh in *The Farming of Bones*. Male bodies, like Sebastien's, carry scars and wounds from the cane pricks, and Wilner has a withered arm. Among four old women, "one was missing an ear. Two had lost fingers. One had her right cheekbone cracked in half, the result of a runaway machete in the fields" (61). How do bodies already damaged and disfigured from dangerous slave-like labor defy death sanctioned by a dictator? Some who are killed, ironically with the very tools of their trade, machetes, resist erasure by the sheer grotesque spectacle of their corpses piled up along the shore. Cadavers floating in the bloody river are also visible evidence of the massacre. Amabelle, while spared harsh working conditions, is nevertheless bitten on the legs by ants, scratched and pricked as she flees through the cane fields only to be brutally attacked by a mob in Dajabón that leaves her battered, bruised, and unable to speak. Her body is transformed into a site of testimony: "Now my flesh was simply a map of scars and bruises, a marred testament" (227). Sylvie, who assumes Amabelle's old job as a handmaid to Valencia, has deep rope burns visible on her neck that testify to the attack.

Another important way to resist annihilation is to recuperate testimony from the survivors, disseminate it, and thereby bring the massacre into the public consciousness. Amabelle urgently desires to bear witness for herself and her lover Sebastien Onius. Her oft-repeated refrain—"His name is Sebastien Onius"—contains the words she would probably utter to identify him in court if given the chance to testify on his behalf. In search of the truth about his and his sister's fate, Amabelle assembles pieces of the story from various characters, representing different sides of the conflict, over a long period of time. Some testimonies she hears during her recuperation at the border clinic, others while waiting on line at the police precinct in Cap Haitien, and still others in individual interviews with Man Denise, Sebastien and Mimi's mother. Wilner and Yves also contribute information. She asks Tibon: "Did you see others being taken?" (173). Twenty-four years after the incident, which coincides with Trujillo's death, Amabelle revisits Alegría where she questions Señora Valencia, her former employer. Amabelle's quest inspires others such as Sylvie, Valencia's servant, who questions her employer about the era for the first time.

Part of Amabelle's arsenal of stories amasses as a result of her temporary voicelessness. At the border clinic, unable to speak because of her serious wounds, she silently listens to the testimony of survivors. Their accounts of torture and the execution of family members; of witnessing hundreds of people forced off a pier or shot and left for dead in a cadaver pit; of people struck with a machete as vultures hovered overhead; along with accounts of ultimate escape, precipitate a visceral reaction in Amabelle. As audience to this *séance*, composed of anonymous speakers, she is already too familiar with what happened in the "country of death" (238).

We conclude that Amabelle converts the oral testimony she gathers into a written document represented by *The Farming of Bones*. Through her, Danticat makes a case for including in the process of history production the oral testimonies of those actually involved in the events, thereby giving voice to those who are typically excluded from this process due to nationality, class, language, gender or censorship. In her role of author, Danticat chooses not to insert into her autofiction a *marqueur de paroles* as does Chamoiseau. Without mediation, her protagonist remembers and speaks for herself. Beverly Bell had similar concerns, recognizing the importance of first-person récits in her *Walking on Fire: Haitian Women's Stories of Survival and Resistance*, a collection that permits peasants and poor urban activists to speak for themselves. In it, she balances commentary with historical context and photographs. Each woman's name appears in capital letters signaling her ownership of her own story and her own eloquence. Following their initial interviews, the women were consulted as part of an extensive editing process, which Bell explains: "After completing a first round of editing, I again traveled south to meet with each storyteller and read back the text that had been created from her words. We worked together, correcting what I had misheard; adding what she had forgotten the first time; deleting what she realized, in retrospect, was dangerous to print. By the time the text had been reshaped to her specifications, every woman was in accord with both the content of her testimony and how it would fit within *Walking on Fire*'s thematic structure" (xv). Collaborative transcribing, editing, and translating brought this project to fruition, making these testimonies accurate and accessible.

According to Edouard Glissant, Haitian painting is the visual representation of an oral sign, and thus, I believe, another site of testimony.[9] Indeed, one cover of *The Farming of Bones* reproduces Gérard Valcin's painting *Lasirèn et Mèt Dlo* in which luxuriant tropical tree tops foreground a waterfall. Lasirèn is a marine Vodun divinity. Mèt Dlo is a Vodun figure from whom one seeks protection, and it is to her that Amabelle dedicates her narrative. Valcin's painting includes a waterfall, which in the novel doubles as a sanctuary for Amabelle and her lover and a *lieu de mémoire* she seeks to revisit. Ernst Prophète commemorates Haitian massacre victims in his painting *1937: Grand-Mère me disait que la riv. Massacre était en sang* [1937: Grandmother used to tell me that the Massacre River was bleeding], reproduced as the cover of *General Sun, My Brother*, Carrol F. Coates English translation of Alexis's *Compère Général Soleil*. Prophète's painting, whose title evokes orality, intergenerational transmission, and an in-trust narrator, depicts a family fleeing across a bridge under which bloodied corpses are carried away by the current.

Glissant's linking of visual and oral signs and the written word with memory and historiography resonates in the typography of *The Farming of Bones*. The lowercase letters in which the title of the first edition is set remind the reader not only of the insignificance officials attached to the testimonies of massacre survivors, but of the exploitation of Haitian cane workers in the Dominican Republic and the collusion of the Haitian government. *The Farming of Bones* is itself an oxymoron, the two principal terms, antithetical. Cultivation evokes life, and bones suggest death. Indeed, the title derives from the Creole expression Sebastien uses as he considers with Amabelle the death of fellow cane worker, Joël: "I considered Joël lucky to no longer be part of the cane life, *travay tè pou zo*, the farming of bones" (55). In other words, those who cultivate the soil are farming their own bones. Danticat's title also suggests that people who till the soil will find the buried bones of previous workers. The expression is articulated in the Creole the *braceros* use among themselves, not in the Spanish they use to communicate with their employers or in the French, the official language of Haiti.[10]

As I have already pointed out, listening is an essential part of témoignage, and Amabelle engages in that activity while she is at work. As a domestic servant to a well-connected Dominican family in Alegría, she has entry not only to the kitchen, but to the parlor and to her employers' bedroom, which gives her access to information she would not ordinarily be privy to. While serving cool water to guests in the front gallery, for example, she hears Béatriz say that Dr. Javier, Sebastien, and Mimi are heading to the border, an indication that the authorities are aware of the planned escape. Amabelle, however, must hide her inside knowledge: "I feigned shock as best I could" (148). On another occasion she overhears Luis, the gardener, tell his wife Juana that Señora Valencia's soldier/husband, while speeding, killed a cane worker. This accident prefigures the indiscriminate killing ordered by the dictator. Yet, visual evidence is still important to Amabelle in confirming her suspicions concerning her friends' fates: "Yves, did you *see* them take Mimi and Sebastien" (164).

Don Ignacio, (Papi), is another avid listener. Every evening, this "exiled patriot" strains to hear the voice of the radio announcer for news about the Spanish Civil War. Like Amabelle, he, too, seeks written confirmation: "On his lap were maps showing different Spanish cities that he consulted with a hand magnifier as he listened" (43). Oblivious to the large enhanced portrait of Trujillo in full military regalia looming above his head, Don Ignacio laments to Amabelle about leaving the scene of a fatal car accident, one in which a Haitian cane worker lost his life. His remark foreshadows the looming massacre, while the portrait in the scene summons up the presence of contemporaneous dictator, Mussolini, who along with Germany and fascist Spain bombed a small defenseless Basque city in April 1937. Pablo Picasso would commemorate that horror in *Guernica*.

Listening is clearly not a passive exercise in *The Farming of Bones*. The sister witness is expected to *relie, relaie, relate* (link, relay, and relate) the information gleaned:

> At times you could sit for a whole evening with such individuals, just listening to their existence unfold, from the house where they were born to the hill where they wanted to be buried. It was their way of returning home, with you as a witness or as someone to bring them back to the present, either with a yawn, a plea to be excused, or the skillful intrusion of your own tale. This is how people left imprints on themselves in each other's memory so that if you left first and went back to the common village, you could carry, if not a letter, a piece of treasured clothing, some message to their loved ones that their place was still among the living (73).

Perhaps relying on that Haitian practice, a dying Hilarion Hilarius in *Compère Général Soleil*, having successfully escaped to Haitian soil in the midst of the slaughter, entrusts his life story to his wife Claire-Heureuse at the close of the novel. Although this is another example of a woman being given the responsibility of passing on an important story, the novel ends without our seeing Claire-Heureuse perform the duties of a curator or a marqueur de paroles. Anthony Lespes's *Les Semences de la colère* (1949) is concerned less with attestations than with the resettlement of 300 Haitian refugee families in Billiguy, one of the government-established "colonies agricoles." At one point in the novel, Solon, who had one arm cut off with a machete and fled Cibao on foot, sparks a discussion of personal stories. While the immediacy of the horror promises a more "authentic" rendering not transformed by distant memory, the public dissemination of the ordeal is limited as the men speak exclusively among themselves. In *The Farming of Bones* testifying about the event is second to remembering it, which "though sometimes painful—can make you strong" (73).

Like the Haitian/Dominican border, the ending of Danticat's novel is ambiguous. It is October, the bloodbath's anniversary month, and Amabelle, removing her dress, immerses herself in the low current of the Massacre River on the Haitian side.[11] I believe that in this image Danticat interrogates the traveler's tree and umbilical cord tropes that draw the individual home. To accommodate those who do not make it back, the location of their burial becomes a site of pilgrimage. Amabelle thus communes with the Massacre River, where her parents drowned: "bound as we are to places where our dead are lain" (290).[12] For the same reason, Kongo decides not to flee Alegría, for he has buried his son Joël there. Valencia, too, respects that tradition: "I don't think I will ever leave here. ... This is the place of my mother's grave, my son's grave. It is likely my father will be buried here. I will never leave here" (150–51).

The Pwofesè is the guardian of the river where so many died. Wandering along the shore and wearing layers of clothing, he is considered a madman. He has "not been the same since the slaughter" (285). The Pwofesè embodies, in Glissant's words, "ces errants, qui aux carrefours moulinent ainsi le tragique de nos déracinements" (those wanderers, who at the crossroads mill the tragic of our uprootings) (*Discours* 362). Glissant reminds us that we pretend to ignore people like the Pwofesè, although we speak the same language; Amabelle, however, identifies with him. Father Romain, too, is psychologically impaired, parroting Trujillo's speeches after surviving torture. He serves not only as an example of invisible scars left by the ordeal, but as a reminder of the destructiveness of hate speech.[13]

The issues raised in *The Farming of Bones* concerning migrants and guest workers in the 1930s are relevant to other eras. The roundup and execution of Haitians in 1937 reconstructs on a much smaller scale the capture of Africans during the centuries-long Atlantic slave trade, the genocide of Jews during the Holocaust, and the genocide of Rwandans in 1994. The flight to freedom depicted in the novel is analogous to that of escaped slaves or maroons trying to evade their pursuers, "frightened maroons that we are" (189). The terror unleashed by the Trujillo regime prefigures that of the dictatorial Duvaliers who over a thirty-year period imprisoned, tortured, executed, and forced thousands of individuals into exile. The drowning of Amabelle's parents, Antoine Désir and Irelle Pradelle, and of Wilner and Odette revives the tragic end of the hundreds of Haitians lost in the waters between the island and Florida. Those who survive the perilous journey today are repatriated or jailed pending a court hearing to prove persecution before they are granted entry as refugees. The illegal trafficking in Haitian cane workers and the horrible conditions in the *bateyes* (shantytowns where cane cutters live) continue today as documented in Michael Régnier's film *Black Sugar*, as well as several reports by Americas Watch. The will to testify about injustices and to convert oral testimony into written documents persists.

The Farming of Bones is a narrative of displacement, separation, rupture, and reconnection, all in relation to home. Amabelle's departure and return to Haiti are involuntary and fraught with peril, leaving her psychologically and physically wounded. Nevertheless, she applies danmyé's principles of resistance, interaction, and balance, and constructs several supportive rondes. Border tensions are still high in 1961 when Amabelle returns to Alegría after Trujillo's death. She must be smuggled in a jeep and bribe the border guards on both sides. She locates neither the waterfall nor Valencia's house where she lived for so many years, a situation that mirrors her earlier, bewildering return to Cap Haitien. This one-day trip is not a nostalgic return nor a quest for lost origins, but a desire to make meaning of her years in her adopted home.

Also an autofiction, *The Farming of Bones* is an account of the early loss of home and the reformation of family in the dyaspora through the retrieval and dissemination of testimony. Amabelle constructs a self in relation to her parents, and to Sebastien, Valencia, and Yves. Not only does she relate her own story, she initiates other narratives. Her questioning of Tibon ("How long have you been traveling, Tibon?" and "Did you see others being taken?") precipitates his harrowing récit of being seized by soldiers in La Romana, made to stand at the edge of a high cliff, and then forced to jump into the rough sea (173–75). Her temporary voicelessness while recovering from her wounds at the clinic puts Amabelle in the position of listening to other survivors' récits, which she adds to her own repertory.

Having lost her belongings in her escape across the border, Amabelle's sole possession is her knowledge of the massacre. As a victim and survivor, she accepts the responsibility not only of being a witness, but of bearing witness and metaphorically passing the baton (*passer le témoin*): "The slaughter is the only thing that is mine enough to pass on" (266). Her priceless first-hand information threatens the established order that prefers to minimize or even ignore this tragic event. Some of those individuals are government officials who are also responsible for translating oral testimony given in Creole into documents in French (and/or Spanish), a concern expressed by Yves, who flees with Amabelle and becomes her companion: "You tell the story, and then it's retold as they wish, written in words you do not understand, in a language that is theirs, and not yours" (246). The question of who ultimately owns a story is thus problematized. Amabelle, however, also functions as a sister witness who does not relinquish power when she retells the story. She spreads the message for those who died so tragically. All in all, *The Farming of Bones* functions as evidence— témoignage—of a tragic event in history that must be acknowledged, remembered, and passed on.

The traveler's tree and umbilical cord resonate in Danticat's other novels as metaphors for return and connection. These images do not so much express nostalgic longing for home, as they do a coming to terms with the new and unstable identities that result from migration and exile. The tension between a present that is rooted in the past is embodied in characters that range from Sophie Caco in *Breath, Eyes, Memory*, a girl who leaves her small town in Haiti to join her mother in New York City, to Bienaimé, the dew breaker/prison guard/torturer under Duvalier, who reinvents himself as a barbershop owner in Brooklyn. On the very first page of the autofiction *Breath, Eyes, Memory*, Danticat investigates the location and meaning of home through twelve-year-old Sophie, who creates a Mother's Day card for her aunt with whom she lives in Croix-des-Rosets. Tante Atie recommends that Sophie send the card instead to her biological mother who has just sent a plane ticket for Sophie to join her in the United States. Danticat suggests at the outset that the responsibility for mothering can shift, can be negotiated between biological and "other mothers," especially when emigration is involved. These kinds of long-distance relationships between parents and children are delicate and difficult to maintain, but they must be preserved. At the same time, Danticat demonstrates Atie's sense of loss, as well as her realization that the child-care arrangement was only temporary. Sophie, in effect, has two mothers, who are also sisters, in two different locations. Representing two motherlands, they raise her and are instrumental in the formation of her identity.

Characters in *The Dew Breaker*, too, are *dyaspora*: though settled in the United States, they maintain various levels of attachment to Haiti, sending money to relatives or traveling between Brooklyn, Port-au-Prince, Tampa, Léogâne, and Manhattan. While inserting themselves into American society—finding jobs, opening businesses, and investing in neighborhoods—they learn the impossibility of concealing a reprehensible past. *The Dew Breaker*, is thus a collage text[île], a cross between a novel and a collection of interconnected short stories with three first-person narrators: Ka Bienaimé, a Brooklyn-born sculptor and substitute teacher; Michel, from Port-au-Prince, who rents the Bienaimé basement apartment with two other men; and Fréda, a twenty-two-year-old funeral singer, who fled Haiti for refusing to sing at the presidential palace. Perhaps appropriately, the torturer of the title does not have access to first-person narration, although his confession to his daughter opens the collection. In fact, Bienaimé's story of evading a past that denied the humanity of his victims frames the text, which centers on the ways his victims cope thirty years after the event.

As we have seen, Danticat's characters, like her, travel and migrate, making identity difficult to assign. Similarly, another Haitian writer, Pascale Blanchard-Glass, who lived in Puerto Rico and the United States for many years before settling in France, creates a Martinican protagonist, Isadora, who falls in love with Tristan, a Haitian in Cuba in *La Comète de Halley*. That the first-person narration passes among four characters in the novel—Ana, Tristan, Hermanse, and

Isadora—also articulates the possibility of multiple subjectivities and positionalities in autofiction. In the next chapter, I examine the work of Maryse Condé, a model for her much-traveled characters. With their varied perspectives, shifts in time and space, anachronisms, and "cannibalizing" of other texts, these narratives qualify as collages text[île]s. Furthermore, Condé's critique of traditional tropes of Caribbean masculinity makes her novels intersect in interesting ways with danmyé.

5

A Roving *I*

Autofiction(s) and Subversions

> *modern black political culture has always been more interested in the relationship of identity to roots and rootedness than in seeing identity as a process of movement and mediation that is more appropriately approached via the homonym routes.*
>
> Paul Gilroy, *The Black Atlantic*

> *Why am I telling this story? I have re-created it with patient research and the power of my imagination, but it may be completely false.*
>
> Maryse Condé, *Land of Many Colors and Nanna-ya*

Maryse Condé elevates autofiction and collage text[île] to yet another level. Provocative and subversive, she rotates narrators within the same text. While Tituba testifies about her own experience in *Moi, Tituba sorcière . . . Noire de Salem* (1986) and Veronica Mercier's inner monologue structures *Hérémakhonon* (1976); while Coco unobtrusively traces the lives of her ancestors beginning with great-grandfather Albert Louis in *La Vie scélérate* (1987) and Maryse recounts her youth in *Le Coeur à rire et à pleurer: contes vrais de mon enfance* (2000), author Condé often subverts autofiction's assumed single narrator discourse, tenets, and outcome. Moreover, the narrative model exemplified by Joseph Zobel and Edwidge Danticat is replaced by a multivoiced configuration in *Traversée de la mangrove* (1989), *Désirada* (1997), and *La Migration des coeurs* (1995), in which diverse first- and third-person narrators preside in rotation. Unlike Pineau in *L'Espérance-macadam*, however, in which the shifts are unanticipated, abrupt, and disconcerting, imitating the vagaries of traumatic memory and simulating the violence of storms and their human counterparts, Condé clearly signals hers, except in *Histoire de la femme cannibale* (2003), in which the shift to first-person is unexpected.

Indicating ownership, in *Traversée de la mangrove*, chapter titles are the personal names of seven women narrators—Mira, Man Sonson, Dinah, Léocadie, Rosa, Vilma, and Dodose—who recount their encounters with Francis Sancher; the men's accounts, with two exceptions, are presented in the third-person. The division along gender lines in *La Migration des coeurs* (1995) also privileges women's voices, with eleven *récits de femmes* and only three by men among its preponderance of first- and third-person narrators. All in all, the *I* in some of Condé's late fiction roves among characters representing different ethnic groups, races, colors, classes, and generations, providing several perspectives on one character or situation, thus disrupting the reader's expectations of a synthesized self. Instead, the *Is* combine to create what could be termed a "split" or "multiple personality," like Francis Sancher, a character whose identity is constructed largely through rumor and conjecture.

I believe that by having several different narrators in her texts Condé interrogates the reliability of single-witness testimony and the contradictory versions it sometimes produces. Instead of corroborating evidence, it can make a story ambiguous and problematic. With this kind of configuration, Condé also challenges the imposition of an all-encompassing identity, illustrating Glissant's notion of the rhizome and the significance of location in identity formation: "C'est comme cela qu'il faut concevoir l'identité, comme un lien que l'on entretient avec un territoire réel ou imaginaire" (qtd. in Sourieau 1096). [That is how identity must be conceived, as a link that one has with a real or imaginary area.] Not confined to representing the clichéd transit between Guadeloupe and the metropole, Condé reconceptualizes traditional boundaries of the Caribbean diaspora, exploring displacement in a broad sense and its effect on identity. Haitians in her oeuvre, for example, are a group that crystallize intra-Caribbean migration, as in *Traversée* where former residents of Jacmel, Les Cayes, and Gonaïves establish a community in Beaugendre, a "colonie des exilés" (colony of exiled Haitians) (200/166).

The breadth and complexity of the Haitian dyaspora is demonstrated with particular force in *Désirada*, in which Ludovic, born in Cuba where his father cut sugarcane, lives in Haiti, the United States, Canada, Belgium, Germany, Mali, Senegal, Mozambique, and France, where his jobs range from a Peace Corps volunteer to musician. These numerous displacements cause him to question his origins: "Ludovic marquait toujours un temps d'hésitation lorsqu'on lui demandait d'où il était." [Ludovic always hesitated a moment when asked where he was born] (38/28). His errance has been an enriching experience in that it increases his ability to communicate. On the one hand, that he speaks five languages illustrates Condé's belief that "la langue n'est pas le phénomène fondamental qui définit une identité" (language is not the fundamental phenomenon that defines identity) (qtd. in Sourieau 1092). On the other hand, those who criticize Ludovic because his Spanish is Cuban and not Castilian and his English is American and not British, refuse Relation.[1]

Condé's Guadeloupean characters travel far from home, too. *Histoire de la femme cannibale* is set primarily in Capetown, but protagonist Rosélie Thibaudin has lived in Japan, the United States, and an unnamed African country. That they embody Glissant's errance, allows Condé to question issues of home, belonging, and ultimately, identity. Resisting the narrow confines of her "île natale," Véronica, in *Hérémakhonon*, undertakes a journey to Africa, which Arlette Smith argues reverses the slave trade route (45–54). Once there, however, she becomes severely disappointed when her strong desire for *enracinement* (rootedness) does not materialize; she does not find the mythical and promised home inherent in the notion of diaspora. Her search for identity ends in failure. Condé's work centers less on the reasons why individuals leave home and more on how they construct identity in a new location. As many of Condé's characters resist geographical fixity, they mimic danmyétistes who avoid establishing a center in the ring in order to avoid their opponent's blows.

Moreover, Condé espouses Suzanne Césaire's notion of cannibal literature as expressed in her January 1942 essay "Misère d'une poésie" in *Tropiques*.[2] After citing several examples from poets who extol in clichés the beauties of the Martinican landscape, Césaire declares: "Nous décrétons la mort de la littérature doudou. Et zut à l'hibiscus, à la frangipane, aux bougainvilliers. La poésie martiniquaise sera cannibale ou ne sera pas" (50). [We decree the death of *doudou* literature (colonial texts in which a Caribbean woman is abandoned by her French lover). And to hibiscus, frangipani, bougainvilleas. Martinican poetry will be cannibal or it will not exist.] In appropriating a negative stereotype assigned to the region's people, Césaire takes a stance parallel to her husband's in his rehabilitation of the word *nègre*. She calls for "une littérature cannibale," in other words, a literature particular to the Caribbean, a region mythologized as savage.[3]

In addition, Condé subverts some of the principles embodied in danmyé that assert a hypermasculinity. For example, her male protagonists are not idealized as they are in négritude texts; instead, they are tormented, like Razyé and Francis Sancher. All of these textual and thematic features—irony, subversion, a questioning of autofiction as a genre, traveling protagonists, and a cannibal poetics—characterize Condé's work that, in my view, epitomizes collages text[îles]. As I argue in this chapter, the collagistes method serves as a metaphor for Condé's critique of unitary or readily identifiable origins. *Traversée de la mangrove* will be the center of my discussion as it epitomizes Condé's subversion of autofiction; here, the roving *I*s, through multiple perspectives, reconstruct the life of a migrating central character whose masculinity, traditionally honored in literature, is undermined. Condé also cannibalizes canonical texts from the *Caribbean*: Roumain's *Gouverneurs de la rosée*, as we shall see, resonates in *Traversée de la mangrove*.

Autofiction in Condé's hands is deceptively simple yet subversive. First-person narrators relate their own stories, offer their takes on events, or are ambivalent about writing history. Maryse Boucolon, the narrator of *Le Coeur à rire et à pleurer: contes vrais de mon enfance,* has the same name as the author (she acquired Condé from her first husband). However, the oxymoronic "true tales," in the title calls into question authenticity and autobiographical resonances that the paperback edition avoids by transforming "true stories" into "childhood memories" ("souvenirs de mon enfance"). In an interview, Condé addresses the tension between truth and memory: "It's a way of saying that every reconstitution of the past is doubtful, becomes a story. One adds, retrenches, embellishes despite oneself where one thinks one is grasping the truth. The problem of truth has always interested me. Where is it? Who holds it?"[4]

The issue of who owns the story is illustrated in *Moi, Tituba sorcière... Noire de Salem*, which is based on a historical figure who was arrested and jailed during the Salem witch trials of 1692. Condé acknowledges Tituba's erasure from history in the title's ellipsis, which is lost in the English translation *I, Tituba, Black Witch of Salem*.[5] Condé counters that invisibility and silencing by having Tituba proudly proclaim the elements that define her identity: gender, vocation, race, and location. Tituba's subjectivity is not only announced in the title. By reproducing Tituba's actual deposition at the center of the text, Condé reasserts her historical testimony. Condé then fills in the gaps by creating a back story, imagining Tituba's situation from the time of her conception—the result of rape by a sailor aboard a slave ship—to her life after death. Inscribing the story, however, gives it a certain legitimacy and adds another dimension: in the end, the popularity of the fictional Tituba has had the effect of restoring the real Tituba to public consciousness.

Prior to Chamoiseau's notion of the sentimenthèque, the remnants of readings that influence a writer, Suzanne Césaire delivered her cannibal poetry manifesto with its more proactive approach to writing. Gone are the days of "Littérature de hamac. Littérature de sucre et de vanille. Tourisme littéraire"; (Hammock literature. Sugar and vanilla literature. Literary tourism) ("Misère" 50). Here, Césaire indirectly censures writers such as John Antoine-Nau, Leconte de Lisle, and José-Maria de Hérédia whose outsider/observer perspectives produce saccharin, bland, and superficial verse. According to Césaire, true Martinican poetry reaches and releases *l'âme nègre* (the black soul). She therefore urges writers to symbolically devour, regurgitate, and thus transform: "la poésie martiniquaise sera cannibale ou ne sera pas" (50).[6] Not only does she imply consuming the flesh of the captured enemy, but she appropriates the term *cannibal* that for centuries denigrated Caribbean people. Aimé Césaire's *Une Tempête* (1968) provides a good example of a cannibal text. It takes Shakespeare's *The Tempest*, shifts its center, gives voice to Caliban, and at one point provides a forum for discussion of Martin Luther King, Jr., and Malcolm X's philosophies.

Suzanne Césaire's poetics for Martinican literature in the 1940s is later adopted by Haitian-born Lucien Lemoine, who has lived in Senegal since the 1960s and has since become a citizen. In a poem entitled "Cannibale, oui!" (Cannibal, yes), the author relishes making a delicious meal out of prominent literary figures:

J'ai pris Paul-Jean Toulet
   Au collet
Et j'ai planté mes dents
   Là-dedans

Avec un appétit
   Pas petit
J'ai dévoré rôti
   Tout Loti

Puis dans un même élan
   Montherlant
Gide et *pois* de mon *riz*
   Valéry

Et tant d'autres Péguy
   René-Guy
Cadou d'Aurevilly
   Et Billy

Garçon un Lamartine
    En tartine
Pouah Tiens remporte vite
    Ce lévite

Oh une côtelette
    De Colette
Deux Lao-tseu un Comte
    J'ai mon compte

Un demi d'Epicure
    Pour ma cure
Du Goethe un bon Shakespeare
    Ou j'expire

Une langue de Dante
    Bien pendante
Huile sel et vinaigre
    Je suis nègre (32–33)

[I grabbed Paul-Jean Toulet
    By the throat
And planted my teeth
    In him

With an appetite
    Not small
I devoured roasted
    All of Loti

Then with the same gusto
    Montherlant
Gide and *peas* in my *rice*
    Valery

And so many others Péguy
    René-Guy
Cadou d'Aurevilly
    And Billy

> Waiter one Lamartine
> > With bread and butter
> Ugh Say take back quickly
> > This Levite
>
> Oh a cutlet
> > Of Colette
> Two Lao-tsu one Comte
> > I've had enough
>
> A half-bottle of Epicure
> > For my cure
> Some Goethe one good Shakespeare
> > Or I die
>
> A tongue of Dante
> > Hanging out
> Oil salt and vinegar
> > I am black] [7]

Both Césaire and Lemoine favor the symbolic consumption and subversion of canonical texts. Condé takes it further by also cannibalizing Caribbean texts that I will discuss in detail below.

Many scholars have commented on the affinities between *La Migration des coeurs* and *Wuthering Heights* without recognizing the theoretical underpinnings of Condé's strategy.[8] More than a rewriting, *La Migration* crystallizes Suzanne Césaire's notion of the cannibal text. Dedicated to Emily Brontë— "qui, je l'espère, agréera cette lecture de son chef-d'oeuvre. Honneur et respect!" (who I hope will approve of this interpretation of her masterpiece. Honour and respect!)—the praise for the canonical text not only borrows its form from orature, but usurps the expectation of the traditional call-and-response. While "respect" normally grants permission to a visitor to enter the house, in this instance, Condé herself provides the rejoinder to the two-part Creole greeting. Not waiting for the invitation, she simply serves notice of her intent, affirming her own *I*.

The borrowings in *La Migration des coeurs* range from transparent to subtle. On the one hand, a passage inspired by a W. H. Auden poem is identified in a footnote, while Aymeric reads an excerpt from Gustave Flaubert's *Salammbô* to Justin-Marie. On the other hand, young Cathy rides a horse named Toussine, who has the same name as the protagonist's grandmother in *Pluie et vent sur Télumée Miracle*. Using an adage about the importance of riding one's own horse, Toussine repeatedly warns Télumée about personal empowerment. Three chapter titles of *La Migration des coeurs* are familiar to readers of French literature: "*Le temps retrouvé*"; "La Mort du loup"; and "Retour au pays natal." Resited, they subvert their original purpose. "*Le temps retrouvé*," of course, is also the title of the last volume of Marcel Proust's *A la recherche du temps perdu*, a book that itself lifts lines from Chateaubriand's *Mémoires d'outre tombe*; thus Condé cannibalizes a cannibalized text. "La Mort du loup" recalls Alfred de Vigny's poem about a father's stoicism and martyrdom in defending his family, qualities that Razyé seriously lacks. In "Retour au pays natal," Razyé's nineteen-year-old son Premier-né returns to Pointe-à-Pitre from Marie-Galante, but not as an enlightened hero as in Aimé Césaire's long poem.

With the exception of *La Migration des coeurs*, Condé's narrative approach most often involves borrowing characters, titles, passages, and structures from texts, sometimes without attribution, by a wide range of writers—Jacques Stéphen Alexis, W. H. Auden, Aimé Césaire, William Faulkner, Nathaniel Hawthorne, Toni Morrison, Marcel Proust, Jacques Roumain, and Alfred de Vigny—whose texts may or may not be set in or even related to the Caribbean. Condé stages an anachronistic encounter between Tituba and Hester Prynne from Nathaniel Hawthorne's *The Scarlet Letter* in order to parody feminist discourse; she puts Hilarion Hilarius's dying lines from Jacques Stéphen Alexis's *Compère Général Soleil* into Tituba's mouth to pay homage to the Haitian writer (Pfaff, "Entretiens" 90, 98). While I agree with Michael Dash's position in *The Other America* that these borrowings are designed to induce "subversive laughter" (118), I also believe that they have broader implications. One is reminded of Hélène Cixous's claim in *Le Rire de la méduse* that writing for women and the dispossessed is a form of resistance.[9] Condé's appropriations invite the reader to be complicit and to participate in the production of the text in which Tituba's *I* "relates" (as in tells her story and in a Glissantian sense) to Hester and to the reader.

Our understanding of the chapter in *Le Coeur à rire et à pleurer* entitled "Chemin d'école" is enhanced if we recognize the nod to two earlier novels about school in Martinique, but with a gender twist. Harking back to Chamoiseau's text of the same name (discussed in chapter 2), "Chemin d'école" also involves *La Rue Cases-Nègres*, a book that is not part of the curriculum at Lycée Fenelon, the school where Maryse is a student. Reading it at age thirteen, she learns for the first time about the slave trade, slavery, color prejudice, colonial oppression, and poverty in the Caribbean, a past that her parents avoid discussing and that school neither acknowledges nor teaches. Identifying with José, she rethinks her past experiences, realizes that discrimination has indeed affected her life, and concludes that she is an example of Frantz Fanon's alienated Antillean in a "peau noire, masque blanc." That her political consciousness is raised by autofiction, not a theoretical tract or history book, attests to the power of *La Rue Cases-Nègres'* advocative discourse.

Maryse's French teacher, Miss Lemarchand, a communist whose ideas conflict with society's values, facilitates her student's *prise de conscience* (awakening) by asking her to do a presentation on a book from her country. That the assignment is relegated to the end of academic year, after the required course work has been completed, reflects the exclusion of perspectives not sanctioned by the state curriculum. Nevertheless, the progressive Miss Lemarchand wants to make Maryse feel more welcome in the classroom. Ashamed to admit that she is unfamiliar with Caribbean authors, Maryse seeks her older brother's advice. Recommending the Zobel text, Sandrino, an activist, lends her his personal copy, thereby initiating Maryse and her classmates into Caribbean literature: "C'était la première fois que je *dévorais* une vie. J'allais bientôt y prendre goût." [It was the first time I *cannibalized* a life. Something I would take a liking to] (120/110; emphasis added). With those two sentences, Maryse conjures up the cannibal image with a wink to the reader, hinting that the future writer will adopt Suzanne Césaire's strategy.[10] For her class presentation, Maryse transforms herself into Josélita, an invented sister or cousin of José Hassam. Imagining hunger and her hair reddened by the implacable sun, she performs a role that her classmates and teacher consider authentic. With her urban middle-class upbringing and perfect French, however, Maryse's knowledge does not come from personal experience, nor does her family in any way conform to Caribbean stereotypes.

In addition to Maryse's learning about Guadeloupean history by reading Martinican autofiction in Paris, other ironies and "targeted borrowings" abound in *Le Coeur à rire et à pleurer*. The chapter entitled "'The bluest eye,'" in English and enclosed in quotation marks to further call attention to itself, focuses on race and color hierarchies as does Toni Morrison's novel from which Condé borrows her title.[11] Condé subverts eleven-year-old Pecola Breedlove's story of obsession with the American standard of beauty through young Maryse, who resists the imposition of that standard in Pointe-à-Pitre. Not recognizing herself in the love letter sent by her light-skinned neighbor Gilbert—"'Maryse adorée, pour moi, tu es la plus belle avec tes yeux bleus'" [My darling Maryse, you are the loveliest of them all with your blue eyes] (65/40)—yet understanding his reference to "ideal" beauty, she becomes confused, sad, and then angry. Author Condé deflates the noble sentiments and the tacitly expected romantic ritual of opposition and resistance by having Maryse later realize that Gilbert has copied the passage from a cheap French novel just as she had her written response to his letter. Condé's borrowing from works by black writers requires readers and characters to exercise diaspora literacy, theorized by Vèvè A. Clark as the ability to recognize those texts. Condé even cannibalizes her own text when "La Belle Créole," a restaurant in *Désirada*, becomes a boat in the novel *La Belle Créole*.

Conde's subversion of autofiction is further achieved in *La Migration des coeurs*, which is composed of récits by three men and ten women, all of whom were ignored by history. Descendants of African slaves and Indian indentured servants, peasants, teachers, and fishermen, their récits dominate, not Récits or master narratives. Similarly, one béké in the novel is not among those whose eighteenth- or nineteenth-century journals would have minimized their exploitation of and complicity in the plantation system; he is genuinely concerned about his workers. *La Migration des coeurs* restores voice to the marginalized in a similar way to Pineau and Abraham's *Femmes des Antilles: traces et voix*.

Traversée de la mangrove, appearing subsequent to Condé's own return to Guadeloupe after many years living abroad, invites a reading in dialogue with Césaire's *Cahier*, which was prompted by his imminent return to Martinique, and with Roumain's *Gouverneurs de la rosée*, whose protagonist returns to his village in Haiti after many years of working in Cuba.[12] Written during a sustained two-year stay in Guadeloupe, she admits "It's the only novel I've written that could be called Guadeloupean" ("Interview" 21). In much of Condé's previous work, the protagonist leaves the island in search of her identity, while in *Traversée* the travel trope is reversed as Francis Sancher returns to Guadeloupe in search of his origins and to die. In this novel, informed by roots and routes, *traversée* (crossing) is represented by the central character who travels from South America, to Africa, to Europe, to the Caribbean, and whose last name reproduces his lack of a fixed location, home, and identity: "Sancher" echoes *sans chez*, meaning "without a home." Moïse, the postman who circulates in his yellow van, represents errance on a smaller scale. This "mosquito" who lives in the *ville-mangrove* interacts with everyone in the community on a daily basis.

Traversée is set during the late 1980s in Rivière au Sel, a small, isolated village in Guadeloupe. Dominated by two powerful families—one of African and European ancestry, the Lameaulnes, and one of East Indian ancestry, the Ramsarans—the town is, nonetheless, forever changed by the arrival and eventual death of a stranger. Opening like a detective story—a dead body is found in the mud on a forest path by Léocadie Timothée, a retired schoolteacher who, while taking her evening walk, diverts from her usual path—the novel, in fact, borrows its structure from the Caribbean *veillée mortuaire* or wake, at which friends and family gather to honor the deceased. Glissant describes "la coutume de la veillée" (the tradition of the wake) as one "où l'on boit et conte, où l'on plaisante où on mime le personnage défunt et se moque de ses défauts tandis que dans la case la famille veille, mais attentive à ce qu'il ne manque rien aux participants qui là dehors se régalent" (where we drink and tell tales, where we make jokes, where we imitate the dead person and laugh at his weaknesses, while in the house the family keeps vigil, yet careful that nothing runs out for the people outside enjoying themselves) (*Discours* 124/59). Part mourning and part celebration, the wake is more than a vigil. It is a site of individual, collective, and reciprocal performance, that is, oral storytelling, music, and dance, the kind of interaction that also resonates in danmyé.[13]

Condé has said that the wake provides a model for the Caribbean novel, and *Traversée de la mangrove* is a fine example. Divided into three sections—dusk, night, and dawn—it spans the favored time for a wake at which storytelling, the *parole de nuit*, is an essential part. Fittingly, each chapter is named after a character who reminisces about Francis Sancher. The seven first-person female narrators—Man Sonson, Dinah, Léocadie Timothée, Rosa, Vilma, Dodose Pélagie, and Mira Lameaulnes (who speaks twice)—alternate with an unnamed third-person narrator who relates how Moïse, Aristide, Sonny, Sylvestre, Cyrille, Carmélien, Désinor, Lucien, and Émile met Sancher.[14] Of the women narrators Suzanne Crosta observes: "Perceived by the other as an object of desire, the women characters of the text subtly reverse this objectification by assuming their own discourse. They recount, and sometimes evaluate very harshly, the discourse of the community at large" ("Narrative" 148). That young Joby and Xantippe, isolated from the rest of the town, also narrate their own story shows that Condé is adamant about allowing marginalized voices to emerge.

This group comprised of people of African, European, Indian, and Chinese descent reconstruct the life of Sancher whose racial and cultural heritage is European, African, and South American. Xantippe, like Médouze in *La Rue Cases-Nègres* and Man Ya in *L'Exil selon Julia*, embodies ancestral memory. Having witnessed changes in the town, he recalls abolition, migration to the city, the opening of schools, the coming of electricity and color television, and mechanization as bananas replaced sugarcane as a cash crop. Xantippe is a founding ancestor like Joab in *L'Espérance-macadam*.

Over the course of the novel, Condé cannibalizes Aimé Césaire's *Cahier d'un retour au pays natal* and Roumain's *Gouverneurs de la rosée*, heeding Suzanne Césaire's Martinican poetics. Echoing the *Cahier*, Moïse articulates his desire to leave Rivière au Sel using *partir* (to depart) as an anaphore, a recognizable structure borrowed from the Césaire poem (48). Carmélien's reminiscence about the impact of reading the Roumain classic in elementary school takes the form of an excerpt from the scene in which Manuel shows Annaïse the *figuier maudit* (strangler fig) tree (174–75/142–43). Determined to discover a spring as Manuel does, Carmélien sets out to the forest where, with his father's machete, he imitates Manuel by trying to bring the water to the surface. At night, he dreams of irrigating the land, but awakes only to find that he has wet the bed. This episode again illustrates Condé's subversion of heroic narratives.

In *Traversée de la mangrove* Condé critiques the literary representation of masculinity in which male characters are associated with trees and tree roots with which they have a special communication. Strong, solid, and sturdy, they provide protection for the entire community. Trees, or *pié-bwa* in Creole, are an important part of the landscape and are invested with historical and cultural significance. According to Jules Faine, Creole *bwa* can also refer to "partie intime de l'homme" (an intimate part of the man) (75). As *bois d'ébène* or ebony wood, they designate captured Africans' bodies laid out like logs in the holds of slave ships.[15]

Forests were often the sites of maroon settlements as well as secret meeting places for planning insurrections, perhaps the most famous being Bois Caïman where in August 1791 Boukman gave a rousing speech that is said to have sparked the slave revolt that marked the beginning the Haitian Revolution. Religious practices are associated with pines, and sacrifices take place underneath the mapou tree. In Guadeloupe, traditions surrounding birth have long been associated with the breadfruit tree, the site where the father of a newborn buried the placenta or *maman-ventre*. The umbilical cord was traditionally buried along with a newly planted coconut palm—a tree known for its robust qualities—forever attaching the person to the land. When a person died, the water used to bathe the corpse was poured at the foot of a tree (Bébel-Gisler, *Léonora* 87).

The all-powerful man as tree is classically embodied in Manuel, who takes on its properties in Roumain's *Gouverneurs de la rosée* (1944). Manuel is likened to the *figuier maudit*, with whom he bonds to save Fonds Rouge. With its strong but soft tentacle-like roots that grow down from the branches to form secondary trunks and above-ground roots that hold water, it provides the necessary sustenance for the drought-stricken Haitian village. When Manuel first comes upon the tree, he is struck by its majesty. The third-person narrator describes it in masculinist terms: "Le figuier géant se dressait là d'un élan de torse puissant; ses branches chargées de mousse flottante couvraient l'espace d'une ombre vénérable et ses racines monstrueuses étendaient une main d'autorité sur la possession et le secret de ce coin de terre." [The giant fig tree proudly lifted its powerful trunk. It's [*sic*] branches, laden with floating moss, covered the spot with venerable shade, and its monstrous roots extended an authoritative hand over the ownership and secret of this corner of the earth] (106/108). Considering it a living being, Manuel and Annaïse marvel at its "head" and "feet," and speak of it with reverence, echoing the way in which Manuel is revered for his actions.

Repairing the *tonnelle* (arbor) by replacing the worm-eaten wood with the trunk of a young logwood—a hard, dark brown tree—Manuel foreshadows his own fate, death at the hands of Gervilen Gervilis: "Il l'avait ébranché, dévêtu de son écorce et mis à sécher. Mais le bois transpirait encore un peu d'humidité rouge." [He had lopped off its branches, stripped its bark, and set it out to dry. But the wood still sweated a bit of reddish moisture] (58/64).[16] The nails Manuel drives into the tender flesh of the tree—"Il enfonçait les clous dans la chair tendre du campêcher" [He was driving nails in the tender flesh of the logwood] (58/64)—lead some critics to consider Manuel a Christ-like figure.[17] Another tree, the calabash, provides support for Manuel's elderly father Bienaimé, his constantly leaning against it mirroring his dependence on his son.

In *Gouverneurs de la rosée* human survival depends on harmony with nature, figured in trees. Returning to Fonds Rouge after a fifteen-year absence, Manuel goes for a walk in order to become reacquainted with his "old friends." Courtesy requires that he greet them in the traditional way, as he would any neighbor whose home he asks permission to enter, a strategy discussed above in *La Migration des coeurs*: "Il avait envie de chanter un salut aux arbres." [He wanted to sing a greeting to the trees] (49/55). This friendship extends to the interaction between trees, their roots, and the rest of nature:

> Un arbre, c'est fait pour vivre en paix dans la couleur du jour et l'amitié du soleil, du vent, de la pluie. Ses racines s'enfoncent dans la fermentation grasse de la terre, aspirant les sucs élémentaires, les jus fortifiants. Il semble

toujours perdu dans un grand rêve tranquille. L'obscure montée de la sève le fait gémir dans les chaudes après-midi. C'est un être-vivant qui connaît la course des nuages et pressent les orages, parce qu'il est plein de nids d'oiseaux. (18)

[A tree is made to live in peace in the color of the day and the friendship of the sun, the wind, the rain. Its roots plunge into the sticky fermentation of the earth, inhaling the essential sap, the fortifying juices. It always seems lost in a deep quiet dream. The dark climb of the sap makes it sigh in the hot afternoon. It is a living being who knows the swift passage of the clouds and senses the storms because it is full of birds' nests.][18]

Ce sont les racines qui font amitié avec la terre et la retiennent: ce sont les manguiers, les bois de chênes, les acajous qui lui donnent les eaux des pluies pour sa grande soif et leur ombrage contre la chaleur de midi. (37)

[It's the roots that make friends with the soil, and hold it. It's the mango tree, the oak, the mahogany that give it rainwater when it's thirsty and shade it from the noonday heat.] (45)

Clearly, trees and their roots can be considered agents like Manuel throughout *Gouverneurs de la rosée*. Drought is the result when they are cut down, leaving the land vulnerable to erosion. Trees with rotten or severed roots, therefore, appear in similes describing characters in precarious positions. Manuel articulates his errance in the following terms: "J'étais comme une souche arrachée, dans le courant de la grand'rivière; j'ai dérivé dans les pays étrangers." [I've been like an uprooted tree in the current of a river. I drifted to foreign lands] (36/44). Old Simidor, who used to lead the *coumbite* (collective labor) before the family feud rendered obsolete his role as the drummer who beat out the rhythm for the workers, "était tout cassé maintenant et branlant comme un arbre pourri à la racine" (was broken and tittering like a tree with rotting roots) (38/46).[19]

Chamoiseau's title character, Solibo Magnifique, who produces a special kind of charcoal, is also favorably compared to trees: "Un charbon dans notre vie: le charbon, c'est le bois, c'est le tronc, c'est les branches et les feuilles, c'est la racine—et le charbon n'est plus le bois car c'est la flamme et le feu, alors imagine cette magie du feu et de la sève, de l'écorce et de la cendre, de la racine et de la poussière." [That's what he was in our lives: the charcoal is the wood, it's the trunk, the branches and the leaves, and also the root—and the charcoal is no longer the wood because it's the flame and the fire, imagine the magic of fire and sap of the bark, of the ash, of the root and the dust] (182/124). In Chamoiseau's novel *L'Esclave le vieil homme et le molosse* (1997), the narrator, pursued by a bloodhound, stops to contemplate the trees and is hypnotized by them. All in all, the rapprochement between masculinity and trees depicted in *Gouverneurs de la rosée* provides a powerful model for subsequent texts.

Echoing their importance in Caribbean culture as well as literature, trees figure prominently in *Traversée de la mangrove*; Condé problematizes their role, however, by associating them with death and destruction as opposed to a heroic masculinity.[20] The massive, dense roots of the swamp's *palétuviers* or mangrove trees prohibit a safe crossing: "On ne traverse pas la mangrove. On s'empale sur les racines des palétuviers. On s'enterre et on étouffe dans la boue saumâtre." [You don't cross a mangrove [swamp]. You'd spike yourself on the roots of the mangrove trees. You'd be sucked down and suffocated by the brackish mud] (192/158). Moïse's dreams "avaient séché comme pié-bwa en Carême" (withered like a tree during the dry season) (30/14). After the breakup of his friendship with Francis Sancher, Moïse feels the trees tighten their hold around him like the walls of a prison (47). Life's problems are compared to trees: "On voit le tronc, on voit les branches et les feuilles. Mais on ne voit pas les racines, cachées dans le fin fond de la terre. Or ce qu'il faudrait connaître, c'est leur forme, leur nature, jusqu'où elles s'enfoncent pour chercher l'eau, le terreau gras." [We see the trunk, we see the branches and the leaves. But we can't see the roots, hidden deep under the ground. And yet it's their shape and nature and how far they dig into the slimy humus to search for water that we need to know] (170/139).

Condé interrogates the association of trees with stereotypically heroic males. For Aristide Lameaulnes, whose obsessive love of his half-sister Mira borders on the incestuous, the forest provides a haven: "Ce n'est que là qu'il se sentait bien, parmi les grands arbres, marbri, châtaignier grande feuille, gommier blanc, acomat-boucan, bois la soie. Il se coulait dans leurs ombres sereines, silencieuses, à peine trouées de pépiements d'oiseaux.... Oui, c'est Loulou qui avait planté en lui cet amour des arbres, des oiseaux." [Only there, among the giant trees, the marbri, châtaignier, candlewood, mastwood and Caribbean pines, did he feel at home. He would slip into their serene and silent shadows, broken here and there by the twittering of birds.... Yes, it was Loulou who had instilled in him this love of trees and birds] (66–67/46–47). Rosa Ramsaran dreads the moment her husband Sylvestre takes each young son to the forest, for it signals the end of her primary relationship with them and their entrance into the masculine domain.

Condé's subversion of the classic association of trees with courageous males is especially evident in the character Francis Sancher. Physically tall and straight—"haut comme un mahogany" (tall as a mahogany tree) (30/15), "ce mahogany d'homme" (this mahogany-tree of a man) (33/17)—he seems to represent Condé's cannibalization of Manuel Jan-Josef in Roumain's *Gouverneurs de la rosée*. Francis Sancher, however, does not arrive in Rivière au Sel to take charge, locate a new water source, or to save the community from itself. Condé positions Francis Sancher on a tree *stump* in the woods at the beginning of the *trace* (path) Saint Charles. That the stump is also the only vestige of his ancestors left in Guadeloupe further indicates that the clan has lost its standing and is powerless. Not only is Sancher not a savior-martyr nor the *marron* to whom the woods are a site of resistance against slavery, he is neither the returning warrior-poet like the one in Aimé Césaire's *Cahier*, who is determined to awaken his countrymen. Francis Sancher returns to Guadeloupe simply to await death.

Condé's representation of what Michael Dash correctly asserts is her "merciless deconstruction of the hegemonic and patriarchal self" (121), which is figured in sturdy trees, is also manifested in Francis Sancher's genealogy, that is, his metaphorical or family tree. Rhizomatic, like the banyan, it stretches around the globe. Born in Medellín, Colombia, to the daughter of one of the wealthiest *cafeiteros* (coffee plantation owners) whose African ancestor is responsible for Francis's skin color—"couleur de maïs bien rôti" (a roasted corn color) (105/80)—Sancher's life is a portrait of loneliness. From his initial abandonment—he is left alone in a corner for forty-eight hours while the midwife tries to save his mother's life—his feeling of isolation increases in a family without love; his father had married Teresa simply because her family was wealthy. Sancher confronts his inherited family curse, the sudden, brutal, and unexplained deaths, in their early fifties, of all the males on his father's side. Ironically, it is Francis Sancher's mother who provides him with information about his father's past. She is the one who gives him papers documenting the Sancher family history, including the 1790 title to a property consisting of 500 hectars at Saint-Calvaire, Petit Bourg, a "Habitation sucrière" issued to François-Régis des Sallins. Because Rivière au Sel is etymologically rooted in "de Sallins," the reader can conclude that the town was probably built on the site of the old Saint-Calvaire sugar plantation. Along with the title to the property, Teresa gives him a thin brochure published anonymously in London in 1862 called *Wonders of the Invisible World*, in which his family's history is recorded by a descendant who thought he could escape the family curse by settling in England. He, too, died mysteriously from a nosebleed at age fifty.

Francis Sancher's name reveals much more than his blood ties. "Francis" reconstructs the name of the founding ancestor, François-Désiré, a wealthy Frenchman who after committing an unnamed crime fled to the Caribbean where he transplanted his "pourriture" (vileness), the first in the "sinistre lignée" (sinister lineage) (155–56/125–26). The family name *Sancher* is particularly appropriate, signaling ancestry but also unraveling some of the strands in the mystery of Sancher's identity. If we divide the surname into two syllables, the first one, "san" echoes *sang*, *sans*, and *cent*. The second syllable, "cher" is a homonym of *chair* and *chaire*. Thus, "san{f}er" makes the following combinations possible—*sang cher* (expensive blood), *sang chair* (blood flesh), *sans chair* (without flesh), *sans chaire* (without a pulpit), *sans chers* (without dear ones), *sans chez* (without a home), *cent chairs* (100 fleshes), *cent chaires* (100 pulpits)—each of which describes some aspect of Sancher's character. *Sans chair* (without flesh) is an apt epithet, in that Sancher, like a ghost, appears mysteriously one day in Rivière au Sel. *Sans chaire* (without a pulpit) suggests Sancher's lack of a site from which to speak. That blood (*sang*) resonates in his name is not a fortuitous link to his ancestors, but, I believe, an echo of Aimé Césaire's *Cahier*: "Que de sang dans ma mémoire! . . . ma mémoire est entourée de sang. Ma mémoire a sa ceinture de cadavres." [How much blood there is in my memory! . . . My memory has its belt of corpses] (35/63–64). With blood in his past—Sancher is haunted by the belief that he is being held responsible for the lynching of one of Xantippe's ancestors—Francis Sancher flees his roots, but the route he takes leads him right back to a site of ignominy.

The different resonances in the various configurations of Francis Sancher's name echo his uncertain identity, an identity made all the more ambiguous when he introduces himself to Moïse, the mailman, as Francisco Alvarez-Sanchez, of which Francis Sancher is merely the French translation. Who exactly is this man? Neither the characters nor the readers are ever sure. Throughout the text, characters hypothesize and spread rumors about him that are sometimes contradictory. He is suspected of being an arms runner, a mercenary, a rapist, and a drug trafficker. At the same time, he is rumored to be a doctor and a healer, having earned the name *curandero* for performing miracles among the poor in war-torn Angola with his magnifying glass and mortar and pestle. A Cuban who fought alongside Fidel Castro, but also a Marielito who fled the revolution; a homosexual and a promiscuous heterosexual, his is indeed an uncertain identity. One thing is sure, however, he has more enemies than friends, and he does not narrate his own story, which is rendered collectively.

Sancher is obsessed with what he believes is the family curse, the premature death of the male ancestors, whose demises follow acts that are neither virtuous nor valorous. Manuel and Médouze, for example, sacrifice their lives for the sake of others. By contrast, Sancher's grandfather dies while returning on horseback from a card game in which he had cheated; his great-grandfather dies after spending the night with his mistress; and his great-great-great-grandfather drowns the day after his second marriage in Louisiana, where he has fled after the abolition of slavery in Guadeloupe in 1848. Sancher himself takes drastic measures in order not to pass on this fatal legacy. He deliberately avoids women in Rivière au Sel, and the two he *does* become involved with, Mira Lameaulnes and Vilma Ramsaran, initiate the relationship. When he learns that Mira is pregnant, he tries to induce an abortion by making her drink tea prepared from leaves he has collected and roots macerated in alcohol. Lying, he tells her it will make her stronger. On the contrary, she becomes weaker, vomiting blood and phlegm. On another occasion, he gives her a very bitter drink that makes her sleep. She awakens to find him trying to insert a long needle between her thighs. On being discovered, he begins to cry, saying that the child cannot be born: "Il ne faut pas que cet enfant-là ouvre ses yeux au jour. Il ne faut pas. Un signe est sur lui, comme sur moi. Il vivra une vie de malheurs et pour finir, il mourra comme un chien, comme je vais bientôt mourir." [That child must never open its eyes to the light of day. Never. An ill omen is upon him as it is upon me. He'll live a life of calamities and he'll end up dying like a dog as I shall soon do] (109/83). When Vilma becomes pregnant, Sancher has a similarly hostile reaction. Contrary to the stereotypical Caribbean man who fathers many children by different women, Sancher declares: "Je ne suis pas venu ici pour planter des enfants et les regarder marcher sur cette terre. Je suis venu mettre un point final, terminer, oui, terminer une race maudite." [I haven't come here to plant children and watch them walk on this earth. I've come to put an end, yes, an end to a race that's cursed] (87/66). Sancher actually dies from a ruptured aneurism.

While most characters cherish family ties, Sancher rejects the kinship offered by Loulou Lameaulnes, who acknowledges only his French heritage, identifying with the colonial plantation owners and their béké descendants and scorning the black women who bore their children. The founding Lameaulnes ancestor, Dieudonné Désiré, shot his slaves in the head for sport. While Sancher treasures his Pléaide edition of Saint-John Perse, the Nobel Prize–winning béké poet, he chooses not to ally himself with Loulou: "Nous ne sommes plus du même camp et je vais te dire que je n'appartiens plus à aucun camp." [We're no longer on the same side and what's more I don't belong to any side] (127/100).²¹ Sancher distances himself from everyone.

Sancher's family's routes and roots traverse Europe, Africa, North and South America, and the Caribbean. On his father's side, the *traversée* involves journeys from France to Guadeloupe and the plantation at Saint-Calvaire, to Louisiana, to London, and to Colombia, where Francis was born. His mother's heritage includes Africans, Europeans, and Indians. He continues this *errance* by traveling to Cuba, Angola, France, Madagascar, and the United States before arriving in Guadeloupe to die. Mira, the mother of his son Quentin, imagines that people will say of him: "C'était un vagabond qui est venu enterrer sa pourriture chez nous! On ne sait même pas si c'était un Blanc, un Nègre, un Zindien. Il avait tous les sangs dans son corps!" [He was a vagabond who came to bury his rotten self here. We don't even know whether he was white, black or Indian. He had every blood in his body] (229/191–92). Francis Sancher's myriad journeys are as important as his family history in forming his identity, ambiguous as it is.

In *Traversée de la mangrove*, roots, read trees, are associated with male characters who are neither courageous nor daring. The *papa-feuilles* (leaf doctor, healer, herbalist), in the guise of *curandero* Francis Sancher, tries to abort his own offspring with a tisane, which in the context of the novel does not qualify as an act of resistance as it did during slavery when, in the words of Patrick Chamoiseau in *Chronique des sept misères*, women out of despair and love killed their own flesh: "Imagines-tu ce qu'il faut de désespoir et d'amour pour tuer sa chair?" [Can you imagine how much love and despair it takes to kill your own flesh and blood?] (159/115). The *trace* Saint Charles, no longer a footpath through the woods carved by *marrons* fleeing slavery, is the place where Francis Sancher awaits death. All in all, the tension between the rhizomatic routes and roots in *Traversée de la mangrove* is not resolved. Francis Sancher remains a mysterious figure, emblematic of Caribbean identity.

Marsye Condé is the consummate example of the Caribbean writer who refuses to be bound by borders of any kind, geographical or literary. She has resided in Guadeloupe, France, Ghana, Ivory Coast, Guinea, Jamaica, the United States, Senegal, and England, and her characters traverse the continents like danmyé performers challenging both the desire and the impulse to establish a center. By examining migration's impact on identity and disputing simple notions of its construction, she undermines négritude's masculinist paradigm. The roving

I in Condé's work also embodies the displaced narrators, who *passent le témoin*, pass the baton, by taking turns transmitting as well as advancing the story. Her autofiction can be strictly autodiegetic, double-voiced, or narrated from several perspectives. Borrowing from European, American, and Caribbean texts, Condé puts into practice Suzanne Césaire's poetics of cannibal literature. Not limiting herself to classic nineteenth-century authors, Condé dares to rewrite Césaire, Roumain, Fanon, Zobel, and Morrison, challenging her readers to recognize disparate but interrelated dimensions and thereby reinterpreting diaspora literacy to include a full range of texts. Author Condé thus interacts with other writers, texts, and the reader, insisting on literary Relation in her multilayered collages text[îles] and advocating for writers' complete freedom.

Conclusion

Qu'est-ce que les Antilles en effet? Une multi-relation.
[What is the Caribbean, really? A multi-relation.]
Edouard Glissant, *Le Discours antillais*

Tu peux danser. [You can dance.]
Yanick Lahens, *Dans la maison du père*

Francophone Caribbean autofiction models authenticity, agency, and advocacy. It is one direct response to the historical circumstances of dispossession that resulted from slavery, colonialism, patriarchy, and their legacy of exploitation. Autofiction also addresses the grave issue of self-representation. Challenging European travelers' discourses, these first-person narratives restore subjectivity to those who were denied it for so long. The privileging of the *I* through témoignage not only provides an insider's perspective, but supplements hegemonic chronicles that ignore these perspectives as well as certain ethnographic studies and cinematic representations that misinterpret insider cultures. In autofiction, when the disenfranchised, positioned as narrators, do not have access to writing, their stories are curated by trustworthy scribes, *marqueurs de paroles* or sister witnesses, who can also be transformed by the experience. Listening, then, is as important as telling, and collaboration is key. Consequently, the narrator relates to an audience inside and outside the text to get around the rule of silence.

The *I* constructs an identity or, more accurately, identities, in various locales: home, school, workplace, plantation, village, L'En-ville, metropole, border towns, lands abroad, or any combination of these. Displacements due to errance or wandering, travel, and migration ultimately make the location of home—a shifting site—debatable. No one place guarantees complete security. The home(land), presumed to be safe, can also be a site of brutality, especially for women, who become physically and psychologically scarred or muted by stress. The masculinist posturing found in négritude texts, therefore, is challenged. School, promising social mobility through expanded career opportunities, is a refuge for those eager to learn, but it is also a site of ignorance, ridicule, and racism, demonstrated in the cultural chauvinism of history instruction and teachers' low expectations for students that can lead to depression and high drop-out rates, especially among boys. On the basis of the autofictions we have considered, we may conclude that nurturing relationships inside or outside of school, especially intergenerational ones where mentors provide encouragement, financial assistance, and alternative lessons in history and culture, encourage the development, maturity, and independence of young charges.

In autofiction, the relational interaction, often reciprocal, coupled with shifts in time, space, and perspective; mixing of genres and settings; fragments of memory; movements between Creole, French, and English, approximate a collage textile, which juxtaposes materials of different textures, colors, shapes, prices, class values, and geographical origins. Not only does the collage provide a model for Caribbean autofiction, but it functions as a metaphor for identity as well. It is fitting that a reproduction of one of Francelise Dawkins's artworks made with contrasting silk and cotton fabric graces the cover of Pineau's *L'Espérance-macadam*. Both artists, one visual and one literary, were born in Paris of Guadeloupean parents and embody multiple origins as well as ongoing migrations: Dawkins resides in the United States, and Pineau, as an adult, lived for many years in Guadeloupe before moving back to France a few years ago. Pineau's work, like Condé's, Chamoiseau's, and Zobel's, along with that of many other contemporary authors, is published by companies located in Paris, while to a lesser degree, local publishers like Jasor, Ibis Rouge, Henri Deschamps, and Desormeaux disseminate Martinican, Guadeloupean, Guyanese, and Haitian literatures. That contemporary Haitian literature is dominated by texts published in the tenth department leads Yanick Lahens to lament that writers living on the island are overshadowed because book distribution networks in the French départements and the metropole are inaccessible to them ("Promotion" 465). At the same time, authors identifying themselves as Haitian create texts in French, Creole, English, German, and Spanish, making their literature a multilingual, transnational one. Ironically, Micheline Dusseck's *Ecos del Caribe* has been translated into Dutch, German, Polish, and Italian, but, so far, not into French or Creole. Geopolitical realities, therefore, expand the literary terrain as well as limit it.

Advocacy, which takes various forms, is intrinsic to Francophone Caribbean writers in general. Some hold elected or appointed office while challenging the status quo: Aimé Césaire served as mayor of Fort-de-France for many years, and Roumain was named chargé d'affaires to Mexico by President Lescot. Glissant denounces the degeneration of Martinique's economy to one that consumes rather than produces goods; Danticat is an outspoken advocate for Haitian refugees; Chamoiseau, a social worker, specializes in helping at-risk adolescents; Bébel-Gisler, an avid supporter of African workers in France, directed a second-chance program for high school dropouts called BWADOUBOUT.

Combining advocacy with autofiction can be dangerous, as authors who position themselves and their characters as *guerriers de l'imaginaire*, warriors of the imaginary, know. Alluding to Marie Chauvet and contesting one of her own mother's gender-specific taboos, Danticat comments on writing in a climate of repression and censorship: "In our world, writers are tortured and killed if they are men. Called lying whores, then raped and killed, if they are women. In our world, if you write, you are a politician, and we know what happens to politicians. They end up in a prison dungeon where their bodies are covered in scalding tar before they're forced to eat their own waste" ("Epilogue" 221). The list of Haitian writers forced into exile is incredibly long.

Still, some women pursuing creative writing as a vocation use their positions to promote social change. In 1934, among the four founding members of the Haiti's Ligue Féminine d'Action Sociale were the novelists Cléanthe Desgraves Valcin and Jeanne Perez, who was also chief editor of *La Voix des femmes*. Poet, novelist, and journalist Marie-Thérèse Colimon-Hall, defining herself as one of the first feminists in Haiti, fought for women's rights, served as president of the Ligue Féminine d'Action Sociale for eleven years, and founded a private school (Condé, *La Parole* 117–18). Marie-Magdeleine Carbet was active in the movement against racism in Martinique, and Guadeloupean novelist Jacqueline Manicom not only wrote two novels in the 1970s, but founded a family-planning organization with her husband, led a movement in favor of legalizing abortion, and cofounded the feminist group, Choisir.

Negotiating the spaces between creativity and advocacy, Francophone Caribbean authors position the *I* as a witness and/or performer who articulates and transmits what he or she saw, heard, experienced, or endured for posterity. In so doing, they restore subjectivity, construct a much-needed archive, disrupt conventional literary and cinematic representations, and change our understanding of Martinican, Guadeloupian, and Haitian communities.

I opened this study by citing the theories of Benitez-Rojo, Nettleford, and Glissant in order to frame my discussion of the performance, communication, and resistance modes of Francophone Caribbean literature and the ways in which danmyé's principles inform autofiction. I would like to conclude by revisiting those issues that are brought together in one single sequence in Lahens's first-person narrative *Dans la maison du père*. Alice Bienaimé's father gives her permission to study ballet, yet out of fear, the teenager conceals from him that she is also taking traditional dance lessons. His alienation from this integral part of Haitian culture is matched by Madame Boural's neighbors, who throw stones at her house when they hear the drums, forcing her to offer lessons in secret. It is 1943, the era when the Catholic Church, allied with the government, launched its antisuperstition campaign in which Vodou practices were banned; this context renders Boural's defiance all the more remarkable. For Alice, learning the Ibo dance is a life-altering experience, especially when she learns that the Ibo captives preferred death to slavery. Performing barefoot, Alice identifies with them, embracing her heritage while opposing patriarchy and the state: "C'est alors que ma vie a changé" (93). [It was then that my life changed.] The subversive spirit that informs Alice's act likewise informs danmyé, the combat dance. After being driven underground, it was revived despite the racial, class, and gender stigmas attached to it. Contingent on the participation of a variety of individuals in relation to one another, this cultural practice embodies and communicates society's complex forces. The oxymoron implicit in combat dance articulates the tensions therein. Moreover, danmyé's principles of interaction, negotiation, improvisation, and positionality offer a powerful framework for reading Francophone Caribbean autofiction.

Notes

Introduction. Caribbean *I*dentity Poetics: Subjectivity, *I-mage*, Collage

1. See Laroche, *Sémiologie des apparences*, and Chamoiseau and Confiant, *Lettres créoles*.

2. To assist reader recognition of Glissant's "la Relation," it remains capitalized throughout my text. I use "Francophone" to refer to those lands/*pays* in which French is the official language—Haiti, Martinique, Guadeloupe, and French Guiana—though Creole is the vernacular of the majority. That Creole is the mother tongue of all Haitians, and that only a tiny percentage of Haiti's citizens actually speak French make inserting it in the Francophone sphere problematic for Déjean (11–13). Although there are differences between Haitian and the Creole spoken in Martinique and Guadeloupe, they are mutually intelligible. *Creolophone* is perhaps a more viable category in the wider Caribbean.

3. The spelling of laghia (*ladja*) varies widely, however, I will use the orthography found in each text quoted. For example, Chamoiseau writes "répondeurs," while in Creole the word is rendered "répondé."

4. My discussion of danmyé draws on and summarizes Gilles, Michalon, Cally, and Bertelli's interview with Dru.

5. Today organized sports provide an outlet for expressions of masculinity. One can make a case that contemporary athletes' tattooing their bodies is another expression of masculinity.

6. See Linden Lewis on "metaphors of masculinity" (115–23).

7. Suzanne Césaire and Paulette Nardal are two prominent examples (see Edwards *The Practice of Diaspora*). Hurley has done extensive work on Marie-Magdeleine Carbet, another writer of the period whose contributions have been slighted. The pattern continues in subsequent literary movements, as Arnold illustrates in "The Gendering of Créolité." It is not surprising then that Chamoiseau and Confiant marginizalize women in *Lettres créoles* whose coverage ends in 1975 just as women writers come to the forefront of and begin to dominate, in some ways, Francophone Caribbean letters.

8. According to Eltis et al., 52,896 embarked from the Bight of Benin (38 percent); 28,446 from West Central Africa (20 percent); 9,568 from the Bight of Biafra (6 per-

cent); 7,583 from Senegambia (5 percent); 6,337 from Gold Coast (4 percent); 2,712 from Sierra Leone; 2,213 from Windward Coast; 786 from Southeast Africa, and 28,110 from unspecified locations (20 percent).

9. According to Saugera, the French slave trade began in La Rochelle in the first half of the sixteenth century and flourished after 1670 (14–17). The major ports were Nantes (with 40 percent of the traffic), Bordeaux, La Rochelle, and Le Havre (38).

10. For information about capoeira, see J. Lowell Lewis.

11. Hearn refers to the mock-fight stick dance called "caleinda" that sometimes deteriorates into a real fight with knives when the men have had too much to drink (146).

12. The raw footage is available in the Dunham archives in Saint Louis. The copy I examined can be located in the Performing Arts Division of the New York Public Library.

13. Clark notes that Dunham wrote under the pseudonym Kaye Dunn in the two *Esquire* articles ("Performing Memory" 195–97). The ballet *L'Ag'Ya*, set in a rural fishing village in 1930s Martinique, includes other Caribbean dance forms as well. For a detailed discussion of the ballet, see Clark, "Tropical Review." For clips of Dunham's ballets, including *L'Ag'Ya*, see <http://lcweb2.loc.gov/cocoon/ihas/html/dunham/dunham-works-browse-back.html>.

14. See danmyé Web sites for drawings, photos, and video, <http://membres.lycos.fr/jla/ledanmye.htm>, and for songs, <http://www.peda.ac-martinique.fr/prem/bele.shtml.

15. Gerstin lists *mayolé, sovéyan*, and *bènaden* in Guadeloupe, *mani* in Cuba, *kokomakuku* in Curaçao, *broma* in Venezuela, and *knocking and kicking* in the Sea Islands (14, n. 15). These particular combat dance traditions exclude stick dancing. For a discussion of the latter, see chapter 8 entitled "Accessing Power: Ritual War and Masquerade," in Warner-Lewis.

16. Danticat revisits the travel narrative in *After the Dance*, but her approach is totally different from the one found in traditional travel literature focused on the Caribbean.

17. I am grateful to Jennifer Morgan for these statistics and for referring me to Eltis's *The Rise of African Slavery* (96–97).

18. I use capitalized "Récit," like Glissant, to refer to the master narrative imposed by imperialist nations and sociopolitical hegemonies upon colonized peoples. It stands in contrast to lowercase "récit," which refers to a story, an account, a tale that is not necessarily part of a master narrative but unfolds above, under, around, in relation to, and also independent of it. As for the silencing or suppression of Caribbean women's narratives and histories, Romero-Cesareo's *Women at Sea* is one attempt to bridge the gender gap.

19. Unless otherwise noted, the translations are mine.

20. See Chamoiseau, *Ecrire en pays dominé*. Aimé Césaire and Maryse Condé also acknowledge these intertextual and extratextual influences. See their interviews with Scarboro. Jacques Stéphen Alexis writes that he was influenced by realist writers Balzac,

Flaubert, Maupassant, and Zola, as well as by Amado, Hemingway, and Roumain ("Où va," 99–100).

21. In his discussion of the pleasure he derives from reading and writing, Chamoiseau recalls with great clarity his first experience touching a book in *Ecrire en pays dominé* (25–35).

22. At a conference a few years ago, one of the panelists was challenged from the floor because she purported to speak about "écrivaines antillaises," but did not include a single Haitian writer.

23. Drawing it from the work of Edwidge Danticat, I use the spelling *dyaspora* to specifically signal the present-day dispersal of Haitians throughout the world. Otherwise, the standard spelling *diaspora* appears. Of the collision of cultures that informs Caribbean identity, Glissant writes: "J'appelle Chaosmonde le choc actuel de tant de cultures qui s'embrasent, se repoussent, disparaissent, subsistent pourtant, s'endorment ou se transforment, lentement ou à vitesse foudroyante" (*Traité* 22). [I call *chaosmonde* the present-day shock of so many cultures that burn, resist each other, disappear, and yet subsist, fall asleep or change, slowly or at lightning speed.]

24. Richard Price and Sally Price also criticize the absence of a Pan-Caribbean sensibility among the créolistes.

25. See also Singaravelou, Moutoussamy, Toumson, ed., and Marceaux. The Paes documentary about the town of Mana in French Guiana entitled *Le Bouillon d'awara* uses a local dish—awara soup—as a metaphor for the residents from diverse backgrounds.

26. The Sunday *New York Times* of February 9, 2003, participates in that kind of discourse, for example. In his travel section article, "The Sweet Essence of Barbados," Wayne Curtis's description of a distillery and sugar plantation tour contains not even one reference to the laborers themselves, indicating a disturbing erasure of people and history.

27. See Douglass's speeches on Haiti in *The Frederick Douglass Papers*. For a detailed discussion of the pavilion, see my "DuSable, Douglass, and *Dessalines*: the Haytian Pavilion and the Narrative of History."

28. Toumson traces the evolution of the word *métis* and warns against the romanticization of métissage as the result of a love relationship. One must not ignore the gender violence associated with slavery, although the enslaved woman is often depicted as a seductress (*Mythologie* 90–95). See also Price and Price "Shadowboxing."

29. Guyanese Penet gives a first-person account of his experiences as a twenty-year-old pilot involved in the liberation of France in *Pilotes de l'empire*.

30. *Négropolitain* is a pun on *métropolitain*, *négzagonal* on *hexagonal*, and *troisième île* on Paris as the third island after Martinique and Guadeloupe.

31. Demme's documentary on Jean Dominique—*The Agronomist*—was released in 2004.

32. See Bensmaïa, "Political Geography of Literature: On Khatibi's 'Professional Traveller.'"

33. Local identities are even more complex. Just as Confiant defines himself as a *chabin*, a person of African and European descent who has light skin and light-brown, tightly curled hair, many writers recognize various combinations based on hair color and texture, eye color, and facial features: *câpresse*, a woman of African descent with dark skin and long, wavy hair, and *couli*, an Antillean of East Indian descent. *Couli*, a derogatory term, has been appropriated and rehabilitated by Khal Torabully who makes a claim for a diasporic consciousness—*coolitude*—in the manner of négritude. See his controversial article "Coolitude." Elisée entitles his novel *Mémoires d'un Chabin*, an example of autofiction in which the protagonist/narrator's experiences are affected by his racial and ethnic background.

34. Durand's journal, acquired by Yale's Sterling Library in 1984, consists of 113 pages of text and 58 leaves of drawings (see Donald Wright's review of Harms's *The Diligent*). Alain Yacou edited *Journaux de bord et de traite de Joseph Crassous de Médeuil*. For information about slavery during this period see Pago, Moitt, and Lara.

35. Forster and Forster translated and edited the four-volume *Pierre Dessalles (1785–1857), la vie d'un colon à la Martinique au XIXe siècle* as *Sugar and Slavery, Family and Race*.

36. Eighteenth- and nineteenth-century French women's perspectives are also lacking, but to a lesser degree. Chronicling his daily life in Saint Domingue during the 1790s, the papers of the French merchant Michel Marsaudon (Georgetown University, special collections) include letters from women. On the other hand, while the verse works of the 19th-century French poet, actress, and singer Marceline Desbordes-Valmore are available, her writings about the French Caribbean are not. More recently, Edwidge Danticat reinvents the travel narrative in *After the Dance: A Walk through Carnival in Jacmel, Haiti*, a chronicle of her *return* to rediscover her cultural heritage. Wideman, too, subverts the conventional travel narrative in *The Island, Martinique* by dedicating it to Fanon. He was hired by National Geographic to keep a diary of his three-week visit from December 2000 to January 2001.

37. The screenplay for the film was written by Patrick Chamoiseau.

38. Césaire wrote: "Ma bouche sera la bouche des malheurs qui n'ont point de bouche, ma voix, la liberté de celles qui s'affaissent au cahot du désespoir." [My mouth shall be the mouth of misfortunes that have no mouth, my voice the freedom of those freedoms that break down in the prison-cell of despair] (22/50). He considers the *Cahier* "un livre autobiographique et en même temps un livre où je tâche de prendre possession de moi-même. En certains sens il est plus vrai que ma biographie" (qtd. in Santa 99); [an autobiographical book and at the same time a book where I tried to take possession of myself. In a certain sense, it is more true than my biography.]

39. Cadet assumes a similarly testimonial and memorializing role for the 250,000 poor children attached to well-to-do families in *Restavec: From Haitian Slave Child to Middle-Class American*, a narrative whose title conceals its first-person perspective. The child of a deceased Haitian coffee factory worker and her white exporter boss, Cadet

grew up in poverty, was beaten and molested. At the other end of the spectrum, Raoul Peck traces his tenure as minister of culture under President Aristide and his growing disillusionment with that administration in *Monsieur le Ministre . . . jusqu'au bout de la patience.*

40. The preface by Strowski was reprinted in the Haitian government's official newspaper, *Le Moniteur.* The introduction cites Lamartine's praise for Demesvar Delorme and Michelet's admiration for Thomas Madiou.

41. See also Forest, who distinguishes autobiography from autofiction in *Le Roman, le Je,* and Gasparini in *Est-il je?* Paquet's monograph *Caribbean Autobiography: Cultural Identity and Self-Representation,* which includes 19th- and 20th-century colonial and postcolonial texts—slave narratives, testimonials, oral narratives, spiritual autobiographies, diaries, and journals—inserts Caribbean autobiography into the Anglophone canon. Furthermore, Paquet's mission hints at the reciprocity that, as we shall see, characterizes Francophone Caribbean autofiction: "to identify strategies of self-representation already in place in Caribbean writing for what they reveal about the fluidity and reciprocity of narrative identity" (8). In addition to Zobel's work, Crosta's *Récits d'enfance antillaise* focuses on Capécia's *Je suis Martiniquaise,* Schwarz-Bart's *Ti-Jean L'Horizon,* Chamoiseau's *Antan d'enfance,* and Confiant's *Ravines du devant jour.*

42. Ollivier realizes the limitations of (re)visitations in that memories are subject to revision and transformation. His self-referential *Mille eaux* (A Thousand Waters), reproduces his nickname, a diminutive for Emile, but refers to the waters of childhood, that is, the liquid into which the adult plunges when one looks to the past (8). In addition, *Mille eaux* combines a modified combination of the author's first and last names (milo), and designates the town, Milot, in which the Citadelle, a stone monument that symbolizes Haitian independence, is located. In this volume in Gallimard's Haute Enfance series, Ollivier's father exists as a silhouette in his memory.

43. One reviewer characterized the text as a collection of short stories, while another said it was a novel.

44. They are: *Comment faire l'amour avec un Nègre sans se fatiguer* (Montréal: VLB Éditeur, 1985); *Éroshima* (Montréal: VLB Éditeur, 1987); *L'odeur du café* (Montréal: VLB Éditeur, 1991); *Le goût des jeunes filles* (Montréal: VLB Éditeur, 1992); *Cette grenade dans la main du jeune Nègre est-elle une arme ou un fruit?* (Montréal: VLB Éditeur, 1993); *Chronique de la dérive douce* (Montréal: VLB Éditeur, 1994); *Pays sans chapeau* (Outremont, Quebec: Lanctôt Éditeur, 1996); *La chair du maître* (Outremont, Quebec: Lanctôt Éditeur, 1997); *Le charme des après-midi sans fin* (Outremont, Quebec: Lanctôt Éditeur, 1997); and *Le cri des oiseaux fous* (Outremont, Quebec: Lanctôt Éditeur, 2000).

45. Blogs are the newest kind of first-person text, a product of the computer age. In an era of corporatized news, some blogs—by debunking propaganda—serve advocative, testimonial function. Danticat's novel *The Dew Breaker* is testimonial; here, bearing witness takes the form of Bienaimé's confession to his daughter, the first-person narrator.

He was a prison guard during the first Duvalier regime, killed several people, fled to Brooklyn, and hid his deeds.

46. See <http://www.vancouver.wsu.edu/fac/peabody/codenoir.htm>.

47. I attended a Théâtre du Grand Large performance of *Le Coeur à rire et à pleurer*—directed by Alain Courivaud, with Martine Maximin, and music by Antoine Bory—at the close of a colloquium in honor of Maryse Condé at Columbia University in November 2002. I also attended the Compagnie Indigo performance of *The Bridge of Beyond: Exploring Clichés in Caribbean Theater*, with Gerty Dambury, Roselaine Bicep-Nanick, and Martine Maximin, at the University of Wisconsin in April 2004. Due to a severe snow storm, I missed the sole performance of *Cahier d'un retour au pays natal* at the French Institute/Alliance Française in Manhattan in fall 2003, but I did attend Sonny Rupaire's interpretation, a montage in French and English with original music, at the Ubu Repertory Theater in May 1998. While not autofiction, Roumain's *Gouverneurs de la rosée* has been adapted for the stage and screen several times. In fact, Darling Legitimus, celebrated for her portrayal of M'man Tine in *Rue Cases-Nègres*, played the role of Délira in a production I saw in Paris. Condé mentions that in Louisiana there was interest in transforming her historical novel *Ségou* into a Mahabharata-like production lasting several days (*Entretiens* 129).

Chapter 1. "To Get Around the Rule of Silence": Performing Masculinity as *Détour*

1. Chamoiseau writes that colonialism gave new names to things: "Elle avait désigné. Elle avait expliqué. Elle avait installé une Histoire qui niait nos trajectoires. Elle s'était inscrite sur nos silences démantelés" (*Ecrire* 97). [It had designated. It had explained. It had installed a History that denied our trajectories. It had inscribed itself on our dismantled silences.] See also Bernabé, Chamoiseau, and Confiant, *Eloge de la créolité*.

2. In her 1982 film based on Zobel's novel, Euzhan Palcy shows danmyétistes performing during a Saturday night celebration after the pay is distributed. Tortilla is one of José's friends.

3. Mayotte Capécia died in 1955 as well.

4. See Rennard, *Tricentenaire des Antilles*, which contains letters, reports, and excerpts from Columbus's journal as well as from texts by missionaries and by Father Jean Baptiste du Tertre.

5. See <http://www.martiniqueshop.com/caribavenue/zobel/biogrph.html>, accessed August 2005.

6. The different species of dragonflies the children chase in *La Rue Cases-Nègres* also reproduce Martinique's pyramidal class structure. The big red ones with straight wings are the most abundant and easy to catch; in the middle are the smaller, agile, brown-winged ones; the rarest are slender, light gold-headed and "aristocratic." For more information about slavery in Martinique, see Moitt and Lara.

7. Article 18 of the Code Noir forbade slaves from selling sugarcane. The penalty for this infraction was a whipping for the slave and a fine for the owner and buyer.

8. In his interview with Ginette Adamson, Jean Métellus said he is moved to tears each time he views the scene in which José is accused of plagiarism. The first time Métellus met Zobel, who makes a cameo appearance in the film as a priest, he shared this experience with him and was surprised to learn that Zobel's son cried on viewing the sequence (375–76). Zobel died in June 2006 at age 91.

9. Eileen Julien considers M'man Tine the real heroine of *La Rue Cases-Nègres*. See her excellent discussion of her hands in "La Métamorphose du réel."

10. Extending the *univers nouveau* theme from *La Rue Casas-Nègres*, Zobel pays homage to specific teachers in his poem "Les Profs," published in the collection *Poèmes d'amour et de silence*. Here, he compares them to des Mages, or Magi kings—"venus par des voies zodiacales / que les nègres marrons / n'empruntaient guère / en ce temps-là" (65). [who came by zodiacal paths / that the fugitive slaves / hardly used then.]

11. Supporting his discussion of the founding and development of the Sainte-Thérèse neighborhood, Laguerre cites Zobel's "valuable description of the landscape" in *Urban Poverty in the Caribbean* (30–31). See also Marlin-Godier, who traces the growth of Fort-de-France between 1884 and 1914.

12. As a student in Paris in 1932, Léopold Senghor had similar problems. Failing a competitive exam, he enrolled in the Ecole Normale Supérieure. At first, he received less money in scholarship money than he expected. Fortunately, the crisis was eventually resolved (Vaillant 102–3).

13. On another level, what Médouze represents—issues of race, class, and resistance and the nation's legacy of slavery and exploitation—is unrecognized and unwelcome in the French classroom.

14. According to André, José's world is too female. See especially 77–103.

15. Carmen's parents name choice echoes the Senegalese custom described by Mariétou Mbaye, author of *Le Baobab fou*, where naming a child *ken bugul* after many miscarriages is believed to ward off bad spirits.

16. See Edwards excellent chapter on *Banjo* (187–240), which, Fabre points out, appeared in the bilingual *La Revue du monde noir* (113–14).

17. Zobel's narrator cites Russian authors Tolstoy and Gorky as among Carmen's favorites. Depestre asserts that his generation also admired these writers in 1942. See "Parler de Jacques Roumain," *Oeuvres complètes*, xxii.

18. See Warner's introduction to *Black Shack Alley* (xiii). Indeed, rereading *Black Boy* I was struck by resemblances between the two texts: the protagonists are born on plantations; as preschoolers, they are left home alone while their guardians work menial jobs; poverty and chronic hunger pervade their early experience; both texts dramatize an accidental fire, the introduction to alcohol, the achievement of literacy, a love of reading, and so on.

19. The verb *latter*—to struggle or wrestle—also means to fight.

Chapter 2. "*I* Spy": Curators, Translators, and In-trust Narrators

1. One can generalize and say that *Chronique des sept misères* and *Solibo Magnifique* comment on the death of a culture, while *Texaco* is about the birth of a neighborhood and the realization that it is not a ghetto but, on the contrary, a balanced ecosystem (*Texaco* 282, 289).

2. In *Ecrire en pays dominé*, Chamoiseau writes: "Je me nommai alors 'Marqueur de paroles'" (256). [I name myself thus 'marker of words.']

3. An analogy could be drawn between the marquer de paroles as a "word scratcher" and hiphop DJs' scratching records.

4. While Coverdale's English translation of the two divisions as the nouns "inspiration" and "expiration" implies motivation and death, I would like to accentuate the storyteller's physical engagement in the process, that is, his performance, by substituting the verb forms "inhaling" and "exhaling."

5. The narrator in *Chronique des sept misères* does not designate himself a marqueur, but positions himself as one of the djobeurs.

6. Ollivier, too, acknowledges his debt to a sentimenthèque: "On est fait de tellement de livres. Nos gènes intellectuels sous l'influence de leur semence ont muté tant de fois" (157). [We are made up of so many books. Under the influence of their seed, our intellectual genes mutated so many times.]

7. Chamoiseau's sentimenthèque crosses boundaries of language, region, nationality, century, continent, and generation: Nabokov, Soljenitsyne, Carroll, Kipling, Shakespeare, Sterne, Swift, Defoe, Stevenson, Ouologuem, Kourouma, Whitman, Naipal, Conrad, Faulkner, Hemingway, Steinbeck, Himes, Baldwin, Morrison, Dib, Khatibi, Yacine, Dante, Joyce, La Fontaine, Racine, Montesquieu, Baudelaire, Hugo, Lamartine, Toqueville, Lautréamont, Segalen, Zola, Camus, Giraudoux, Beckett, Breton, Gide, Le Clézio, Proust, Saint-John Perse, André Schwarz-Bart, Damas, Roumain, Ollivier, Aimé Césaire, Fanon, Glissant, Gratiant, Pépin, Rupaire, Delsham, Brathwaite, Cervantes, Goytisolo, Cortazar, Asturias, Garcia Marquez, Unamuno, Neruda, Paz, Plato, Petrarch, Nietzche, Rabemananjara, Rabearivelo, Carpentier, Marti, Guillén, Brecht, Machado, the Koran, the Bible.

8. Likewise, Ollivier's grandmother is responsible for his earliest contact with books. She keeps some of her husband's volumes along with old issues of *Historia* and *La Revue des Deux Mondes* in the house, launching her grandson's life-long love of reading: "Le livre se présenta donc d'abord comme un palliatif à ma solitude. Très vite, j'y ai découvert une voie étroite de salut" (15). [Books presented themselves first as a palliative to my solitude. I quickly discovered a straight path to health.] Later using his allowance to make purchases at a bookstore alone, he is "frappé d'une bulimie de lectures" (struck by a bulimia of readings) (158). Exchanging books with classmates takes him out of his immediate environment and teaches him about other eras, customs, and places: "J'ai compris alors que les livres ne viennent pas seuls, nus et bruts, s'aligner sur des étagères.

Ils sont escortés de voix ténues, de rumeurs, de bruit, de jugements imperceptibles qui les relient autrement que les fils et la colle. Ils sont tissés de lumières et d'émotions, chargés de combats secrets ou de joies sans motifs" (159). [I understood then that books do not come alone, naked and bare, lined up in stacks. They are escorted by subtle voices, rumors, noise, imperceptible judgments that link them far more than string or glue. They are woven with light and emotions, charged with secret combats or joys without motive.] Ollivier balances the pleasurable with the instructive and transformative functions of books: "Les livres m'aéraient et me fascinaient. J'ai compris très tôt que les mots, gonflés de sève, marchent au-dessus de l'humanité. J'avais au fond découvert que les mots avaient une mission: ils devaient nous apprendre à vivre" (160). [Books aerated me and fascinated me. I understood very early that words, bursting with sap, walk above humanity. I discovered deep down that words had a mission: they were supposed to teach us to live.]

9. See Yerro and Rey. Confiant explores these urban mangroves in his novels, many of which are situated in Morne Pichevin. In *L'Image des quartiers populaires dans le roman antillais*, Cauna studies the representation of these neighborhoods in Chamoiseau's *Texaco*, Confiant's *Mamzelle Libellule* and *Chimères d'en ville*, Lucie Julia's *Mélody des faubourgs*, and Pineau's *L'Espérance-macadam*.

10. See the four functions of the conteur in Chamoiseau and Confiant's *Lettres créoles*. They applaud the conteur as a self-effacing figure of resistance to slavery (56–64). Also see the introduction to Chamoiseau's *Au temps de l'antan* (x–xiv, 10–11). In his interview with Lucien Taylor, Confiant adamantly insists, in a tone bordering on the hostile, that only men are "conteurs" (268). Juminer instead honors the product, "la parole de nuit," as an "oeuvre de désaliénation, de réintégration" (work of disaliénation, of reintegration), for consumers in a dominant culture (139).

11. Bouafesse disparages Solibo's intelligence, asserting that his knowledge comes from consulting the illustrated *Larousse* dictionary (176).

12. I am grateful to the anonymous reader who pointed out this aspect of the *bête-longue*'s history and its resonance in my analysis.

13. The nickname *Congo* also reproduces the character's origins and the persistence of hierarchal racial categorizations despite the process of creolization, which transforms formerly distinct groups into Martinicans, an inclusive identity. Alleyne cites Revert's statistics: "in 1877, there were 6,500 Africans from the Congo in Martinique. In 1901, this number fell to 5,345; and in 1910 only 837 could be identified. They settled in the Commune of François, and in Morne l'Afrique in the Commune of Diamant, where the African phenotype still dominates. They are referred to as *Nègres Guinée* (Congo being another pejorative designation) and, ironically, they are viewed by some Martinicans as having preserved features from the period of slavery. They provide a focus for the distancing of Martinicans from the black African phenotype.... They have at the present time disappeared as a group, having been absorbed into the general population.... The term *nègre Congo* still exists and is used injuriously, to insult" (172).

14. Originally published by Gallimard, *Antan d'enfance* and *Chemin-d'école* were issued in paperback by Folio under the titles *Une enfance créole 1* and *2*, their original titles becoming subordinate. *A bout d'enfance*, published in 2005, is being promoted as the third part of a trilogy.

15. Evariste Pilon, the detective in charge of the investigation into Solibo's death, represents the in-betweenness attributable to his having been born in Martinique, his graduation from school, and his travels to the metropole. While he uses scientific methods and is in favor of the use of Creole in the schools, he is startled when his own children speak it. He admires Césaire, yet has never read his work. He wears shoes and socks as well as a *bakoua*, the straw hat worn by rural men that graces the cover of the first edition of *Solibo Magnifique*. The coexistence of these contradictory indicators in Pilon (his name is the word for "pestle" in "mortar and pestle") reflects the complexities of identity.

16. For a thorough discussion of literary treatments of African childrens' encounter with the colonial school, see Gadjigo's *Ecole blanche, Afrique noire*.

17. Kane's quotation continues: "De l'aimant, l'école tient son rayonnement. Elle est solidaire d'un ordre nouveau, comme un noyau magnétique est solidaire d'un champ. Le bouleversement de la vie des hommes à l'intérieur de cet ordre nouveau est semblable aux bouleversements de certaines lois physiques à l'intérieur d'un champ magnétique. On voit les hommes se disperser, conquis, le long de lignes de forces invisibles et impérieuses." [From the magnet, the school takes its radiating force. It is bound up with a new order, as a magnetic stone is bound up with a field. The upheaval of the life of man within this new order is similar to the overturn of certain physical laws in a magnetic field. Men are seen to be composing themselves, conquered, along the lines of invisible and imperious forces] (60–61/45–46). There is an echo of Kane's magnet trope—"aimant"—in *Chemin-d'école*, where it is Gros Lombric (Big Bellybutton) "qui *aimantait* les tirs immanquables que le Maître décochait du tableau, ou les railleries massives des autres petites-personnes" (who drew all the inevitable jibes shot off by the Teacher from the blackboard or the massed scorn of the other children) (107 emphasis added/76).

18. *La Rue Cases-Nègres* and *Chemin-d'école* are both connected to 1950s Martinique. Chamoiseau's narrative is set during those years, while Zobel's *La Rue Cases-Nègres* was published in 1950. Another similarity between the two works is the centrality of a mother figure to each young hero's success in school. In fact, Man Ninotte and José would belong to the same generation and in the 1950s (*La Rue* is set in the 1930s) would possibly be the same age. Chamoiseau's négrillon, however, embodies a revision of José's positive school experience with teacher Stéphen Roc. The connection between the two texts was not lost on the publishers of the paperback who placed on the cover of the Folio edition a still photograph of Henri Melon in his role of Stéphen Roc in Palcy's film *Rue Cases-Nègres*.

19. Women writers also recognize school as an important site/rite of passage. One of the chapters in Condé's *Le Coeur à rire et à pleurer* is entitled "Chemin d'école," and the

second chapter of Bébel-Gisler's *Léonora* is called "Sur le chemin de l'école." Condé's experiences are not analogous to those of a migrant entering a new-language environment; her mother was a school teacher, her father, a banker, and the family spoke French exclusively at home. On the other hand, Léonora's school experience more closely resembles the négrillon's in that in 1928, when she enrolled, French was a new language to her.

20. In *Urban Poverty in the Caribbean*, Laguerre discusses the ways in which school is a vehicle for maintaining social order (13–14).

21. The definition of *creole* is informed by time and place, its meaning fluid. Glissant provides a clear and useful distinction between métissage and creolization in *Poétique de la Relation*: "Si nous posons le métissage comme en général une rencontre et une synthèse entre deux différents, la créolisation nous apparaît comme le métissage sans limites, dont les éléments sont démultipliés, les résultantes imprévisibles. La créolisation diffracte, quand certains modes du métissage peuvent concentrer une fois encore." [If we posit métissage as, generally speaking, the meeting of and synthesis of two differences, creolization seems to be a limitless métissage, its elements diffracted and its consequences unforeseeable. Creolization diffracts, whereas certain forms of métissage can concentrate one more time] (46/34). Glissant articulates this distinction again in *Introduction*, writing that the end result of métissage is predictable, while the outcome of créolisation is not (19).

22. The translator, Linda Coverdale, includes an "appendix of out-takes," suggesting supplementary material not germane to the story (216).

Chapter 3. Secrets and Silence, Displacement and *Délivrance*

1. Other texts that treat domestic violence are Pineau's *La Grande drive des esprits*, Bébel-Gisler's *Léonora*, Schwarz-Bart's *Pluie et vent sur Télumée Miracle*, and Condé's "La Châtaigne et le fruit à pain."

2. Beverly Bell filled more than one hundred tapes with interviews of peasant and poor urban women that formed the basis for *Writing on Fire: Haitian Women's Stories of Survival and Resistance*. Her goal was to let her respondents control their own stories. After transcribing the tapes, she traveled back to Haiti so that the subjects could listen to their own words and edit their texts for accuracy. This method, while accentuating collaboration, is actually more concerned with foregrounding the women's voices.

3. This period also gave rise to what would become the *beur* generation, that is, the generation comprised of the children of North Africans living in France.

4. Anselin's *L'Emigration antillaise en France* includes interviews, but none from a child's point of view.

5. One of the shortcomings of *créolité* is that its foundation is language, a language that Pineau did not grow up speaking. Her mother tongue is French as is Condé's.

6. Glissant goes on to suggest that Creole, the language of the plantation system, will disappear if it does not find another function.

7. Wright made France his adopted home. In fact, his cremains, which include a copy of *Black Boy*, are interred in Père Lachaise cemetery. When he died in 1960, Pineau was four years old. Ironically, Wright writes about his impressions of racial freedom in France (see Stovall 138–41, 183, and 190–97). The Pineau family experienced otherwise.

8. For example, Ega's *Le Temps des madras* formulates 1920s and 1930s Martinique from a child's point of view and her posthumous *Lettres à une Noire*, from the point of view of an exploited immigrant domestic worker in Marseille. In Capécia's *Je suis Martiniquaise*, the title character moves to Guadeloupe and France. Lacrosil's *Cajou* settles in France. Warner-Vieyra's *Juletane* moves to France and Senegal.

9. Stovall calls this period the "golden age of African American literature in Paris." See especially chapter 5. Also see Edwards's *The Practice of Diaspora*.

10. Julia also returns to Guadeloupe separately on a steamship, accompanied by a relative.

11. For an in-depth discussion of Pineau's "culinary geography of diaspora," see Mehta.

12. Condé's *Hugo le terrible* is a children's story, in diary form, in which a boy not only survives the hurricane, but is transformed by it. Maximin's *L'île et une nuit*, alternating autofiction and third-person narrative, is set during the seven hours of the hurricane. Maximin's first novel *L'Isolé soleil* intersects in other interesting ways with *L'Espérance-macadam*. For example, a young girl, Angela loses her voice after witnessing a traumatic event. In *L'Espérance-macadam*, Eliette temporarily loses her voice after her rape.

13. The hurricane season in the Caribbean runs from July to December. Due to its geographical location, the region is susceptible to violent weather. The 1780 storm killed 22,000 people. The 1928 hurricane hit Guadeloupe and poor black communities in Texas particularly hard. See Saffache, Marc, and Belrose, *Les Cyclones en Guadeloupe*.

14. Before the era of television meteorologists' forecasts, storm-tracking, and analyses with the aid of satellites and Doppler radar, information about hurricanes was supplied by a range of witnesses, who had access to historical accounts, such as Christopher Columbus's observations on a Caribbean hurricane.

15. Trauma visits another eight-year-old, Sarah Jansson, in Raoul Peck's film *L'Homme sur les quais*. Sarah's memory of seeing her godfather Sorel, a suspected opponent of the Duvalier regime, tortured by the Tontons Macoutes while her father, an army captain, looks on helplessly, surfaces intermittently. This horrific memory is replayed as a nightmare three times in the film, which is presented through the eyes of an adult Sarah, who has tried hard to forget the experience. Nevertheless, she sometimes still wakes up at night in a cold sweat to hear her grandmother Madame Camille Desrouillères reassure her that the whole experience isn't real: "Ce n'est qu'un mauvais rêve, ma chérie." [It is only a bad dream, my dear.] "Twa fèy" (three leaves), sung in Creole in the background by Toto Bissainthe embodies the forgetting and remembering dialectic.

16. Rosette's reaction is shaped by guilt and the memory of her own mother Gilda's warnings about neighbor Rosan's untrustworthiness—advice she ignored that has come to haunt her.

17. Eliette is also linked to the incest theme through her "floral" last name, Florentine. Unlike Rosan et Rosette, however, she is a victim.

18. I am grateful to Aletha Stahl for information about this dish.

Chapter 4. Travelers' Trees and Umbilical Cords: Embodying Dyaspora, Renegotiating Home

1. Coincidentally, after choosing to center this chapter around the trope of the traveler's tree, I came across Fermor's *The Traveller's Tree: A Journey through the Caribbean Islands* with individual chapters on Guadeloupe, Martinique, Haiti, Jamaica, Dominica, Barbados, and Trinidad.

2. For a discussion of Danticat's sentimenthèque, see the interview with Shea (386–87). She acknowledges borrowing a line from Alexis's *Compère Général Soleil* for *The Dew Breaker* (*Dew Breaker* 243). The line is "Tu deviens un véritable bourreau" (you are a real executioner).

3. For a detailed discussion of Haitian/Dominican relations and the 1937 massacre, see chapters 12 and 13 of *Blood in the Streets: The Life and Rule of Trujillo*, in which Hicks provides graphic details originally reported by Quentin Reynolds, the reporter sent to investigate rumors of a slaughter; Price-Mars's *La République haïtienne et la République dominicaine*, which lists more than sixty towns where Haitians were killed; and volume 1 of Vega's *Trujillo y Haiti*, which includes summaries of testimonies taken from survivors at the border. See also Logan, Castor, Garcia, Derby, and Roorda. The publication of studies on Haitian/Dominican relations and migration continues apace: for the Dominican Republic, see Silie and Segura, ed., *Una isla para dos* and Bissainthe, *Paradigma de la migracion haitiana en Republica Dominica*; for France, see Thédat, *Haiti République Dominicaine: une île pour deux, 1804–1916*; and for the United States, see Matibag, *Haiti-Dominican Counterpoint: Nation, State, and Race on Hispaniola*, chapter 6 especially.

4. Lipski asserts that "Haitian Creole has always maintained a vigorous presence in rural villages, and has affected regional varieties of Spanish as well" (15). He cites a report asserting that in 1922 not only was the population of Dajabón 40 percent Haitian, but that Dominicans in the area also spoke Haitian Creole (18).

5. Castillo refers to the offspring of Haitian and Dominican couples as "catizos" (65).

6. The large number of Haitians residing in other countries prompted the creation of the cabinet-level Ministère des Haïtiens Vivant à l'Etranger (Ministry for Haitians Living Abroad) in 1994 under President Aristide. The official section in France has its own set of officers and is the object of Fleurimond's *La Communauté haïtienne de France: dix ans d'histoire 1991–2001*.

7. For a long time, the defeat of Napoleon's troops was not mentioned at all in French history textbooks.

8. The novel was translated in 2005 under the title *Massacre River*.

9. "Une peinture qui signifie la matière mémorielle en la symbolisant: l'essentiel d'une sorte d'historiographie dont la communauté serait l'objet." [A painting that makes memory significant through symbols: the essentials of a kind of historiography of the community] (*Discours* 269/155).

10. The title, translated into French as *La Récolte douce des larmes* [The Sweet Harvest of Tears], eclipses the idea of death.

11. Some critics interpret the scene as a suicide (see Brice-Finch and Clithandre). Shemak sees it as a "ritual cleansing not unlike the scene before the massacre in which Haitians cleansed the residue of their labor from their bodies in the stream" (105). Chancy adds that Amabelle is protected by Metrès Dlo ("Recovering" 27).

12. In "Nineteen Thirty-Seven," women who lost their mothers in the slaughter make an annual pilgrimage to the Massacre River on November 1st.

13. In Peck's film *L'Homme sur les quais*, narrator Sarah's godfather Sorel is tortured into mental illness and then nicknamed Gracieux. For a discussion of the intersection of Peck's film and *The Farming of Bones*, see my article "Girl by the Shore" (50).

Chapter 5. A Roving *I*: Autofiction(s) and Subversions

1. This is by no means an exhaustive list of Haitian characters in Condé's work.

2. Condé institutionalized Suzanne Césaire's concept by offering courses on "cannibal texts" at Columbia University and Cornell's annual summer theory seminar in 2004.

3. Lestringant traces the connotative evolution of the word *cannibal*, since its coinage by Christopher Columbus to designate Amerindians, to its rehabilitation under Montaigne, to its negative associations in the late eighteenth century.

4. The Web site where I originally located this interview in August 2005 <http://www.culture-developpement.assoc.fr/o_home/conde/html> is no longer operative and reroutes the reader to a new .net location for the National Association for Culture and Development, Grenoble, France, at <http://culture-developpement.fluid-image.net/>. Although the Condé interview is currently unavailable there, the new site is still under construction.

5. The title of the English translation also slightly alters the original, which would be "I, Tituba, witch, black woman of Salem."

6. One can only speculate as to whether or not Suzanne Césaire was aware of a similar notion circulating in Brazil. In *The Caribbean Postcolonial: Social Equality, Post-Nationalism, and Cultural Hybridity*, Puri discusses Oswald de Andrade, "the earliest influential proponent of cultural cannibalism as a metaphor and model for Brazilian national culture. His 'Anthropophagite Manifesto,' published in 1928 in the inaugural journal of *Revista de Antropofagia* (Cannibal Review), like several elaborations of *mestizaje* and *jibarismo*, aims to articulate an original Brazilian culture in the context of dependent capitalism and uneven development" (71) Puri goes on to describe Oswald's

"1924 'Manifesto da Poesia Pau-Brasil' ('Manifesto of Brazil-wood Poetry') or 'poetry for export'" and to explain that in the pair of manifestos, Oswald opposes "both Brazil's neocolonial economic dependence on imports and its cultural dependence (i.e. the importation and imitation of European culture)" (71). Andrade preceded Césaire by two decades.

7. Lemoine dedicates the poem to two Haitian writers, Emile Roumer and Léon Laleau.

8. Most studies on *La Migration des coeurs*, in the form of conference papers and articles, compare the two novels.

9. Cixous writes: "Ecrire était réservé aux élus. Cela devrait se passer dans un espace inaccessible aux petits, aux humbles, aux femmes" (Caws 328). [Writing was reserved for the chosen few. That should take place in a space inaccessible to children, to the humble, to women.]

10. Condé quotes the passage describing M'man Tine's hands in *La Rue Cases-Nègres* and cited in Julien's essay.

11. Condé prefers this Morrison novel to *Beloved* and *Jazz* (Pfaff 155–56).

12. In Palcy's three-part film *Aimé Césaire: une voix pour l'histoire*, Césaire discusses the genesis of the *Cahier*, which began with the view of a European mountain range that reminded him of Martinique's landscape.

13. *Gouverneurs de la rosée*, *La Rue Cases-Nègres*, *Solibo Magnifique*, *Léonora*, *La Migration des coeurs*, *La Grande drive des esprits*, *L'Odeur de café*, and *Pluie et vent sur Télumée Miracle* are a few texts that depict a wake.

14. Embedded within the chapter on Aristide is Sancher's interaction with Isaure, a prostitute.

15. See for example, Roumain's poem "Bois d'ébène, in *Oeuvres complètes*."

16. The Hughes/Cook translation overlooks the resonances of *dévêtu* when they render it as "stripped." The verb *dévêtir* means to undress and thus reinforces my assertion that trees have the stature and importance of humans in the text.

17. For a discussion of Manuel as a Christ-like figure, see Serres, Gazarien-Gautier, and Ormerod (17–35).

18. Curiously, the Hughes/Cook translation omits this passage.

19. For the next generation of Francophone Caribbean writers, trees also represent masculine subjectivity. The title tree in Glissant's *Mahagony* marks the site where the stories of the three main characters, separated by many years—Maho (1935), Gani (1831), Mani (1978)—converge. In *Tambour-Babel*, Pépin's trees are more than decorative objects. With leaves as hands, the forest trees make a sound that resembles the juggling of a large key chain, an important male adornment signaling power. The imposing kapok tree keeps watch in the forest and seems to sway to the rhythm of the drum. Protagonist Napo embraces the trunk, imploring it to give him the talent so that he may become a master drummer like his father.

20. In *La Migration des coeurs*, Condé once again cannibalizes and subverts *Gouver-*

neurs de la rosée. Razyé, "haut comme un arbre de la forêt mésophile, musclé sans lourdeur" (tall, as a tree from the rain forest, a muscular athletic build) (118/115), who returns after three years in Cuba to avenge the loss of his beloved, contrasts with Manuel, who learned in Cuba how to organize workers for collective action in order to revive Fond Rouge. Razyé participates in the labor movement in Guadeloupe not for the greater good, but in order to exact revenge on Aymeric de Linsseuil, who married Cathy. Selfish and a batterer, Razyé represents a perverted masculinity, while Manuel, stabbed to death by Gervilen, is a tragic hero whose martyrdom is celebrated with a *coumbite*.

21. That Sancher purchases the Alexis property, a small house built in 1920 and eventually sold to Jules Alexis, a teacher in Petit-Bourg, who abandoned it for many years (the house is believed to be haunted), is another one of Condé's winks at the reader. Saint-John Perse is the pen name of Alexis Saint Léger, the béké poet who, in effect, abandoned Guadeloupe.

Bibliography

Adamson, Ginette. "Jean Métellus ou l'écrivain en partage: une esthétique de vie et d'écriture." *Ecrire en pays assiégé, Haiti Writing Under Siege*. Edited by Marie-Agnès Sourieau and Kathleen M. Balutansky. Amsterdam and New York: Rodopi, 2004, 361–88.

Alexis, Jacques Stéphen. *Compère Général Soleil*. Paris: Gallimard/L'Imaginaire, 1982. Translated by Carrol F. Coates as *General Sun, My Brother*. Charlottesville: University of Virginia Press, 1999.

———. "Où va le roman?" *Présence Africaine* 13 (avril–mai 1957): 81–101.

———. *Romancero aux étoiles*. Paris: Gallimard, 1960.

Alleyne, Mervyn C. *The Construction and Representation of Race and Ethnicity in the Caribbean and the World*. Barbados: University of the West Indies Press, 2002.

Alvarez, Julia. *In the Time of the Butterflies*. Chapel Hill, N.C.: Algonquin Books, 1994.

André, Jacques. *Caraïbales: études sur la littérature antillaise*. Paris: Editions Caribéennes, 1981.

Anselin, Alain. *L'Emigration antillaise en France*. Paris: Karthala, 1990.

Antoine, Régis. *La littérature franco-antillaise*. Paris: Karthala, 1992.

Arnold, A. James. "The Erotics of Colonialism in Contemporary French West Indian Literary Culture." *NWIG* 68 (1994): 5–22.

———. "The Gendering of *Créolité*." *Penser la créolité*. Edited by Maryse Condé and Madeleine Cottenet-Hage. Paris: Karthala, 1995, 21–40.

———. *Modernism and Negritude: The Poetry of Aimé Césaire*. Cambridge, Mass.: Harvard University Press, 1981.

Arnold, A. James, et al., eds. *A History of Literature in the Caribbean*. Vol. 1. Amsterdam and Philadelphia, Pa.: J. Benjamins, 1994.

Balutansky, Kathleen M., and Marie-Agnès Sourieau, eds. *Caribbean Creolization: Reflections on the Cultural Dynamics of Language, Literature, and Identity*. Gainesville: University Press of Florida, 1998.

Baude, Théodore. *La Martinique à l'exposition coloniale internationale de Paris 1931*. Paris: De Plas and G. Alexandre, 1932.

Bébel-Gisler, Dany. *Le Défi culturel guadeloupéen: devenir ce que nous sommes*. Paris: Editions Caribéennes, 1989.

———. *Léonora: l'histoire enfouie de la Guadeloupe*. Paris: Seghers, 1985. Translated by

Andrea Leskes as *Leonora: The Buried Story of Guadeloupe*. Charlottesville: University of Virginia Press, 1994.

Bell, Beverly. *Walking on Fire: Haitian Women's Stories of Survival and Resistance*. Ithaca, N.Y.: Cornell University Press, 2001.

Bellegarde-Smith, Patrick. *Haiti: The Breached Citadelle*. Boulder, Colo.: Westview Press, 1990.

Belugue, Geneviève. "Entre ombre et lumière, l'écriture engagée de Gisèle Pineau." *Notre Librairie* 138–39 (septembre 1999–mars 2000): 84–90.

Benitez-Rojo, Antonio. *The Repeating Island: The Caribbean and the Postmodern Perspective*. Translated by James E. Maraniss. Durham, N.C.: Duke University Press, 1992.

Benoît, Catherine. *Corps, jardins, mémoires: anthropologie du corps et de l'espace à la Guadeloupe*. Paris: Editions de la Maison des Sciences et l'Homme, 2000.

Bensmaïa, Réda. "Political Geography of Literature: On Khatibi's 'Professional Traveller.'" *French Cultural Studies: Criticism at the Crossroads*. Edited by Marie-Pierre Le Hir and Dana Strand. Albany, N.Y.: SUNY Press, 2000, 295–308.

Bernabé, Jean, Patrick Chamoiseau, and Raphaël Confiant. *Eloge de la créolité*. Paris: Gallimard, 1989. Translated by Mohamed B. Taleb Khyar as "In Praise of Creoleness." *Callaloo* 13.4 (Fall 1990): 866–909.

Bertelli, Cristina. "Entretien avec Pierre Dru. Inspirations, pratiques et origines du danmyé: de l'ancienne Egypte à la Martinique." *Les Périphériques* 13 (printemps 2000): 18–30. <http://www.lesperipheriques.org/article.php3?id_article=155>, accessed August 2005.

Bethel, Elizabeth. "Images of Haiti: The Construction of an African-American Lieu de Memoire." *Callaloo* 15.3 (Summer 1992): 827–41.

Bissainthe, Jean Ghasman. *Paradigma de la migracion haitiana en República Dominicana*. Santo Domingo: Instituto Tecnológica de Santo Domingo, 2002.

Blanchard-Glass, Pascale. *La Comète de Halley*. Paris: L'Harmattan, 2000.

Bouson, J. Brooks. *Quiet As It's Kept: Shame, Trauma, and Race in the Novels of Toni Morrison*. Albany, N.Y.: SUNY Press, 2000.

Brice-Finch, Jacqueline. "Memories of Mafa." *MaComère: Journal of the Association of Caribbean Women Writers and Scholars* 4 (2001): 146–54.

Browne, Katherine E. *Creole Economics: Caribbean Cunning Under the French Flag*. Austin: University of Texas Press, 2004.

Burton, Richard D. E. *Le Roman marron: études sur la littérature martiniquaise contemporaine*. Paris: L'Harmattan, 1997.

Burton, Richard D. E., and Fred Reno, eds. *French and West Indian: Martinique, Guadeloupe, and French Guiana Today*. Charlottesville: University of Virginia Press, 1995.

Cadet, Jean-Robert. *Restavec: From Haitian Slave Child to Middle-Class American*. Austin: University of Texas Press, 1998.

Cally, Sully. *Musiques et danses afro-caraïbes*. Gros Morne, Martinique: Sully Cally/Lezin, 1990.

Capécia, Mayotte. *Je suis Martiniquaise*. Paris: Corréa, 1948. Translated by Beatrice Stith Clark as *I Am a Martinican Woman/The White Negress*. Pueblo, Colo.: Passeggiata Press, 1997.

Caruth, Cathy. *Unclaimed Experience: Trauma, Narrative, and History*. Baltimore, Md.: Johns Hopkins University Press, 1996.

Castillo, Freddy Prestol. *El Másacre se pasa a pie*. Santo Domingo: Taller, 1973.

Castor, Suzy. *Migraciones y relaciones internationales: el caso haitiano-dominicano*. Mexico City: Facultad de ciencias politicas y sociales, 1983.

Cauna, Alexandra de. *L'Image des quartiers populaires dans le roman antillais*. Paris: Karthala, 2003.

Caws, Mary Ann, et al., eds. *Ecritures de femmes: nouvelles cartographies*. New Haven, Conn.: Yale University Press, 1996.

Césaire, Aimé. *Aimé Césaire: Poet and Statesman*. Interview with Ann Scarboro. Dir. Susan Wilcox. Videocassette. Cinema Guild, 2002.

———. *Cahier d'un retour au pays natal*. Paris: Présence Africaine, 1983. Translated by John Berger and Anna Bostock as *Return to My Native Land*. Middlesex, England: Penguin Books, 1969.

———. *Corps perdu*. Paris: Editions Fragrance, 1950.

———. *Discours sur le colonialisme*. 5th ed. Paris: Présence Africaine, 1970. Translated by Joan Pinkham as *Discourse on Colonialism*. New York: Monthly Review Press, 1972.

———. *Soleil cou-coupé*. Paris: Editions K, 1948.

———. *La Tragédie du roi Christophe*. Paris: Présence Africaine, 1970. Translated by Ralph Manheim as *The Tragedy of King Christophe*. New York: Grove Press, 1969.

———, ed. *Tropiques: 1941–1945. Collection complète*. Paris: Jean-Michel Place, 1978.

Césaire, Suzanne. "Le Grand camouflage." Edited by A. Césaire, *Tropiques: 1941–1945*. 267–73.

———. "Malaise d'une civilisation." Edited by A. Césaire, *Tropiques: 1941–1945*, 43–49.

———. "Misère d'une poésie: John Antoine-Nau." Edited by A. Césaire, *Tropiques: 1941–1945*, 48–50.

Chamoiseau, Patrick. *A bout d'enfance*. Paris: Gallimard, 2005.

———. *Au temps de l'antan*. Paris: Hatier, 1988. Translated by Linda Coverdale as *Creole Folktales*. New York: New Press, 1994.

———. *Biblique des derniers gestes*. Paris: Gallimard, 2002.

———. *Chronique des sept misères*. Paris: Folio, 1996. Translated by Linda Coverdale as *Chronicle of Seven Sorrows*. Lincoln: University of Nebraska Press, 1999.

———. *Ecrire en pays dominé*. Paris: Gallimard, 1997.

———. *Une enfance créole 1. Antan d'enfance*. Paris: Folio, 1998.

———. *Une enfance créole 2. Chemin-d'école*. Paris: Folio, 1996. Translated by Linda Coverdale as *School Days. A Creole Childhood*. Lincoln: University of Nebraska Press, 1997.

———. *Solibo Magnifique*. Paris: Folio, 1993. Translated by Rose-Myriam Réjouis and Val Vinokurov as *Solibo Magnificent*. New York: Pantheon Books, 1999.

———. *Texaco*. Paris: Gallimard, 1992. Translated by Rose-Myriam Réjouis and Val Vinokurov as *Texaco*. New York: Pantheon Books, 1997.

Chamoiseau, Patrick, and Raphaël Confiant. *Lettres créoles: tracées antillaises et continentales de la littérature 1655–1975*, Paris: Hatier, 1991.

Chancy, Myriam J. A. *Framing Silence: Revolutionary Novels by Haitian Women*. New Brunswick, N.J.: Rutgers University Press, 1997.

———. "Recovering History 'Bone by Bone': Conversation with Edwidge Danticat." *Calabash* 1 (Summer 2001): 15–38.

Clark, Vèvè A. "Developing Diaspora Literacy and *Marasa* Consciousness." *Comparative American Identities: Race, Sex, and Nationality in the Modern Text*. Edited by Hortense Spillers. New York: Routledge, 1991, 40–61.

———. "Katherine Dunham's Tropical Review." *Caribbean Dance from Abakua to Zouk: How Movement Shapes Identity*. Edited by Susanna Sloat. Gainesville: University Press of Florida, 2002, 305–19.

———. "Performing Memory of Difference in Afro-Caribbean Dance: Katherine Dunham's Choreography." *History and Memory in African American Culture*. Edited by Geneviève Fabre and Robert O'Meally. New York: Oxford University Press, 1994, 188–204.

Clitandre, Nadege. "Body and Voice as Sites of Oppression: The Psychological Condition of the Displaced Post-colonial Haitian Subject in Edwidge Danticat's *The Farming of Bones*." *Journal of Haitian Studies* 7.2 (Fall 2001): 28–49.

Coates, Carrol F. "Interview with Dany Laferrière." *Callaloo* 22.4 (Autumn 1999): 910–21.

Condé, Maryse. *La Belle Créole*. Paris: Mercure de France, 2001.

———. "La Châtaigne et le fruit á pain." *Parallèles: Anthologie de la nouvelle féminine de langue fransaise*. Eds. Madeleine Cottenet-Hage and Jean-Philippe Imbert. Quebec: Editions de L'instant même, 1996, 211–26.

———. *Le Coeur à rire et à pleurer: souvenirs de mon enfance*. Paris: Presses Pocket, 2001. Translated by Richard Philcox as *Tales from the Heart: True Stories from My Childhood*. New York: Soho Press, 2001.

———. *Desirada*. Paris: Robert Laffont, 1997. Translated by Richard Philcox. New York: Soho Press, 2000.

———. *Histoire de la femme cannibale*. Paris: Mercure de France, 2003.

———. *Hugo le terrible*. Paris: Sepia, 1990.

———. Interview with Viola G. Thomas. *Belles Lettres* 11.1 (January 1996): 20–22.

———. *Maryse Condé Speaks from the Heart*. Interview with Ann Scarboro. Dir. Susan Wilcox. Videocassette. Cinema Guild, Inc., 2002.

———. *La Migration des coeurs*. Paris: Robert Laffont, 1995. Translated by Richard Philcox as *Windward Heights*. New York: Soho Press, 1998.

———. *Moi, Tituba, sorcière . . . Noire de Salem*. Paris: Folio, 1994.

———. "Order, Disorder, Freedom, and the West Indian Writer." *Yale French Studies* 83 (1993): 121–35.

———. *La Parole des femmes: essai sur des romancières des Antilles de langue française.* Paris: L'Harmattan, 1979.

———. *Pays mêlé suivi de Nanna-ya.* Paris: Robert Laffont, 1997. Translated by Nicole Ball as *Land of Many Colors and Nanna-ya.* Lincoln: University of Nebraska Press, 1999.

———. *Traversée de la mangrove.* Paris: Folio, 1994. Translated by Richard Philcox as *Crossing the Mangrove.* New York: Anchor Books, 1995.

———. *La Vie scélérate.* Paris: Seghers, 1987. Translated by Victoria Reiter as *Tree of Life.* New York: Ballantine, 1992.

Confiant, Raphaël. *Bassin des ouragans.* Paris: Mille et Une Nuits, 1994.

———. *Chimères d'En-Ville.* Translated by Jean-Pierre Arsaye. Paris: Ramsay, 1997.

———. *Le Meurtre du Samedi-Gloria.* Paris: Mercure de France, 1997.

Coridun, Victor. *Mon pays Martinique, Martinique!* Paris: Editions de Paris, 1937.

Crosta, Suzanne. "Narrative and Discursive Strategies in Maryse Condé's *Traversée de la mangrove*." *Callaloo* 15.1 (1992): 147–55.

———. *Récits d'enfance antillaise.* Sainte-Foy, Québec: GRELCA, 1998.

Curtis, Wayne. "The Sweet Essence of Barbados." *New York Times* 9 Feb. 2003, travel section. <http://query.nytimes.com/gst/fullpage.html?res=9D0DE1D91F38F93AA3575 1C0A9659C8B63&sec=travel>, accessed Jan. 4, 2006.

Damas, Léon Gontran. *Pigments/Névralgies.* Paris: Présence Africaine, 1978.

Danticat, Edwidge. *After the Dance: A Walk through Carnival in Jacmel, Haiti.* New York: Crown Journeys, 2002.

———. "AHA!" *Becoming American: Personal Essays by First Generation Immigrant Women.* Edited by Meri Nana-Ama Danquah. New York: Hyperion, 2000, 39–44.

———. *Behind the Mountain.* New York: Orchard Books, 2003.

———. *Breath, Eyes, Memory.* New York: Vintage Books, 1995.

———. *The Dew Breaker.* New York: Alfred A. Knopf, 2004.

———. "Epilogue: Women Like Us." *Krik? Krak!* New York: Vintage Books, 1996, 219–24.

———. *The Farming of Bones.* New York: Soho Press, 1998.

———, ed. *The Butterfly's Way: Voices from the Haitian Dyaspora in the United States.* New York: Soho Press, 2001.

Dash, J. Michael. *The Other America: Caribbean Literature in a New World Context.* Charlottesville: University of Virginia Press, 1998.

Davies, Carole Boyce. *Black Women, Writing and Identity: Migrations of the Subject.* London and New York: Routledge, 1994.

Dejean, Yves. *Dilemne en Haïti: français en péril ou péril français.* New York: Connaissance d'Haïti, 1975.

Delawarde, Jean-Baptiste. *La Vie paysanne à la Martinique: essai de géographie humaine.* Fort-de-France, Martinique: Imprimerie Officielle, 1937.

Demme, Jonathan, dir. *The Agronomist.* DVD. New Line Home Entertainment, 2005.

Depestre, René. "Le Multiple ailleurs d'Haïti." *Boutures* 1.4 (March–August 2001): 42.

Derby, Lauren. "Haitians, Magic, and Money: 'Raza' and Society in the Haitian-Domini-

can Borderlands, 1906–1937." *Comparative Studies in Society and History* 36.3 (1994): 488–526.
Desch-Obi, T. J. "Combat and the Crossing of the 'Kalunga.'" *Central Africans and Cultural Transformations in the American Diaspora*. Edited by Linda M Heywood. Cambridge: Cambridge University Press, 2002, 353–70.
Deslauriers, Guy, dir. *Le Passage du milieu*. Screenplay by Guy Deslauriers and Patrick Chamoiseau. Réseau France Outre-mer (RFO). Les Films du Raphia, France, 1999.
Des Rosiers, Joël. *Théories caraïbes: poétique du déracinement*. Montreal: Triptyque, 1996.
Doubrovsky, Serge. "Analyse et autofiction." *Ecriture de soi et psychanalyse*. Edited by Jean-François Chiantaretto. Paris: L'Harmattan, 1996, 263–82.
Douglass, Frederick. *The Frederick Douglass Papers. Series One. Speeches, Debates, and Interviews*. Vol. 5, *1881–95*. Eds. John W. Blassingame and John R. McKivigan. New Haven: Yale University Press, 1992.
Dove, Rita. *Museums: Poems*. Pittsburgh, Pa.: Carnegie-Mellon University Press, 1983.
Dunham, Katherine. *L'Ag'Ya*. Ballet. Federal Theater, Chicago. January 27, 1938.
Dusseck, Mícheline. *Ecos del Caribe*. Barcelona: Femenino Lumen, 1996.
Edwards, Brent Hayes. *The Practice of Diaspora: Literature, Translation, and the Rise of Black Internationalism*. Cambridge: Harvard University Press, 2003.
Ega, Françoise. *Lettres à une Noire*. Paris: L'Harmattan, 1978.
———. *Le Temps des madras*. Paris: Editions Maritimes et d'Outre-Mer, 1966.
Elisée, Max. *Mémoires d'un Chabin*. Paris: Elma, 2000.
Eltis, David. *The Rise of African Slavery in the Americas*. Cambridge: Cambridge University Press, 2000.
Eltis, David, David Richardson, Stephen D. Behrendt, and Herbert S. Klein, eds. *The Trans-Atlantic Slave Trade: A Database on CD-ROM*. New York and Cambridge: Cambridge University Press, 1999.
Fabre, Michel. *La Rive Noire: de Harlem à la Seine*. Paris: Lieu Commun, 1985. Translated by Michel Fabre as *From Harlem to Paris: Black American Writers in France 1840–1980*. Urbana: University of Illinois Press, 1991.
Faine, Jules. *Dictionnaire français-créole*. Ottawa, Canada: Leméac, 1974.
Fanon, Frantz. *Peau noire, masques blancs*. Paris: Seuil, 1952. Translated by Charles Lam Markmann as *Black Skin, White Masks*. New York: Grove Press, 1967.
Farred, Grant. *What's My Name? Black Vernacular Intellectuals*. Minneapolis: University of Minnesota Press, 2003.
Fauquenoy, Marguerite. "Dimensions de la guyanité ou langue et identité en Guyane." *Contemporary French Civilization* (Summer/Fall 1990): 256–74.
Fermor, Patrick Leigh. *The Traveller's Tree: A Journey through the Caribbean Islands*. London: John Murray, 1950.
Fleurimond, Wiener Kerns. *La Communauté haïtienne de France: dix ans d'histoire 1991–2001*. Paris: L'Harmattan, 2003.
Forest, Philippe. *Le Roman, le Je*. Paris: Pleins Feux, 2001.

Forster, Elborg, and Robert Forster, eds. and trans. *Sugar and Slavery, Family and Race: The Letters and Diary of Pierre Dessalles, Planter in Martinique, 1808–1856*. Baltimore, Md.: Johns Hopkins University Press, 1996.

Gadjigo, Samba. *Ecole blanche, Afrique noire: l'école coloniale dans le roman d'Afrique noire*. Paris: L'Harmattan, 1990.

Garcia, Juan Manuel. *La Matanza de los haitianos: genocidio de Trujillo, 1937*. Santo Domingo: Editora Alfa and Omega, 1983.

Gasparini, Philippe. *Est-il je? Roman autobiographique et autofiction*. Paris: Seuil, 2004.

Gautier, Arlette. *Les Soeurs de Solitude: la condition féminine dans l'esclavage aux Antilles du XVIIe au XIXe siècle*. Paris: Editions Caribéennes, 1985.

Gazarien-Gautier, Marie-Lise. "Le symbolisme religieux dans *Gouverneurs de la rosée* de Jacques Roumain." *Présence Francophone* 7 (Automne 1974): 19–23.

Gerstin, Julian. "Kalenda and Other Neo-African Dances." *NWIG* 78.1–2 (2004): 5–41.

Gilles, Clotilde. *Un univers musical martiniquais: les swarès bèlè du Nord Atlantique*. Paris: L'Harmattan, 2001.

Gilroy, Paul *The Black Atlantic: Modernity and Double Consciousness*. Cambridge, Mass.: Harvard University Press, 1993.

Glissant, Edouard. *Le Discours antillais*. Paris: Seuil, 1981. Translated by J. Michael Dash as *Caribbean Discourse: Selected Essays*. Charlottesville: University of Virginia Press, 1992.

———. *Introduction à une poétique du divers*. Paris: Gallimard, 1996.

———. *Mahagony*. Paris: Seuil, 1987.

———. *Poétique de la Relation*. Paris: Gallimard, 1990. Translated by Betty Wing as *Poetics of Relation*. Ann Arbor: University of Michigan Press, 1997.

———. *Traité du Tout-monde*. Paris: Gallimard, 1997.

Hall, Stuart. "Negotiating Caribbean Identities." *New Caribbean Thought: A Reader*. Edited by Brian Meeks and Folke Lindahl. Mona, Jamaica: University of the West Indies Press, 2001, 24–39.

———. "What is this 'Black' in Black Popular Culture?" *Black Popular Culture*. Edited by Gina Dent. Seattle, Wash.: Bay Press, 1992, 21–33.

Harms, Robert. *The Diligent: A Voyage Through the Worlds of the Slave Trade*. Oxford: The Perseus Press, 2002.

Hearn, Lafcadio. *Two Years in the French West Indies*. New York: Harper and Bros., 1890.

Hellerstein, Nina. "Violence, mythe et destin dans l'univers antillais de Gisèle Pineau." *Littéréalité* 10.1 (Spring/Summer 1998): 47–58.

Hicks, Albert. *Blood in the Streets: The Life and Rule of Trujillo*. New York: Creative Age Press, 1946.

Hine, Darlene Clark, and Earnestine Jenkins. "Introduction: Black Men's History: Toward a Gendered Perspective." *A Question of Manhood: A Reader in U.S. Black Men's History and Masculinity*. Vol. 1. Bloomington: Indiana University Press, 1999, 1–58.

Howard, David. *Coloring the Nation: Race and Ethnicity in the Dominican Republic*. Oxford: Signal Books; Boulder, Colo.: Lynne Reiner, 2001.

Hurley, E. Anthony. "Choosing Her Own Name, Or Who is Carbet?" *CLA Journal* 41.4 (June 1998): 387–404.

"Joseph Zobel, Biographie." <http://www.martiniqueshop.com/caribavenue/zobel/biogrph.html>, accessed June 2005.

Julien, Eileen. "La Métamorphose du réel dans *La Rue Cases-Nègres.*" *French Review* 60.6 (May 1986): 781–87.

Juminer, Bertène. "La Parole de nuit." *Ecrire la 'parole de nuit:' la nouvelle littérature antillaise*. Edited by Ralph Ludwig. Paris: Folio, 1997, 131–49.

Kali. "Reggae DOM-TOM." By Jean-Marc Monnerville (Kali) and Rémi Bellenchombre. *Débranché*. Déclic Communication, 1995.

Kane, Cheikh Hamidou. *L'Aventure ambiguë*. Paris: Julliard, 1961. Translated by Katherine Woods as *Ambiguous Adventure*. New York: Collier Books, 1969.

Labat, Jean-Baptiste. *Voyage aux îles de l'Amérique*. Paris: L'Harmattan, 2005.

Lacrosil, Michèle. *Cajou*. Paris: Gallimard, 1961.

Laferrière, Dany. *J'écris comme je vis. Entretien avec Bernard Magnier*. Genouilleux, France: Editions La Passe du vent, 2000.

Lafond, Jean-Daniel, dir. *Tropique Nord*. Production ACPAV, Canada, 1994.

Laguerre, Michel S. *Urban Poverty in the Caribbean: French Martinique as a Social Laboratory*. New York: St. Martin's Press, 1990.

Lahens, Yanick. *Dans la maison du père*. Paris: Le Serpent à Plumes, 2000.

———. *L'Exil entre l'ancrage et la fuite, l'écrivain haïtien*. Port-au-Prince, Haiti: Deschamps, 1990. Translated by Cheryl Thomas and Paulette Richards as "Exile: Between Writing and Place." *Callaloo* 15.3 (1992): 735–46.

———. "La Promotion du livre et de l'écrit." *La République haïtienne: état des lieux et perspectives*. Edited by Gérard Barthélémy and Christian Girault. Paris: ADEC-Karthala, 1993, 449–65.

Lara, Oruno D. *Caraïbes en construction: espace, colonisation, résistance*. Epinay sur Seine, France: CERCAM, 1992.

———. *De l'oubli à l'histoire: espace et identité caraïbes: Guadeloupe, Guyane, Haïti, Martinique*. Paris: Maisonneuve et Larose, 1998.

Laroche, Maximilien. *Sémiologie des apparences*. Sainte-Foy, Quebec: GRELCA, 1994.

Larrier, Renée. "DuSable, Douglass and *Dessalines*: the Haytian Pavilion and the Narrative of History." *Ecrire en pays assiégé, Haïti Writing Under Siege*. Edited by Marie-Agnès Sourieau and Kathleen M. Balutansky. Amsterdam and New York: Rodopi, 2004, 39–56.

———. "'Girl by the Shore': Gender and Testimony in Edwidge Danticat's *the farming of bones*." *Journal of Haitian Studies* 7.2 (Fall 2001): 50–60.

Laye, Camara. *L'Enfant noir*. Paris: Presses Pocket, 1981.

Légitimus, Pascal, dir. *Antilles sur Seine*. DVD. CPZ and TF1 Films Productions, 2000.

Leiris, Michel. *Contacts de civilisations en Martinique et Guadeloupe*. Paris: UNESCO/Gallimard, 1955.

Lejeune, Philippe. *Je est un autre: l'autobiographie de la littérature aux médias*. Paris: Seuil, 1980.

Lemoine, Lucien. *Douta Seck ou la Tragédie du roi Christophe*. Paris: Présence Africaine, 1993.

———. *Veilleur de Jour*. Dakar, Senegal: Nouvelles Editions Africaines, 1980.

Lemoine, Patrick. *Fort-Dimanche, Fort-la-mort*. 2nd ed. Port-au-Prince, Haiti: Editions Regain, 1996.

Lepine, Edouard. *La Crise de février 1935 à la Martinique: la marche de la faim sur Fort-de-France*. Paris: L'Harmattan, 1980.

Lespes, Anthony. *Les Semences de la colère*. Port-au-Prince, Haiti: Deschamps, 1949.

Lestringant, Frank. *Le Cannibal: grandeur et décadence*. Paris: Perrin, 1994.

Léti, Geneviève. *L'Immigration indienne à la Martinique 1853–1900*. Fort-de-France, Martinique: Archives dépot, 2003.

Lewis, J. Lowell. *Ring of Liberation*. Chicago: University of Chicago Press, 1992.

Lewis, Linden. "Caribbean Masculinity: Unpacking the Narrative." *The Culture of Gender and Sexuality in the Caribbean*. Edited by Linden Lewis. Gainesville: University Press of Florida, 2003, 94–125.

Lionnet, Françoise. *Autobiographical Voices: Race, Gender, Self-Portraiture*. Ithaca, N.Y.: Cornell University Press, 1989.

Lipski, John M. *A New Perspective on Afro-Dominican Spanish: The Haitian Contribution*. Albuquerque: Latin American Institute, University of New Mexico, 1994.

Logan, Rayford W. *Haiti and the Dominican Republic*. New York: Oxford University Press, 1968.

Ludwig, Ralph, ed. *Ecrire la parole de nuit: la nouvelle littérature antillaise*. Paris: Folio, 1997.

Marceaux, Michel. *Les Hmong de Guyane*. Matoury, French Guiana: Ibis Rouge, 1996.

Marlin-Godier, Micheline. *Fort-de-France: la ville et la municipalité de 1884 à 1914*. Petit Bourg, Guadeloupe: Ibis Rouge, 2000.

Marshall, Paule. *Browngirl, Brownstones*. New York: Random House, 1959.

Matibag, Eugenio. *Haitian-Dominican Counterpoint: Nation, State, and Race on Hispaniola*. New York: Palgrave, 2003.

Maximin, Daniel. *L'île et une nuit*. Paris: Seuil, 1995.

———. *L'Isolé soleil*. Paris: Points, 1987.

Mehta, Brinda J. "Culinary Diasporas: Identity and the Language of Food in Gisèle Pineau's *Un papillon dans la cité* and *L'Exil selon Julia*." *Journal of International Francophone Studies* 8.1 (Spring 2005): 23–51.

Michalon, Josy. *Le Ladjia : origine et pratiques*. Paris: Editions Caribéennes, 1987.

Milne, Lorna. "Patrick Chamoiseau and the Erotics of Colonialism." *Paragraph* 24.3 (November 2001): 59–75.

Minatchy-Bogat, Arlette. *Terre d'exil et d'adoption*. Matoury, French Guiana: Ibis Rouge, 2001.

Moitt, Bernard. "In the Shadow of the Plantation: Women of Color and the *Libres de fait* of Martinique and Guadeloupe, 1685–1848." *Beyond Bondage: Free Women of Color in the Americas*. Edited by David Barry Gaspar and Darlene Clark Hine. Urbana: University of Illinois Press, 2004, 37–59.

———. *Women and Slavery in the French Antilles, 1635–1848*. Bloomington: Indiana University Press, 2001.

Morpeau, Louis, ed. *Anthologie d'un siècle de poésie haïtienne 1816–1925*. Paris: Editions Brossard, 1925.

Moutoussamy, Ernest. "Indianness in the French West Indies." *Indenture and Exile: The Indo-Caribbean Experience*. Edited by Frank Birbalsingh. Toronto: TSAR, 1989, 26–36.

Murdoch, H. Adlai. *Creole Identity in the French Caribbean Novel*. Gainesville: University Press of Florida, 2001.

———. "Negotiating the Metropole: Patterns of Exile and Cultural Survival in Gisèle Pineau and Suzanne Dracius-Pinalie." *Immigrant Narratives in Contemporary France*. Edited by Susan Ireland and Patrice J. Proulx. Westport, Conn.: Greenwood Press, 2001, 129–39.

Ngugi wa Thiong'o. *Decolonising the Mind*. Portsmouth, N.H.: Heinemann, 1992.

Nora, Pierre. "Between Memory and History: *Les Lieux de Mémoire*." *Representations* 26 (1989): 7–25.

Ollivier, Emile. *Mille eaux*. Paris: Gallimard, 1999.

Ormerod, Beverley. *Introduction to the French Caribbean Novel*. London: Heinemann, 1985.

———. "The Martinican Concept of "Creoleness": A Multiracial Redefinition of Culture." *Mots Pluriels* 7 (1998): 1–7. <http://www.arts.uwa.edu.au/MotsPluriels/MP798bo.html>.

Paes, César, dir. *Le Bouillon d'awara*. Videocassette. California Newsreel, 1995.

Pagès, Eric, dir. *Combat damyé*. Films Concept Associés, 2001.

Pago, Gilbert. *Les Femmes et la liquidation du système esclavagiste à la Martinique, 1848–1852*. Matoury, French Guiana: Ibis Rouge, 1998.

Palcy, Euzhan, dir. *Aimé Césaire: une voix pour l'histoire*. Videocassette. California Newsreel, 1994.

———, dir. *Rue Cases-Nègres*. 1982. Videocassette. Cinématèque, 1985.

Paquet, Sandra Pouchet. *Caribbean Autobiography: Cultural Identity and Self-Representation*. Madison: University of Wisconsin Press, 2002.

Paravisini-Gebert, Lizabeth, and Ivette Romero-Cesareo, eds. *Women at Sea*. New York: Palgrave, 2001.

Peck, Raoul, dir. *L'Homme sur les quais*. Videocassette. KJM3 Entertainment Group, 1993.

———, dir. *Lumumba*. Videocassette. Zeigeist Films, 2002.

———. *Monsieur le Ministre . . . jusqu'au bout de la patience*. Port-au-Prince: Editions Velvet, 1998.

———, dir. *Lumumba: la mort du Prophète*. Videocassette. California Newsreel, 1992.
Penet, Auguste-Robert. *Pilotes de l'empire*. Matoury, French Guiana: Ibis Rouge, 2000.
Pepin, Ernest. *Tambour-Babel*. Paris: Gallimard, 1996.
Perret, Delphine. *La Créolité: espace de création*. Matoury, French Guiana: Ibis Rouge, 2001.
Pfaff, Françoise. *Entretiens avec Maryse Condé*. Paris: Karthala, 1993. Translated by Françoise Pfaff as *Conversations with Maryse Condé*. Lincoln: University of Nebraska Press, 1996.
Philip, M. Nourbese. *Genealogy of Resistance and Other Essays*. Toronto: Mercury Press, 1997.
Philoctète, René. *Le peuple des terres mêlées*. Port-au-Prince, Haiti: Henri Deschamps, 1989. Translated by Linda J. Coverdale as *Massacre River*. New York: New Directions, 2005.
Pineau, Gisèle. *L'Âme prêtée aux oiseaux*. Paris: Stock, 1998.
———. *Chair piment*. Paris: Folio, 2004.
———. "Ecrire en tant que noire." *Penser la créolité*. Edited by Maryse Condé and Madeleine Cottenet-Hage. Paris: Karthala, 1995, 289–95.
———. *L'Espérance-macadam*. Paris: Stock, 1995. Translated by C. Dickson as *Macadam Dreams*. Lincoln: University of Nebraska Press, 2003.
———. *L'Exil selon Julia*. Paris: Livre de poche, 1996. Translated by Betty Wilson as *Exile According to Julia*. Charlottesville: University of Virginia Press, 2003.
———. *La Grande drive des esprits*. Paris: Le Serpent à Plumes, 1993.
———. "L'Identité, la créolité et la francité." *La Culture française vue d'ici et d'ailleurs*. Edited by Thomas C. Spear. Paris: Karthala, 2002, 219–24.
———. *Un papillon dans la cité*. Paris: Sepia, 1992.
———, and Marie Abraham. *Femmes des Antilles, traces et voix*. Paris: Stock, 1998.
Pratt, Mary Louise. *Imperial Eyes: Travel Writing and Transculturation*. New York: Routledge, 1992.
Price, Richard, and Sally Price. "Shadowboxing in the Mangrove: The Politics of Identity in Postcolonial Martinique." *Caribbean Romances: The Politics of Regional Representation*. Edited by Belinda Edmondson. Charlottesville: University of Virginia Press, 1999, 123–62.
Price-Mars, Jean. *La République haïtienne et la République dominicaine: les aspects divers d'un problème d'histoire, de géographie et d'ethnologie*. 2 vols. Port-au-Prince, Haiti: Deschamps, 1953.
Puri, Shalini. *The Caribbean Postcolonial: Social Equality, Post-Nationalism, and Cultural Hybridity*. New York: Palgrave MacMillan, 2004.
Racine, Marie M. B. *Like the Dew that Waters the Grass: Words from Haitian Women*. Washington, D.C.: EPICA, 1999.
Rapon, Maurice-François. *Ladja*. Vol. 2 of *Mystère à White-House*. Trinité, Martinique: Kolibri, 2003.
Régnier, Michael, dir. *Black Sugar*. National Film Board of Canada and Indiana University Audio Visual Center, 1989.

Rennard, Joseph. *Tricentenaire des Antilles: Guadeloupe, Martinique, 1635–1935*. 1935. Microfilm. Fort-de-France, Martinique: René Cottrel.
Revert, Eugène. *La Martinique: étude géographique et humaine*. Paris: Nouvelles Editions Latines, 1949.
Rey, Nicolas. *Lakou and Ghetto: les quartiers périphériques aux Antilles françaises*. Paris: L'Harmattan, 2001.
Roorda, Eric Paul. "Genocide Next Door: The Good Neighbor Policy, the Trujillo Regime, and the Haitian Massacre of 1937." *Diplomatic History* 20.3 (1996): 301–19.
Roumain, Jacques. *Gouverneurs de la rosée*. Paris: Messidor, 1986. Translated by Langston Hughes and Mercer Cook as *Masters of the Dew*. London: Heinemann, 1978.
———. *Oeuvres complètes*. Coord. Léon-François Hoffmann. Madrid: Editions UNESCO-ALLCA 22 (Collection Archivos), 2003.
Ruprecht, Alvina. "'L'Amérique c'est moi': Dany Laferrière and the Borderless Text." *Reordering of Culture: Latin America, the Caribbean, and Canada*. Edited by Alvina Ruprecht and Cecilia Taiana. Carleton, Ontario: Carleton University Press, 1995, 251–67.
Sadji, Abdoulaye. *Maïmouna*. Paris: Présence Africaine, 1958.
———. *Nini, mûlatresse du Sénégal*. 3rd ed. Paris: Présence Africaine, 1988.
Saffache, Pascal, Jean Valéry Marc, and Vincent Huygues Belrose. *Les Cyclones en Guadeloupe*. Matoury, French Guiana: Ibis Rouge, 2003.
Said, Edward. *Culture and Imperialism*. New York: Knopf, 1993.
Saint-Amand, Edriss. *Bon Dieu rit*. Paris: Domat, 1952.
Sainville, Leonard. *Dominique, nègre esclave*. Paris: Présence Africaine, 1951.
Santa, Angels. "*Cahier d'un retour au pays natal* et le problème autobiographique." *Aimé Césaire, du singulier à l'universel: actes du colloque de Fort-de-France, 28–30 juin 1993*. *Oeuvres et critiques* 19.2 (1994): 97–106.
Saugera, Eric. *Bordeaux, port négrier: chronique, économie, idéologie XVIIe-XIXe siècles*. Paris: Karthala, 1995.
Schwarz-Bart, Simone. *Pluie et vent sur Télumée Miracle*. Paris: Seuil, 1972.
Serres, Michel. "Christ noir." *Critique* 29 (1973): 13–25.
Seyhan, Azade. *Writing Outside the Nation*. Princeton, N.J.: Princeton University Press, 2001.
Shea, Renée H. "The Dangerous Job of Edwidge Danticat: An Interview." *Callaloo*. 19.2 (Spring 1996): 382–89.
Shemak, April. "Re-membering Hispaniola: Edwidge Danticat's *The Farming of Bones*. *Modern Fiction Studies* 48.1 (September 2002): 83–112.
Silie, Ruben, and Carlos Segura, eds. *Una isla para dos*. Santo Domingo: FLASCO, 2002.
Singaravelou, E. I. *Les Indiens de la Caraïbe*. 3 vols. Paris: L'Harmattan, 1987.
Slater, Mariam. *The Caribbean Family: Legitimacy in Martinique*. New York: St. Martin's Press, 1977.
Smith, Arlette. "Maryse Condé's *Hérémakhonon*: A Triangular Structure of Alienation." *CLA Journal* 32.1 (September 1988): 45–54.

Sourieau, Marie-Agnès. "Entretien avec Maryse Condé, de l'identité culturelle." *French Review* 72.6 (May 1999): 1091–98.
Sroka, Ghila. *Femmes haitiennes: paroles de négresse*. Montréal: Editions de la Parole Métèque, 1995.
Stovall, Tyler. *Paris noir: African Americans in the City of Light*. Boston: Houghton Mifflin, 1996.
Strachan, Ian Gregory. *Paradise and Plantation: Tourism and Culture in the Anglophone Caribbean*. Charlottesville: University of Virginia Press, 2002.
Tardon, Raphaël. *La Caldeira*. Paris: Fasquelle, 1948.
Taylor, Lucien. "Mediating Martinique: The 'Paradoxical Trajectory' of Raphaël Confiant." *Cultural Producers in Perilous States: Editing Events, Documenting Change*. Edited by George E. Marcus. Chicago: University of Chicago Press, 1997, 259–329.
Taylor, Patrick, ed. *Nation Dance: Religion, Identity and Cultural Difference in the Caribbean*. Bloomington: Indiana University Press, 2001.
Thédat, Jean-Marie. *Haiti République Dominicaine: une île pour deux, 1804–1916*. Paris: Karthala, 2003.
Torabully, Khal. "Coolitude: Prémisses historique d'une non-parole." *Notre Librairie* 128 (octobre–décembre 1996): 59–71.
Toumson, Roger. *Mythologie du métissage*. Paris: PUF, 1998.
———. *La Transgression des couleurs: littérature et langage des Antilles (XVIIIe, XIXe, XXe siècles)*. Vol. 1. Paris: Editions Caribéennes, 1989.
———, ed. *Les Indes antillaises: présence et situation des communautés indiennes en milieu caribéen*. Paris: L'Harmattan, 1995.
Trouillot, Evelyn. *Rosalie L'Infâme*. Paris: Editions Dapper, 2003.
Trouillot, Michel-Rolph. *Silencing the Past: Power and the Production of History*. Boston: Beacon Press, 1995.
Vaillant, Janet G. *Black, French, and African: A Life of Léopold Sédar Senghor*. Cambridge, Mass.: Harvard University Press, 1990.
Vargas Llosa, Mario. *The Feast of the Goat*. New York: Farrar, Straus and Giroux, 2001.
Vega, Bernardo. *Trujillo y Haiti*. Vol. 1, *1930–37*. Santo Domingo: Fundacion Cultural Dominicana, 1988.
Veldwachter, Nadège. "An Interview with Gisèle Pineau." *Research in African Literatures* 35.1 (Spring 2004): 180–86.
Walker, Alice. Forward. *A Piece of Mine: Short Stories by J. California Cooper*. Navarro, Calif.: Wild Trees Press, 1984. vii-ix.
Wallace, Maurice O. *Constructing the Black Masculine: Identity and Ideality in African American Men's Literature and Culture, 1775–1985*. Durham, N.C.: Duke University Press, 2002.
Warner, Keith Q. "Emasculation on the Plantation: A Reading of Joseph Zobel's *La Rue Cases-Nègres*." *CLA Journal* 32.1 (September 1988): 38–44.

Warner-Lewis, Maureen. *Central Africa in the Caribbean: Transcending Time, Transforming Cultures*. Kingston, Jamaica: University of the West Indies Press, 2003.

Warner-Vieyra, Myriam. "Depuis mon navire." *Maryse Condé: une nomade inconvenante: mélanges offerts à Maryse Condé*. Edited by Madeleine Cottenet-Hage and Lydie Moudileno. Matoury, French Guiana: Ibis Rouge, 2002, 53–56.

———. *Juletane*. Paris: Présence Africaine, 1982.

Wideman, John Edgar. *The Island: Martinique*. National Geographic Directions, 2003.

Wilson, Victor-Emmanuel Roberto. "The Forgotten Eighth Wonder of the World." *Callaloo* 15.3 (1992): 849–56.

Wright, Donald R. Rev. of *The Diligent: A Voyage Through the Worlds of the Slave Trade*. *African Studies Review* 46 (April 2003). <http://www.findarticles.com/p/articles/mi_qa4106/is_200304/ai_n9219107>, accessed Jan. 11, 2006.

Wright, Richard. *Black Boy*. New York: Harper Perennial, 1993.

———. *Native Son*. New York: Perennial Classics, 1998.

Yacou, Alain. *Journaux de bord et de traite de Joseph Crassous de Médevil: de La Rochelle á la côte de Guinée et aux Antilles, 1772–1776*. Paris: Karthala, 2001.

Yerro, Philippe Alain. "Where Life is Born: Experiencing Texaco's Urban Mangrove." Translated by Wanda Mills Bocachica. *The Indigenous Planning Times* 1.4 (2003): 69–71.

Zobel, Joseph. *Diab'la*. Paris: Nouvelles Editions Latines, 1946.

———. *La Fête à Paris*. Paris: La Table Ronde, 1953. Republished as *Quand la neige aura fondue*. Paris: Editions Caribéennes, 1979.

———. *Gertal et autres nouvelles*. Matoury, French Guiana: Ibis Rouge, 2002.

———. *Les Jours immobiles*. Fort-de-France, Martinique: 1946. Republished as *Les Mains pleines d'oiseaux*. Paris: Nouvelles Editions Latines, 1978.

———. *Laghia de la mort*. Paris: Présence Africaine, 1978.

———. *Poèmes d'amour et de silence*. Fréjus, France: Librairie Prosveta, 1994.

———. *La Rue Cases-Nègres*. Paris: Jean Froissard, 1950. Paris: Présence Africaine, 1974. Translated by Keith Q. Warner as *Black Shack Alley*. Boulder, Colo.: Lynne Rienner, 1997.

———. *Le Soleil partagé*. Paris: Présence Africaine, 1964.

Index

Advocacy, 20, 72; and autofiction, 9, 54; danger of, 148; documenting history, 58; forms of, 147–48; and literature, 20, 134; and writers, 24, 78, 79–81, 100, 104, 134, 145, 146, 147–48, 155n45

Africa, 49, 71, 86, 87, 97, 128; African heritage, 2–3, 67–68, 141, 149; and Africans, 4, 6, 9, 11, 19, 34, 67, 93, 122; film dedicated to, 19

Alexis, Jacques Stéphen, 34, 55, 104, 114, 119, 121, 133, 152n20, 163n2

Alienation, 14, 30, 42, 77, 80, 84–85, 91, 149; resistance to, 31; and violence, 95

Alvarez, Julia, 114

André, Jacques, 47, 50, 157n14

Anselin, Alain, 81, 161n4

Archive, 7, 23, 90, 113, 116, 148

Arnold, A. James, 10, 151n7

Assimilation, 30, 33, 81–82; consequences of, 33; French policy of, 10, 70, 74–77, 81; resistance to, 52, 77

Autofiction, 55, 125; and advocacy, 54, 77–78, 148; and authenticity, 21, 92, 146; as challenge to European travelers' discourse, 6–7, 32, 146; and Chamoiseau, 56–57, 77; characteristics of, 21–24, 32, 34, 55–56, 114, 129, 146–47; and *collage text[île]*, 147; and Condé, 129, 134, 145; and Danticat, 100, 104, 114, 119, 123–24; multi-voiced narrative discourse, 28–29, 128–29, 135; and Pineau, 27, 80, 84, 99; raising political consciousness, 134; and testimony, 21–29; and Zobel, 32. *See also* First-person perspective

Balutansky, Kathleen and Marie-Agnès Sourieau, 37

Baudelaire, Charles, 89, 158n7

Bébel-Gisler, Dany, 27, 34, 56, 84, 90, 113, 148, 160n19, 161n1, 165n13

béké, 38, 41, 42, 45–46, 51, 61, 87

Bell, Beverly, 18, 25–26, 119, 161n2

Benitez-Rojo, Antonio, 1, 148

Bouson, J. Brooks, 98

Browne, Katherine, 62

BUMIDOM (Bureau pour le développement des migrations d'outre-mer), 15, 61, 65, 81, 93

Cadet, Jean-Robert, 35, 154n39

Capécia, Mayotte, 15, 21, 32, 84, 155n41, 156n3, 162n8

Caribbean: culture, 10–11, 14, 21, 25, 29, 43–44, 67–68, 75, 88, 140, 149; definition of, 9–10, 102; history, 60; population, 11, 14–18, 45, 66, 81; tourism, 12–13. *See also* Identity

Caruth, Cathy, 93, 96. *See also* Trauma

Castillo, Freddy Prestol, 114, 163n5

Césaire, Aimé, 28, 60, 102, 111, 133, 145, 147, 152n20, 154n38, 158n7, 160n15; *Cahier d'un retour au pays natal*, 3, 9–10, 20, 29, 32, 72, 133, 135, 137, 141, 142, 156n47, 165n12; *Discours sur le colonialisme*, 19–20, 33, 82, 87, 152n20; poetry collections, 33; *La Tragédie du roi Christophe*, 111; *Une tempête*, 130

Césaire, Suzanne, 9, 17, 21, 151n7; and cannibal poetics, 29, 123, 128, 130, 132, 134, 137, 145, 164nn2,6

Chamoiseau, Patrick, 5, 6, 15, 24, 27, 29, 34, 56, 81, 82, 83, 99, 147, 148, 154n37; *A bout d'enfance*, 56, 70, 85, 160n14; *Antan d'enfance*, 155n41, 160n14; *Biblique des derniers gestes*, 56; *Chemin-d'école*, 8, 27, 56, 57, 58, 59, 60, 70–77, 85, 89, 133, 160nn14,17,18; *Chronique des sept misères*, 27, 56, 58, 60, 63, 77, 85, 144, 158nn1,5; *Ecrire en pays dominé*, 15, 53, 152n20, 153n21, 156n1, 158n2; *L'Esclave le vieil homme et le molosse*, 139–40; *Lettres créoles*, 151n7; *Solibo Magnifique*, 8, 27, 56, 58, 59, 60–70, 77, 85, 139, 158n1, 159nn11,13, 160n15, 165n13; *Texaco*, 8, 21, 22, 27, 56, 57, 58, 60, 63, 77, 85, 98, 158n1, 159n9. *See also* *Créolistes*; *Marqueur de paroles*; *Sentimenthèque*

Chauvet, Marie Vieux, 16, 84, 104, 148
Clark, Vèvè, 135, 145, 152n13
Class and color differences, 35, 43, 44, 46, 59, 106, 109, 156n6; prejudice, 42, 50, 68, 81, 82, 86
Collage text[île], 8, 18, 22, 28, 57; definition of, 26–27, 147; examples of, 80, 94, 124, 125, 126, 128–29, 145; and performance, 29
Colonialism, 3, 10, 21, 34, 35, 36, 47, 52, 77, 82, 98, 134, 156n1
Combat dance traditions, 2, 4, 6, 152nn10,11,15. See also *Danmyé*; *Laghia*
Condé, Maryse, 17, 24, 28, 30, 31, 84, 98, 125, 126–29, 147; *La Belle Créole*, 28, 135; and cannibal poetics, 28–29, 128–29, 132–35, 137, 141, 145, 164n2; "La Châtaigne et le fruit à pain," 21, 161n1; *Le Coeur à rire et à pleurer*, 29, 30, 32, 126, 129, 133–35, 156n47, 160n19; *Desirada*, 17, 97, 126, 127–28, 135; *Hérémakhonon*, 126, 128; *Histoire de la femme cannibale*, 17, 28, 126, 128; *Hugo le terrible*, 92, 162n12; *La Migration des coeurs*, 28, 126, 127, 132–33, 135, 138, 165nn8,13,20; *Moi, Tituba sorcière*, 28, 126, 129, 133, 164n5; *Traversée de la mangrove*, 28, 126, 127, 129, 135–44, 165n14; *La Vie scélérate*, 126
Confiant, Raphaël, 5, 9, 10, 14, 15, 22, 53, 81, 151n7, 154n33, 159nn9,10
Coridun, Victor, 32
Creole language, 2, 88, 151n2, 161n6; as cultural archive, 76, 90; Haitian, 8, 103, 104, 105, 106, 107, 117, 120, 123, 151n2, 163n4; and identity, 82–83; low status of, 42, 43, 61, 66; Martinican, 57; origins of, 83; and race and class, 2; and school, 31, 72, 74–77; speakers, 70, 75, 87, 104; varieties of, 69; words and nicknames, 68–69, 75, 89, 120, 137
Créolistes, 7, 8, 14, 61, 64, 84, 161n5; critique of, 11, 14, 153nn24,28, 161n5; and *Eloge de la créolité*, 14, 61
Creolization, 4, 11, 14, 75, 81, 159n13; and *métissage*, 17, 161n21
Crosta, Suzanne, 136, 155n41

Damas, Léon, 19, 158n7
Dance, 1–2, 4, 5, 29, 136, 149. See also *Danmyé*
Danmyé, 8, 14, 29, 36, 104, 136, 144, 149, 152n14, 156n2; and Chamoiseau, 56–57, 64–65, 70, 77; and Condé, 125, 128, 144–45; and Danticat, 101, 105, 122; definition and history of, 2–5; and fiction, 5–6, 8, 26–29; intersection with autofiction, 7, 26–29; and metaphor, 4, 30; and Pineau, 80, 99, 101; principles of, 6, 28, 36, 47, 101, 105, 122, 149; and survival, 63–64; and Zobel, 26, 31, 35–36, 47, 53, 54. See also *Laghia*
Danticat, Edwidge, 6, 24, 28, 100, 102, 104, 120, 126, 148, 163n2; *After the Dance*, 152n16; *Behind the Mountain*, 104; *Breath, Eyes, Memory*, 104, 124; *The Dew Breaker*, 22, 104, 124, 155nn43,45, 163n2; *Farming of Bones*, 28, 100–101, 102, 104–23, 164nn10,11; *Krik? Krak!*, 104, 115; "Nineteen Thirty-Seven," 115–16, 164n12
Dash, Michael, 133, 141
Davies, Carole Boyce, 84–85, 89, 103
Dawkins, Françoise, 26, 147
Depestre, René, 16, 17, 90, 157n17
Deslauriers, Guy, 19
Des Rosiers, Joël, 14, 17, 103, 110
Desroy, Annie, 84
Displacement, 15–17, 27, 28, 80, 84, 91, 99, 108, 127; and alienation, 80, 91; and exile, 15–16, 85–86, 90, 102, 105, 109, 122; and identity, 36, 108, 127; men's, 60, 65, 66, 67–68, 69; narrative of, 122; ruptures of, 104; tensions of, 60; women's, 29. See also *La drive*
Dominique, J. J., 84
Dove, Rita, 114
La Drive, 63, 64–65, 70, 78
Dunham, Katherine, 4, 5, 152nn12,13
Dusseck, Micheline, 147
Dyaspora, 10, 16, 101, 102, 123, 124, 127, 153n23, 163n6

Education, 20; access to, 46–47; colonial system of, 30, 48; instrument of French domination, 82; and literacy, 35, 36, 43, 52–53, 59, 68, 69, 72, 89, 158n8; oral, 48–49, 53, 83, 88, 91, 147; and racism, 82, 147; school experiences, 42, 70–77, 84, 87–89, 133–34, 160n16; and socialization, 42, 161n20; and upward mobility, 35, 69, 86, 146; and women, 160n19
Edwards, Brent Hayes, 15, 34, 52, 151n7, 157n16, 162n9
Ega, Françoise, 32, 84, 162n8
L'En-ville, (city), 44, 46–47, 52, 61, 68, 70, 146;

and *la drive*, 63; and peripheral communities, 45–46, 62–64, 65, 69, 98, 159n9

Family and kinship: dysfunctional, 95, 97–98, 141–42, 143–44; effect of slavery on, 97; intergenerational relations, 49, 82–83, 84, 85, 104, 147; reformation of, 48, 109, 123, 124
Fanon, Frantz, 21, 60, 72, 80, 81, 82, 83, 145, 158n7; *Peau noire, masques blancs*, 7, 14, 33, 42, 77, 87, 134
Farred, Grant, 49
Firmin, Anténor, 17
First-person perspective, 114, 124; fictional narrators, 27, 79, 85, 100, 116, 153n29, 154n39, 155n45; function of, 6–9; and narrative shifts, 22, 26, 57, 80, 94, 101, 124–25, 126–27, 136, 144–45; in poetry, film, and nonfiction prose, 19–20; testimonial dimension of, 23–25. *See also* Autofiction; *Témoignage*
French Guiana, 11, 12, 34, 79

Gender, 51, 53, 79, 80, 81, 82, 89, 90, 106, 114, 119, 129, 153n28; differences, 81, 97; equality, 25, 48; and identity, 51–52, 129; oppression, 3; relations, 80, 89; restrictions, 42, 60, 148; and socialization, 42, 51; stereotypes, 16
Glissant, Edouard, 1–2, 7, 8, 10–11, 14, 24, 27, 28, 34, 36, 60, 61, 70, 81, 83, 89–90, 109, 110, 119, 127, 128, 136, 147–48, 153n23, 158n7, 161n6, 164n9; creolization, 4; *chaosmonde*, 10–11, 153n23; *détour*, 1, 2, 10; *Le Discours antillais*, 112, 122; *Mahagony*, 165n19; *Poétique de la Relation*, 4, 7–8, 79, 99; *relie, relaie, relate*, 7–8, 58, 72, 79, 99, 121; and slavery, 7, 23–24, 34. *See also Relation*
Guadeloupe, 79, 85, 87, 88, 90, 91, 92, 95, 99, 127, 128, 147, 163n1; departmentalization, 34; heritage, 26, 84; hurricane, 92–93; population, 11; and tourism, 89; and the Western imaginary, 11

Haiti, 26, 81, 101–6, 163n1; the Citadelle, 110–12, 113; and the Dominican Republic, 16, 34, 55, 101, 102, 104–10, 112, 114–22, 163n3; and exile, 15–16, 28, 102; Haitian Revolution, 113, 137; image of, 13, 20; transnationalism, 102–4. *See also Dyaspora*
Hall, Stuart, 10
Hearn, Lafcadio, 4, 6–7, 18, 31–32, 50, 152n11

History, construction of, 30, 113, 163n7; documenting of, 58; and *histoire*, 72, 78, 99, 129; oral, 91, 113; recuperation of, 113–14, 129; silences of, 7, 80, 113, 163n7
Howard, David, 109
Hurricane Hugo, 92–93, 94, 95, 98, 108, 162nn12,13

I, 38, 56, 132, 133; appropriation of, 6–7, 17, 21, 32; and identity construction, 146; privileging of, 6–7, 19–20, 21–22, 58, 146; relational, 8, 19, 21–23, 27, 28, 57–58; shifts of, 27, 56, 80
Identity, 8, 31, 82, 84–85, 90, 110, 127, 128, 154n33, 159n13; ambiguity of, 142; appropriation of, 90; articulations of, 14–21; complexities of, 10, 21, 103, 115, 127, 142, 154n33, 159n13, 160n15; fluidity of, 87–88, 109, 123; formation of, 33, 36, 84, 91, 110, 124, 127, 146; gender, 70, 129; Guadeloupean, 82–83; imposition of, 91, 124; in-betweenness, 81, 102, 160n15; and location, 9–11, 36–47, 127, 128, 144, 146; masculine, 3; metaphors of, 147; perceptions of, 87–88; regional, 9, 14; renegotiating of, 85, 102, 104, 110; sexual, 47, 157n14
Indo-Caribbeans, 11, 14, 17, 75, 87–88, 93, 136, 154n33
In-trust narrator, 27, 55–58, 119; and curated texts, 27, 80, 85, 99, 146. *See also Marqueur de paroles*

Julia, Lucie, 84
Juminer, Bertène, 10, 159n10

Kali, 14–15
Kane, Cheikh Hamidou, 71, 72, 160n17

Laclos, Choderlos de, 89
Lacrosil, Michèle, 84
Lafayette, Madame de, 89
Laferrière, Dany, 22–23, 79–80, 155n44
Laghia, 2–4, 47, 151n3, 152n12; *laghia de la mort*, 2, 5, 31. *See also Danmyé*
Laguerre, Michel, 45, 62–63, 157n11, 161n20
Lahens, Yanick, 103, 147, 148–49
Language: access to culture, 83; and communication, 106–7; and identity, 128; and origins, 69; and prejudice, 82; tensions, 8, 58, 61, 72–77, 83, 106, 123, 147. *See also* Creole

Lara, Oruno, 9, 11, 82
Laroche, Maximilien, 56, 58, 151n1
Laye, Camara, 34, 83, 84
Lemoine, Lucien, 130–32, 156n7, 165n7
Lemoine, Patrick, 20
Lespès, Anthony, 33, 114, 121

Maran, René, 52
Marqueur de paroles, 21–22, 56–59, 68, 69, 70, 77, 119, 146, 158nn2,3,5. *See also* Chamoiseau
Marshall, Paule, 83–84, 104
Martinique, 10, 30–35, 49, 57, 60–71, 72, 74, 75, 76, 78, 81, 87, 102, 134, 163n1; and *danmyé*, 5; departmentalization, 32; at the Exposition Coloniale, 12; and slavery, 11; and tourism, 40, 61; visitors to, 4, 31; and the Western imaginary, 11–12; and Zobel, 27
Masculinity, 60, 125, 128, 129, 165n19; constraints on, 31, 47; construction of, 3; critique of, 125, 128, 137, 140–41, 144; distortion of, 46; impact of urbanization on, 60; models of, 48–53; and *négritude*, 3–4, 137–40; performance of, 3–4, 26, 31, 43, 49–51, 146, 151n5
Maximin, Daniel, 92, 162n12
McKay, Claude, 52
Memory: ancestral, 7, 10, 34, 49, 90, 136; childhood, 99; collective, 10, 91; cultural, 46, 67; fragments of, 28; recounting from, 19; repressed, 94, 101; resurgence of, 94, 99; transmission of, 8, 94, 95, 129; and trauma, 93–99, 126; unpredictability of, 94
Métissage, 14, 15, 153n28, 161n21
Michalon, Josy, 4
Middle Passage, 17–18, 19, 80, 87, 92–93
Migration, 28, 52, 81, 91, 92, 98, 104, 123; circular, 127; forced, 104; and home, 84–85, 88, 90, 100, 103–4, 109, 110, 112, 122, 124, 135, 146; and identity 15–17, 28, 81, 84, 144; promotion of, 61; and school, 70; transatlantic, 78; urban, 44. *See also* BUMIDOM
Milne, Lorna, 58
Moitt, Bernard, 4, 48, 69
Morrison, Toni, 60, 98, 104, 133, 134, 145, 158n7, 165n11
Murdoch, H. Adlai, 26, 56, 82

Nardal, Paulette, 15, 53, 151n7
Négritude, 3–4, 14, 15, 33, 35, 82, 128, 144, 146, 154n33, 155n42, 158n6

Nettleford, Rex, 1–2, 148
Ngugi wa Thiongo, 71

Ollivier, Emile, 21, 32, 99, 155n42, 158nn6,7,8
Orality/oral tradition, 70, 73, 84, 85, 90, 93, 114. *See also* Storytelling
Ormerod, Beverley, 36

Pagès, Eric, 4
Palcy, Euzhan, 40–41, 111, 156n47(intro), 156n2(chap.1), 157n8, 160n18, 165n12
Peck, Raoul, 16, 24, 155n39, 162n15, 164n13
Performance, 1, 3, 5, 49, 57–58, 68, 70, 111
Philip, M. Norbese, 8
Philoctète, René, 114–15, 163n8
Pineau, Gisèle, 6, 11, 22, 24, 25, 27, 79–84, 147, 162n7; *L'Âme prêtée aux oiseaux*, 79, 80; *Chair piment*, 79, 80; and *danmyé*, 26, 27; *L'Espérance-macadam*, 26, 27, 79, 83, 89, 91–99, 101, 126, 137, 147, 159n9, 162n12; *L'Exil selon Julia*, 27, 29, 79, 80, 84, 85–92, 97, 99, 136; *Femmes des Antilles*, 18, 25, 79, 80–81, 95, 135, 162n11; *La Grande drive des esprits*, 79, 80, 161n1, 165n13; *Un papillon dans la cité*, 10, 79, 80, 162n11
Plantation, 27, 42, 46, 48, 49, 50, 51, 53, 92, 95, 141, 153n26; and creolization, 4; exploited workers on, 30, 34–41, 108, 109, 112, 120, 122, 135; and Glissant, 4, 36; harsh life on, 31, 33, 45, 52, 80–81, 95; and tourism, 12–13, 39–40, 153n26; women on, 35, 41
Positionality, 6, 78, 84, 91, 105, 125
Présence Africaine, 33, 34, 35
Price, Richard, and Sally Price, 11, 153nn24,28
Price-Mars, Jean, 14, 17
Puri, Shalini, 62, 81, 164n6

Race and color: issue in literature, 32–33, 35; prejudice, 11, 26, 81, 82, 91, 107–8, 134; stereotypes, 6; stratifications, 2, 11, 36, 44, 59, 63, 82, 86, 87, 89, 159n13
Récit/master narrative, 6, 7, 18, 32; as opposed to *récit*, 20, 27, 29, 41, 49, 55, 85, 92, 101, 119, 127, 135; silences of, 58, 114, 119, 123, 152n18
Relation, theory of, 2, 14, 26, 53, 83, 85, 102, 107, 128, 145, 151n2
Répondeurs, 2, 8, 27, 57, 70, 77, 151n3
Representation, 8, 11–12, 13, 20, 26, 81, 86, 91, 103, 146

Roumain, Jacques, 28, 34, 129, 133, 137–39, 143, 145, 147, 156n47, 158n7, 165nn13,15,17,20

Sadji, Abdoulaye, 33
Sainville, Léonard, 33
Schwarz-Bart, Simone, 24, 27, 29, 55, 84, 133, 155n41, 156n47, 161n1, 165n13
Senegal, 15, 71, 86, 102, 111, 130, 144, 157n15
Senghor, Léopold, 33, 157n12
Sentimenthèque, 8, 29, 59–60, 83, 98, 104, 129–30, 158nn6,7, 163n2
Seyhan, Azade, 16, 103
Silence and silencing, 4, 21, 64, 80, 93, 115, 129. *See also* Trouillot
Slavery, 9, 10, 11, 12, 17–18, 24, 27, 30, 34, 69, 91, 98, 113, 134; abolition of, 34, 37, 80, 143; *Code noir*, 17, 24–25, 63, 157n7, 159n10; legacy of, 6, 27, 34, 36–41, 62, 69, 95, 97, 146, 157n13; resistance to, 66, 112–13, 141, 144, 149; silences around, 7; and suffering, 28
Slave trade, 4, 17–18, 19, 30, 122, 128, 134, 151n8, 152n9
Storytelling, 8, 56, 57, 58, 61, 66, 73, 119; *conteur*, prowess of, 56, 60, 66, 70, 73, 159n10; *parole de nuit*, 8, 61; and writing, 53–54
Strachan, Gregory, 13
Subjectivity, 7, 8, 31, 80, 125, 129; asserting of, 21, 59; and autofiction, 32, 148; men's, 165n19; women's, 84, 85

Tardon, Raphaël, 44–45

Témoignage/testimony: and advocacy, 79, 100, 155n49; bearing witness, 7–8, 18, 20, 21, 23–26, 28, 55, 68, 70, 79, 100, 101, 123, 155n45; dissemination of, 123; and documenting violence, 20, 96, 113; *I*-witness, 19–20, 39, 77, 148; and listening, 24–25, 114, 117, 120–21, 123, 146; potential, 55, 96–97; sister witness, 25, 55–56, 77, 121, 123, 146; sites of, 116–19; subversion of, 127; and witnesses, 68, 92, 127, 129; and women, 24–25, 79, 121
Toumson, Roger, 9, 42, 153nn25,28
Transnationalism, 53, 103, 104, 147

Trauma, 27–28, 80, 91–92, 93, 94, 95–96, 98, 100, 104, 105, 162n15. *See also* Caruth, Cathy
Travel narrative, 6–7, 31, 39, 152n16; ships' journals, logs, and settlers' letters, 6, 17–18, 19, 21, 31, 32, 39–40, 92, 135, 146, 154nn34,35, 156n4. *See also* Hearn, Lafcadio
Trouillot, Michel-Rolph, 7, 11, 113, 116. *See also* Silence

Valcin, Cléanthe, 84
Veillée/wake, 18, 53–54, 65, 66–67, 136, 165n13
Violence, 91–92, 146; child abuse, 95, 97; colonial, 10–11; domestic, 27, 80, 86, 89, 95, 161n1; incest, 27, 80, 93–96, 101, 140, 163n17; massacre, 101, 105–7, 109, 112, 113–18, 163n3; murder, 95; and poverty, 98; rape, 27, 41, 80, 92, 97, 129, 153n2; of slavery, 18, 80–81; torture, 24, 122; and trauma, 95, 104. *See also* Hurricane Hugo

Walker, Alice, 25
Warner, Keith, 41, 47, 157n18
Warner-Vieyra, Myriam, 15, 28, 84, 89, 162n8
Women: erasure of, 26, 30; gender equality of, 41; mothers and surrogates, 39, 41, 42, 44, 46, 48, 110, 115, 124; and slavery, 18, 48, 80–81, 98; storytellers, 56, 57, 60, 66; witnesses, 24, 25–26; writers, 85, 148
Wright, Richard, 33–34, 83–84, 157n18, 162n7

Yerro, Philippe, 45, 62, 159n9

Zobel, Joseph, 5, 6, 15, 28, 40, 60, 63, 82, 83, 126, 145, 147; *Diab'la*, 32; *La Fête à Paris*, 5–6, 32; *Gertal et les autres*, 40; *Les Jours immobiles*, 32; *Laghia de la mort*, 5, 32; poetry, 157n10, 165n10; *La Rue Cases-Nègres*, 26–27, 30–54, 63, 71–72, 77, 83, 85, 86, 96, 101, 111, 133, 134, 136, 143, 155n 156n47(intro), 156n6(chap. 1), 157nn 13,17, 160n18, 165nn10,13; *Le Soleil partagé*, 43–44
Zola, Emile, 83, 158n7

Renée Larrier is professor of French at Rutgers University. Author of *Francophone Women Writers of Africa and the Caribbean* and coeditor with E. Anthony Hurley and Joseph McLaren of *Migrating Words and Worlds: Pan-Africanism Updated*, she has also published dozens of articles in scholarly journals and essay collections.

www.ingramcontent.com/pod-product-compliance
Lightning Source LLC
Chambersburg PA
CBHW020845160426
43192CB00007B/797